PRAISE FOR *HUCKABEE*

"Scott Lamb brilliantly captures the remarkable journey of Mike Huckabee. When Mike worked for me as a young adult, I witnessed his commitment to God, his understanding of freedom, and his unique gift to communicate. Through the Reagan years, with the collapse of the Soviet Union, end of the Cold War, and economic recovery, Mike didn't just watch—he contributed. He went on to lead in Arkansas and now continues to lead nationally, constantly inspiring people and influencing the culture in a positive way."

—JAMES ROBISON
FOUNDER AND PRESIDENT, LIFE OUTREACH INTERNATIONAL
FOUNDER AND PUBLISHER, THE STREAM

"I have known and respected Mike and Janet Huckabee for many years. Mike's many gifts, common sense, sense of humor, and strong convictions are nationally known. His foundation is his Christian faith. His strength is his faith that people and countries can change. This book will give a greater understanding of this good man to every reader."

—REX M. HORNE JR.
FORMER PRESIDENT OF OUACHITA BAPTIST UNIVERSITY
PRESIDENT OF ARKANSAS' INDEPENDENT COLLEGES AND UNIVERSITIES

"Scott Lamb's *Huckabee: The Authorized Biography* provides an objective but sympathetic introduction to the colorful life of Governor Mike Huckabee. Lamb has caught the essence of the man, the essence of his character, and has revealed the gentle spirit of a great man. One may not agree with all of Lamb's conclusions, but what is important is that he has provided us with an accurate portrayal of a man whose Christianity has permeated the deepest levels of his life. This book is a great read for this year."

—PAIGE PATTERSON
PRESIDENT OF SOUTHWESTERN BAPTIST THEOLOGICAL SEMINARY
FORT WORTH, TX

"Whenever we're around 'the Gov' our spines are stiffened and our hearts are strengthened to stand courageously at a time in our nation's history when cowardice is so contagious. You will feel your own spine stiffen with resolve as you read this enjoyable biography of Huckabee, written by our friend Scott Lamb."

—DAVID AND JASON BENHAM
SPEAKERS AND AUTHORS OF *WHATEVER THE COST*

"A compelling account of one man's unlikely ascent from rural Arkansas to national prominence. If you thought you knew the governor before reading this book, think again! Lamb transparently takes you into the very character of the man, from the Baptist pulpit to the governor's mansion. This book provides a gripping account of Huckabee's remarkable journey of faith, family, and politics that took place within one of the most fascinating eras of recent American political history."

—STU EPPERSON JR.
AUTHOR OF *LAST WORDS OF JESUS*
PRESIDENT OF THE TRUTH NETWORK

HUCKABEE

c-2

HUCKABEE

The Authorized Biography

SCOTT LAMB

W PUBLISHING GROUP

AN IMPRINT OF THOMAS NELSON

Published in Nashville, Tennessee, by W Publishing, an imprint of Thomas Nelson.

Thomas Nelson titles may be purchased in bulk for educational, business, fund-raising, or sales promotional use. For information, please e-mail SpecialMarkets@ThomasNelson.com.

Any Internet addresses, phone numbers, or company or product information printed in this book are offered as a resource and are not intended in any way to be or to imply an endorsement by Thomas Nelson, nor does Thomas Nelson vouch for the existence, content, or services of these sites, phone numbers, companies, or products beyond the life of this book.

Unless otherwise noted, photos are from the Huckabee family photo archives.

Unless otherwise noted, Scripture quotations are taken from the Holy Bible, New International Version®, NIV®. Copyright © 1973, 1978, 1984, 2011 by Biblica, Inc.® Used by permission of Zondervan. All rights reserved worldwide. www.zondervan.com. The "NIV" and "New International Version" are trademarks registered in the United States Patent and Trademark Office by Biblica, Inc.®

Scripture quotations marked ESV are from the ESV® Bible (The Holy Bible, English Standard Version®). Copyright © 2001 by Crossway, a publishing ministry of Good News Publishers. Used by permission. All rights reserved.

Scripture quotations marked KJV are from the King James Version. Public domain.

Scripture quotations marked NASB are from New American Standard Bible®. Copyright © 1960, 1962, 1963, 1968, 1971, 1972, 1973, 1975, 1977, 1995 by The Lockman Foundation. Used by permission. (www.Lockman.org)

Scripture quotations marked NKJV are from the New King James Version®. © 1982 by Thomas Nelson. Used by permission. All rights reserved.

ISBN 978-0-7180-3914-1 (eBook)

ISBN 978-0-7180-3915-8 (HC)

Library of Congress Cataloging-in-Publication Data

Library of Congress Control Number: 2015909808

Printed in the United States of America

15 16 17 18 19   RRD   10 9 8 7 6 5 4 3 2 1

This book is dedicated in memory of Jesse David Clanton Jr.—the beloved father of my wife, a friend of Jesus, and an American patriot who knew the beauty of integrity and the honor of civic duty.

He died in 2013 on the birthday of Mike Huckabee, a man he never met but would have enjoyed talking to because of their shared zeal for God and country.

Mr. Clanton's death also fell on the seventeenth anniversary of my wedding to his daughter. Her soul bears the indelible fingerprint of his affection and provision.

God is a poet, writing verse with our lives and into our lives. One year to the day after Mr. Clanton's death, Pearl delivered our sixth child into the world. We named him Aaron Jesse in honor of a grandfather he would never meet on this side of glory.

The LORD gave, and the LORD has taken away; blessed be the name of the LORD. . . .

For I know that my Redeemer lives,
and at the last he will stand upon the earth.

—JOB 1:21; 19:25 ESV

Thus says the LORD of hosts, the God of Israel, to all the exiles
whom I have sent into exile from Jerusalem to Babylon: Build
houses and live in them; plant gardens and eat their produce.
Take wives and have sons and daughters; take wives for your sons,
and give your daughters in marriage, that they may bear sons
and daughters; multiply there, and do not decrease. But seek the
welfare of the city where I have sent you into exile, and pray to the
LORD on its behalf, for in its welfare you will find your welfare.

—JEREMIAH 29:4–7 ESV

For here we have no lasting city, but we
seek the city that is to come.

—HEBREWS 13:14 ESV

Pray then like this:

Our Father in heaven,
hallowed be your name.
Your kingdom come,
your will be done,
on earth as it is in heaven.

—MATTHEW 6:9–10 ESV

CONTENTS

Contents

Part 4—The City of Man

EMPIRE STATE OF MIND

> Do you like bacon?
>
> —MIKE HUCKABEE

AFTER NEARLY RUNNING OVER A DOZEN NEW YORK CITY pedestrians who all seemed oblivious to their near-death experiences, the taxi driver pulled his Midwestern passenger, me, up to the Renaissance Hotel in Times Square. Given the location of the hotel, it now seemed strange that my driver had not immediately known how to get there and had taken a few wrong turns, all on the meter.

Note to self: when a taxi driver in New York asks, "Have you ever been there?" or "Do you know where it is?" always answer in the affirmative.

As we pulled up to the curb, Mike Huckabee approached the cab.

"Scott Lamb?" he asked. This was our first time meeting in person.

I said yes, and he got in.

I didn't know how much time he'd have available, but I had hoped for at least an hour of interviewing. He had been on various FOX programs that afternoon, and his schedule the next day involved taping his own television show before an immediate flight out of the city.

It was a beautiful Friday night in April 2014. I had already begun fairly extensive background research for this biography, and I was eager to begin the more formal interview sessions. Though still months away from any serious speculation in the newspapers regarding Huckabee's 2016 plans, it was never too early for critics to begin dismantling potential candidates. Some recent pieces I had read attacked him because of his weight. Indeed, he wasn't the skin-and-bones he had been almost a decade earlier. He ran the New York marathon in 2006 but hurt his knee ligaments doing so, and the injury now kept him away from any regimented preparation for marathons. He had put on about 30 pounds since then, but because he had lost 105 pounds to begin with, the idea that he had "put it all back on" seemed less than truthful.

I wanted to ask him about that, but since this was our first interview I decided against it, fearing he might be sensitive about the topic. I'd save that for another day, once I had been able to gauge how open and transparent he was when under the lens of biographical investigation.

"West Side Steakhouse," Huckabee said, and then told the driver exactly how best to get there.

On the drive he pointed out to me one "don't miss" spot after another, commenting on how exciting the city of New York was to him. "It's just such a center of culture and humanity. Energy and people coming together. Incredible city."

"On a different scale than Hope, Arkansas?" I joked.

"Yeah, the pace is a bit faster," he said.

We arrived at the restaurant and were greeted warmly by a man whom Huckabee seemed to know very well.

"Scott, this is Nick. He owns the place. Nick, Scott is a new friend from out of town. I'm here to show him why I love your place—one of my favorites in the city."

Nick beamed like a craftsman who is proud of having built something special—in this case, a restaurant people enjoyed bringing new friends to.

He turned Huckabee aside for a minute and talked to him about "what they're doing in Washington"—the kind of political small talk that is Huckabee's stock-in-trade. He talked to Nick with excitement, as if it were the first time he had been called on to give his opinion on that particular subject that week. As far as Nick was concerned, it was.

We took our seats and scanned the menu. That's when Huckabee leaned toward me from across the table, wide-eyed and grinning. "Do you like bacon?" he asked.

"Well, sure. Everyone likes bacon," I said.

"Nick, bring us out an appetizer. Make it a double order of slab bacon. Thanks." He turned back to me. "Oh, you're going to love this."

I did. The smell alone would have driven a vegetarian to recant for one night. Thick-cut (hence the word *slab* printed on the menu) bacon had been grilled like steak, and it came with Nick's special sauce on the side.

After the bacon came a steak-and-broccoli entrée. I laughed a bit as I realized this was the finest meal I had ever eaten with someone who had written a book titled *Quit Digging Your Grave with a Knife and Fork.* Huckabee knew he had one chance to take a new friend out for a memorable meal—and he did so with joy.

Just over one year later, on May 5, 2015, Huckabee came to his hometown of Hope, Arkansas, to announce his candidacy for the president of the United States. Local high school students joined with campaign supporters, national media, and mere curiosity seekers to fill every available seat on the main floor, in the balcony, and in an overflow room. Classic rock and country boomed from the sound system. Large screens positioned on stage read, "From Hope to Higher Ground" and "Mike Huckabee 2016."

When it was time to begin, a line of Boy Scouts marched in the side door and filed onto a runway platform, poled flags in hand. Lester Sitzes, the local Scout leader and best friend of Huckabee since they had played marbles together in first grade, directed the young men. They responded in tight formation just as they had been drilled and led the audience in the pledge:

> I pledge allegiance to the Flag of the United States of America, and to the Republic for which it stands, one Nation under God, indivisible, with liberty and justice for all.

The phrase "under God" is a late addition to the pledge, added in through an act of Congress in 1954—one year before Sitzes and Huckabee were born. As he signed the bill, President Eisenhower stated, "From this day forward, the millions of our schoolchildren will daily proclaim in every city and town, every village and rural schoolhouse, the dedication of our nation and our people to the Almighty."[1] Those additional two words signified to the world that American citizens, unlike their counterparts living under Soviet Communism and its official doctrine of atheism, did not pledge ultimate allegiance to the state. U.S. citizens do pledge allegiance to the state, but only as it exists "under God." Eisenhower's pastor said that without those two words, "it could be the pledge of any republic."[2]

Next on the program in Hope, a pair of teens came onstage to sing the national anthem. The girl, styled like Taylor Swift, smiled as if born without the ability to be nervous. The boy, equally gregarious, wore high tops and looked like an early-years Justin Bieber. You might have assumed that this duo, like the Scouts, were locals. But after singing only a few notes, their *American Idol* caliber of talent and confident stage presence let you know they had done this kind of thing before. And you also realized that they probably didn't come from Hope—at least, not both of them. Lightning doesn't strike twice in the same place, and small towns don't produce two people of such talent and execution.[3]

Then again, this *is* Hope, Arkansas.

Backstage, Huckabee reflected on his life's journey. At fourteen—the same age as these teens—Huckabee had gotten his own big break when he was hired as a DJ for the local radio station, where he fell in love with music, especially all the pop and rock songs of the era. Behind the microphone, he lost the last vestige of his childhood shyness and honed his gifts of humor and gab passed down from his parents. It was also at KXAR that Huckabee received mentoring from the station manager, one of the few Republicans in all of Hempstead County. More importantly, the manager was a Christian statesman who taught Huckabee the importance of serving one's community as a natural outworking of one's Christian faith.

Nearly five decades later, Huckabee was back in Hope to continue the vision his mentor had given to him. Still hidden from the eyes of the audience and cameras, he knew that by the end of the hour, he would once again officially be a candidate for the president of the United States of America.

He was jumping into this public arena along with a whole host of Republicans and Democrats. But out of all of them, only Huckabee and Democrat Hillary Clinton had also waged war for their parties' 2008 nominations. Obviously, neither had won that year. Huckabee needed more time and money in order to gain name recognition. You can't just shift from being unknown to ubiquitous overnight.

That was a joke. Of course you can—this is America.

In 2007, one week before Huckabee announced his first presidential campaign, a single mother in Canada uploaded to YouTube a poorly lit video of her twelve-year-old son singing "So Sick" in a local talent contest.[4] A music studio executive came across the video and signed the kid, who would soon become a household name: Justin Bieber.

The founders of the social media platforms that now facilitate people's rise to fame—YouTube, Facebook, Twitter, and the like—are mostly Gen Xers, contemporaries of Huckabee's three children (born in 1976, 1980, and 1982). But Huckabee and his wife, Janet, were born in 1955, the same year as Bill Gates and Steve Jobs—baby boomers who created the computer hardware and software infrastructure that make social media possible.

Given the speed of generational turnover in leadership, Mike Huckabee is either past his prime or ready for prime time—depending on which aspects of a person's biography serve as the best gauge for choosing a leader of the United States of America. Will one more member of the baby boomer generation be called on to lead the nation? Or will a Gen-X candidate be given the keys to the White House?

———

Every new generation of evangelical leaders wrestles with the question of how Christians should relate to government and political involvement. The pendulum swings back and forth—and sometimes swings too far. There has never been a consensus opinion on that issue, not even during the height of the Moral Majority and the Religious Right in the 1980s. Certainly, no consensus currently exists.

Christians talk about the "city of God" and the "city of man"—to employ language used by Luther, Augustine, Paul, and Jesus. Some evangelicals mix and jumble these cities in unhelpful ways. Other evangelicals split them apart, in equally unhelpful ways. However, on neither side of the debate do I find evangelicals holding an earthly empire state of mind. Christians believe that "we do not have an enduring city, but we are looking for the city that is to come" (Hebrews 13:14). Both sides know that Jesus taught, "My kingdom is not of this world" (John 18:36), *and* that God told His people, "Seek the welfare of the city where I have sent you into exile, and pray to the LORD on its behalf, for in its welfare you will find your welfare" (Jeremiah 29:7 NASB).

This biography does not attempt to resolve the issue. Nor does it look to change your political affiliations or cause you to vote for a candidate. The goal here is much more modest: I want to serve you well by telling the story of a man who desires to lead the United States. Huckabee says that he does what he does in order to leave the world in better condition than when he found it—like one of Lester Sitzes' Boy Scouts. Huckabee would rather be criticized and make mistakes along the way than to sit on the sidelines making commentary and cash but not making a difference. He wants to live like the "man in the arena" described by Theodore Roosevelt, one of Huckabee's favorite presidents:

> It is not the critic who counts; not the man who points out how the strong man stumbles, or where the doer of deeds could have done them better. The credit belongs to the man who is actually in the arena, whose face is marred by dust and sweat and blood; who strives valiantly; who errs, who comes short again and again, because there is no effort without error and shortcoming; but who does actually strive to do the deeds; who knows great enthusiasms, the great devotions; who spends himself in a worthy cause; who at the best knows in the end the triumph of high achievement, and who at the worst, if he fails, at least fails while daring greatly, so that his place shall never be with those cold and timid souls who neither know victory nor defeat.[5]

Any political party or world religion could form such a "man in the arena." Huckabee happens to be conservative and Republican—and, as he would say, "by the grace of God," he is Christian. But in addition to those credentials, Huckabee is a "what you see is what you get" kind of man. He says what he means and he means what he says. He is comfortable in his own skin, and he doesn't rely on manipulating people's perception of him. He is a sinner and a saint—he knows it, and he knows that you know it too. Because of Huckabee's transparency throughout our interview sessions, this biography was a joy to write. To the extent that I have captured his life on paper, I hope you find it a joy to read.

No matter your political persuasion, you've got to appreciate a man who gets fat-shamed by the media but still orders up a double slab of bacon for a new friend.

Is there an incognito New York Times *reporter nearby, observing my consumption of pork product?* That type of question doesn't seem to be of concern for Huckabee. He knows that game; he just refuses to play it. Once you begin down the path of being somebody you're not, nobody will know who you really are—including yourself.

"Who cares what the *New York Times* prints about me," he said to me on a later occasion. "I'm from Hope, Arkansas. New York's not my home."

PART 1

BACKSTORY, BIRTH, AND BOYHOOD

CHAPTER 1

LAND OF HOPE AND DREAMS

1830–1901

> What doth the LORD require of thee, but to do justly, and
> to love mercy, and to walk humbly with thy God?
>
> **—MICAH 6:8** KJV

RANDY SIMS RECALLS THE FIRST TIME HE MET HIS remarkable friend. As first-semester freshmen entering Ouachita Baptist University together, they enrolled in the same class, Introduction to Political Science. Legendary professor Jim Ranchino taught the course. Ranchino pioneered poll-driven political-demographic work throughout Arkansas, and, like just about every other person in the state of Arkansas, he was a Democrat.

"Ranchino was asking all these crazy questions, really challenging us—but nobody would say anything back," Sims recalled.

"That's when some guy in the back spoke up and said, 'You know, I don't agree with you at all.'" The room of eighteen-year-olds sat in silence, waiting for the professor to turn their classmate into a heap of academic ashes.

"This guy was the only one who had the nerve to do it. He started arguing back and forth with Ranchino. I thought, *Who is that guy? He's smart and knows how to speak clearly.*" Later that day, Sims met the guy—"Hi. I'm Mike Huckabee"—and discovered they were hall mates in the now-nonexistent dorm known as Daniel Hall, named after the Old Testament character. Sims thought, *This Huckabee guy is going to either be the next Billy Graham or he's going to be a politician. He is clearly headed somewhere.*[1]

In 1853, the State of Arkansas commissioned the Cairo and Fulton Railroad to build a line of track across the state from Missouri to Texas. Delayed by the Civil War and poor finances, it was not completed until the early 1870s. Missouri rail bosses had built a line from St. Louis downward through the state to reach the iron ore deposits in what was aptly named Iron Mountain. Jesse James robbed one of these trains in 1874 but refused to take items from men who had "working man's hands." He was after the Yankee money of bankers and businessmen. Revenge for the so-called War of Northern Aggression made good motivation for robbing trains.

That rail line coming out of St. Louis eventually extended all the way down to the Arkansas-Texas border. And for good reason. Connecting an entire state's worth of Southern neighbors to the excitement of St. Louis and Chicago made good business sense. In a time when horseback travel through some sections of Arkansas might take you a mere seven miles per day, the railroads advertised their line with this claim: "This is positively the only line that runs its entire trains from St. Louis to Texas without change."[2]

In addition to creating the quickest path from Missouri to Texas, the railroads planned their specific route through Arkansas due to the lay of the land. For the sake of simplicity, geologists divide Arkansas diagonally from the northeast corner all the way down to the southwest corner where Arkansas meets Texas, culminating in a town called Texarkana. North of the geological divide is called "highlands," and south of the divide they call "lowlands." When people envision Arkansas "hillbilly" culture and history, it is the mountainous Ozark region of the northwest to which they are referring. But when talking about Old South realities present within Arkansas culture—sharecropping, agriculture dependence, plantations, and Memphis blues—that refers to the lowlands of the Delta and Gulf Coastal Plains. Therefore, central Arkansas sits at the intersection of three cultural regions, as embodied by the cities one would travel to upon leaving Little Rock in opposite directions: St. Louis (Midwest), Memphis (Deep South), and Dallas

(Southwest). And heading northwest out of Arkansas would take you into "Indian Territory," now known to us as the state of Oklahoma. Arkansas was a crossroads and a land of untapped potential. The railroads were about to change that.

Texarkana came into existence as a railroad supply town. As the railroad companies in Texas and Arkansas each laid down their tracks, they joined up on the state line. Early city planners decided to obtain one hundred feet from the railroads—fifty feet from each company—to create the main street of the town that would straddle the state line. On the Arkansas side of the dealings, it was Joseph A. Longborough, an executive with the St. Louis and Iron Mountain Railroad, who granted them their fifty feet.[3]

Of course, Texarkana wasn't the only town springing into existence along the route of the new railroad lines. Thirty miles up from Texarkana, Longborough's team decided to build a train depot, a stopping point for people to board the trains that would soon be coming through. They built the train depot in 1874.[4] But people who waited for trains often needed food, lodging, and supplies. So businesses cropped up, the first ones being on land purchased from the railroad companies. Residential houses came after that, followed by churches, a school, and a post office. In a short amount of time, an entire town had sprung up around the original depot and rail lines. But no matter how humble its beginnings, every town needs a name. Mr. Longborough decided this particular train-depot town was worthy of being named after his daughter, Hope.

On January 16, 1901, Virgil Huckabee entered the world in Hempstead County, Arkansas. The Huckabees had called Hempstead County their home for a few generations, long before it even had the name. They trickled over from North Carolina and Georgia and settled in the region almost two hundred years ago. Just south of Hope, you'll find a cemetery with a fresh sign at the entrance: "Huckabee Cemetery, est. 1830." Keep in mind that Arkansas didn't become a state until 1836, so the Huckabee tribe can lay claim to deep roots in the region. Dozens of Mike Huckabee's relatives are buried here, though his own parents are buried in town. The cemetery sits adjacent to

Huckabee Road. If you've got enough Huckabees around to have a cemetery and a road named after you, then you must have a lot of kinfolk in that "neck of the woods," as they say.

Over the years, the local newspaper, the *Hope Star*, printed stories about "the recent biennial Huckabee family reunion." They would include the many names of the Huckabee adults in attendance, along with a description of the meat, side items, and desserts served. Local newspapers sell copies when local people know their name is in print, so these kinds of stories fill up the pages of small-town papers in the early twentieth century. Now, of course, there is Facebook.

The best that research can tell, it was Berryman William Huckabee—Mike's great-great-grandpa—who brought his family over to Arkansas from North Carolina. He was the father of eleven children. The third child, a son they named Lucius Elmore, came along in 1876. In 1898, Lucius married a local girl named Lula, who bore Lucius seven children, then died in 1944 at the age of sixty-six—not a short life span for the time. But though the average life span for a man born in the 1870s was forty-five,[5] Lucius lived to be almost ninety-four. That is to say, when Lucius died in 1970, not only had he outlived his wife by twenty-six years, but he also had lived more than twice as long as the average baby boy from the 1870s. In fact, he died only eight years ahead of his son Virgil. When friends of Mike Huckabee talk about his physical stamina, his work ethic, and the short amount of sleep he requires, they ask, "I wonder if that runs in his family." The longevity of his great-grandpa Lucius, along with many other Huckabees named on the gravestones at Huckabee Cemetery—with eighty- and ninety-year life spans—indicates as much.

As other Huckabees would also do, Virgil Huckabee chose a wife from the Betts family, marrying Ernie Jerome Betts in the early 1920s. The couple became parents to a son, Dorsey Wiles Huckabee—Mike's father—in 1923. Fifteen years later, in 1938, they gave Dorsey a sister, Alta Joyce. So after coming from a family of eleven children, Virgil fathered just two. That explains why, when asked about his relatives who remain in the area, Huckabee answers, "Distant cousins mostly . . . second and third cousins."[6]

William Thomas Elder, Huckabee's maternal grandfather, was born in 1868, three years after the assassination of President Lincoln. Huckabee did not know this grandfather, however, because he died in 1945 at age seventy-eight. The bare facts of William's adult life are fascinating enough to leave us wishing for more of the story. Here is what we do know: William served during the Spanish-American War. Then, in 1903, at the age of thirty-five, he married a local girl from his native Kentucky. Mary L. "Mollie" Murrell bore him two children in the first two years of their marriage and died at some point between 1910 and 1920.

Now a widower living in Arkansas with his two sons, William married a second wife, Eva Lorene Whitney. We're not sure exactly when they tied the knot, but we do know their first baby, Mae Elder—Mike Huckabee's mother—arrived in 1925. Eva, a native of Illinois, was born in 1904, the same year as William's oldest son from his late wife. William was fifty-seven and Eva was twenty-one when she gave birth to Mae. They would go on to have seven children altogether. This means that William spent his first thirty-five years as a bachelor, but then died forty-two years later as the father of nine.

Though Mike never met his maternal grandfather, he wrote about him based on his mother's description:

> She didn't talk about him much, and when she did, it was not with affection, but rather with a level of contempt that probably hid a lot of stuff I didn't need to know. She did tell me that he was an alcoholic and that he could often be harsh, even abusive. But in general, my mother buried her memories of her father deep within her soul and never, to my knowledge, talked about them to anyone.[7]

Huckabee also wrote about the two sons William sired by his first wife, the boys old enough to be a father to Huckabee's mother. One of those brothers, "Uncle Garvin," became a significant presence in the Huckabee household. Huckabee describes him as "the closest thing to an actual father figure she (Mae) had."[8] Though Garvin spent his adult life as a bachelor in Houston, Texas, he died of cancer in the Huckabees' home and is buried in the Huckabee cemetery.

After William's death in 1945, Eva eventually remarried, to a "Mr. Garner," and lived until 1989. In August 1973, as Mike Huckabee left for college, the *Hope Star* highlighted Eva, then sixty-nine, in its Celebrity Corner column. It says a lot about her, but also about the family and the times in which Mike Huckabee came of age. Here is an excerpt:

> Eva Lorene Elder Garner . . . known as "Miz Elder" or "Miz Garner" to so many friends, is better known to her 15 grandchildren as "Go-Go", not a frivolous term, but one derived by being a person constantly on the go, whether she feels like it or not.
>
> Go, go, go has been her lot in life, not from choice actually, but something she has accepted without grumbling and with grace. Walking and the ability to walk has been a mainstay in this spunky lady's life, she has never driven an automobile. The scripture, Micah 6:8—". . . and what doth the Lord require of thee, but to do justly, and to love mercy, and to walk humbly with thy God?" could best depict her long, busy, useful life.[9]

Suffice it to say, Eva was a strong woman who gave her children and grandchildren an example to live by. And her "go, go, go" manner of life foreshadowed an oft-used description of her famous grandson, Mike Huckabee—always on the go.

———

An individual cannot take credit for the moral strength and stability of the family into which he was born. But he can only be grateful for what he has received.

All six direct ancestors of Mike Huckabee written about in this chapter are buried in Hempstead County, Arkansas. However much the world changed during the last 150 years, the Huckabees from which Mike Huckabee descended gave him the inheritance of family stability. His grandparents remained married for more than fifty years, supporting their family with everyday work in an obscure little town in order to give their children's children a sturdy foundation for the future.

Geography and economic realities have a strong influence on our lives. Had the trains not cut through the Arkansas landscape in the 1870s, life would have gone on for the Huckabees. Life, liberty, and the pursuit of happiness were theirs even without trains. But the fact that the trains did, in fact, come to Arkansas, and that geographical terrain guided the railroad executives to lay down track just north of where the Huckabee tribes had *already* established their roots forty years earlier—this all seems providential.

To be sure, the first generation of Huckabees felt the influence of the trains chiefly because of the new flow of products, in and out, that the trains provided. But then, over the next hundred years, the machines of modernity took the residents of Hope places they would never have gone otherwise. Because of the trains—and later on, the interstate system that followed the same path—the sons and daughters of Hope gained access to a world that may have eluded them if they had been born elsewhere, like up in the Ozark Mountains, where transport did not come easily.

But along with the positive advances of modernity also came the scourge of efficient evil. Leaders who desired to inflict either joy or sorrow upon the world could now do so with greater speed and in greater quantity. By 1940, the dominant nations of the world took advantage of the major leaps in technological advancement, creating war machines unimaginable at the time of the birth of William Elder (1868) or Lucius Huckabee (1876). The nineteenth-century doctrine of Charles Darwin's "survival of the fittest" began bearing its fruit in the 1930s, as evil men like Adolf Hitler sought to ensure their own nations would be the fittest and survive. People deemed as "unworthy of life" were simply eliminated. The same train lines in Europe that had brought families together in previous years now stripped them apart, as millions were sent by rail line to concentration camps in far reaches of land under a tyrant's control. The world marched into another global war.

Meanwhile, half a world away in Hope, Arkansas, two generations of Mike Huckabee's forefathers picked up the Saturday, June 7, 1941, *Hope Star* and saw in massive font at the top of the front page: "HOPE OBTAINS BIG WAR-PLANT." The effects of Hitler's killing machine were headed for Hope. Nothing would ever be the same again.[10]

CHAPTER 2

SMALL TOWN

c. 1920–1955

> The bride was becomingly attired in a two piece suit of chocolate
> brown covert with winter white and green accessories.
>
> —*HOPE STAR* DESCRIPTION OF MAE HUCKABEE, NOVEMBER 3, 1948

JUST MONTHS BEFORE THE BOMBING OF PEARL HARBOR,
the War Department sent eviction notices to four hundred families near
Hope, Arkansas. The government had chosen six locations in Arkansas as
sites for the building of ordnance plants, and residents of the acquired lands
were given a one-month notice to vacate.[1] With war on the way, time was of
the essence. The construction of the ammunition testing facility began with
a fury of manpower and funding: 40,000 to 50,000 acres seized, $15 million
(1941 dollars), 4,000 to 5,000 temporary construction jobs, and 500 permanent
jobs until the end of the war.[2] The installation was called the Southwestern
Proving Grounds, or SPG for short.

When first constructed, the runways of the SPG airport were the third
largest in the nation. The War Department had needed them on that scale
so that the large bombers could take off on trial bombing raids over the
Gulf of Mexico.[3] After the war the city of Hope obtained the airport, and
it continues to be used as a municipal airport to this day. Undoubtedly,

Hope's immense runways are the envy of every other town of ten thousand people. Although the testing of ammunition ceased with the end of the war, the economic and cultural impact of the SPG would continue for a generation.

Nonnatives of Hope who worked at SPG also stamped a lasting fingerprint on the town by bringing their experience and education to the city. For example, engineer Paul Klipsch served as a lieutenant colonel at SPG. People took note of his tinkering around with designs for a brilliant new form of loudspeaker, a "corner horn speaker design." He obtained a patent for the design in 1945 and began manufacturing the world-renowned speakers right there in Hope. Though endless changes have occurred in every area of audio technology since then, the company is proud to note that "the Klipschorn is the only speaker in the world that has been in continuous production, relatively unchanged, for over 65 years."[4] Klipsch died in 2002 at the age of ninety-eight, but not before publishing a new article in the *Journal of the Audio Engineering Society*—he kept influencing the industry right up to the end. "Paul was a verifiable genius who could have chosen any number of vocations," said his cousin, a chairman of the company. "But the world sounds a lot better because he chose audio."[5]

Everyone comes from somewhere, and Mike Huckabee's somewhere was Hope, the same childhood home of former president Bill Clinton. Although his family later moved north to Hot Springs, Arkansas, Clinton lived in Hope until he was eight. The Huckabees knew Clinton's grandparents, but they did not know much, if anything, about Bill until he first ran for Congress in 1974. His name had been in the *Hope Star* a few times, but nothing stood out as memorable to place him as being from Hope. Huckabee noted that it wasn't until Clinton's rise to national prominence that he started to link himself to the town. "Of course, it sounds better," Huckabee said. "You know, 'I believe in a place called Hope,' and Hope certainly embraced him."[6] If Mike Huckabee had been born first, ahead of Clinton, he could have used the line for his own campaigns. Huckabee did title his 2007 pre-campaign book *From Hope to Higher Ground*, showing that even if you're the second man to run for president from the same small town of ten thousand, a bit of creativity will allow you to tap into your small-town roots.

In 2014, when asked whether or not she thought her son Jeb should run for president, former first lady Barbara Bush said, "If we can't find more than two or three families to run for higher office, that's silly."[7] Though she later reversed herself on the issue, she had made a good point. With 100 million families in the United States, it seems strange to keep pulling from the same tribe. Of course, the same thing could be said for a little town in the southwest corner of Arkansas. If the November 2016 presidential ballot reads "Clinton" and "Huckabee," then three out of four (including spouses) of the people campaigning to move into the White House spent their childhood years in Hope, Arkansas.

And Clinton and Huckabee are not alone as prominent officials originating from Hope. Two other men connected with Clinton's administration also originated from Hope: Vince Foster served as deputy counsel to the White House, and Mack McLarty served as Clinton's chief of staff. One might argue that these men were made by Clinton, but not so. They had their own successes and career attainments before Clinton called on them for duty in Washington. Also included in the list of Hope natives is Kelly Bryant, who served as the Arkansas secretary of state from 1963 to 1975. And Melinda Dillon, the actress who played the mother in the Christmas cult classic *A Christmas Story*, came from Hope. Also, two famous singers, Patsy Montana and Ketty Lester, both originated from Hope.

One more Hope-born politician worth mentioning is Mike Ross, a Democratic member of the U.S. House of Representatives for the Arkansas Fourth District from 2001 to 2013. In 2014, Ross ran for governor of Arkansas and held a political rally in his hometown during the lead-up to the election. He called in the big guns for help. Bill Clinton arrived in Hope, marking his first campaign visit to the town since 1999, when he still resided in the White House.

Clinton rallied the Hempstead County citizens to turn out and vote Ross into the governor's mansion. If Ross had won, then Hope would have seen a third native son elected governor in a span of thirty-five years. Of course, out of all the politicians from Hope mentioned in this chapter, Huckabee stands as the lone Republican among the bunch. Huckabee came to Arkansas and campaigned for Asa Hutchinson, the Republican candidate for governor. Hutchinson defeated Ross by a spread of thirteen points, and Ross even lost his native Hempstead County by a squeaker (2,637 to 2,603).[8]

―――――

"A Slice of the Good Life" has served as a motto for Hope for about as long as anyone can remember. Which is to say, it seems somebody thought it up in the 1980s. The digitized newspaper archives of the *Hope Star* (1930–1977) never once used the phrase. But one word the old newspapers did print a lot— more than five thousand times in that same time span—was *watermelon*.[9] Big watermelons—record-setting watermelons—are one of the hallmarks of Hope. Hence, the town motto.

To get close to the record books, you need to raise a melon of at least two hundred pounds, and folks in southwest Arkansas have been perfecting the art for a century. The town inaugurated an annual watermelon festival in 1926, complete with a parade, a "Watermelon Festival Queen," truckfuls of the melons on hand to eat, and yes, a "biggest watermelon" contest.[10] The watermelon festival continues to the present day. So if anyone asks, "Which came first, the melon festival or the motto?" now you know.

A January 1930 issue of the *Hope Star* explained the widespread popularity Hope's melons had achieved the previous year: "Hempstead county, in particular, gained national fame through the gigantic proportions reached by its watermelons. Many carloads of these were shipped to points ranging from coast to coast."[11] An op-ed that same week urged the farmers to band together and solidify the branding of the county's watermelons. Here's how this master of melon marketing explained "branding" to his fellow citizens: "The value of a brand is simply this. It establishes a staple as a luxury product. Sometimes there is greater excellence in the product itself. More often it is simply a good product, well advertised, and wrapped up in a standardized package."[12]

―――――

As was true throughout much of the rural South during the 1920s and 1930s, neither Prohibition nor the Great Depression had a profound effect on everyday life. Hempstead County had shut down liquor in 1854, closing saloons and outlawing stills. It is hard to pinpoint whether the law kept the county dry from 1854 through Prohibition, but the issue certainly never went away during that time. The passage of the Volstead Act (1919) did not fundamentally change the dynamic between law and liquor in Hempstead County, nor did its repeal (1933). If anything, Volstead simply made the knowledge of how to make moonshine more widespread, as people got into the business of it as a means of earning money

The "dry county" debate is best illustrated in a 1935 op-ed piece written by an older resident of Hope: "I have been in Hempstead County over 60 years, and there has been whiskey here since I have. . . . I never saw the time when whiskey was not sold in Hope. . . . When the Eighteenth Amendment was passed there was not one man out of fifty, that knew how to make whiskey, or had seen any made. Today, 95 out of 100 know how it is made, or have seen it made."[13]

Even today, thirty-five of seventy-five Arkansas counties are dry, though cities within a county may opt for allowing alcohol sales. On the other hand, Huckabee has never even tasted beer. He claims his teetotalism isn't merely a moral high ground but is due to being repelled by the smell. Within the Bible Belt of Huckabee's youth, however, total abstinence from alcohol cannot be separated from Protestant piety. Only in the past few years have a slight minority of younger Baptist ministers and churches opened to the acceptance of drinking alcohol in moderation. But that position would have been completely out of bounds for a young pastor-in-training in the 1970s, or even for a layperson in the pew. Of course, many "good Baptists" tipped the bottle in private. Hence, the old saw: "Lutherans drink on the front porch. Baptists drink on the back."

The Great Depression did not affect Hope, Arkansas, in the same way as it did urban cities and industrial centers. As many people who grew up in the rural South have said, "We were so poor we didn't notice any Great Depression." Two other factors come into play as well. First, rural areas would be hit less by food shortages because they were already accustomed to growing so much of their food close by—or in their own yards. Eva Huckabee, Mike's grandmother, was known for having canned eight hundred jars of vegetables in one season.

Second, in response to the economic depression, the federal government poured money into public works projects. Hope benefited from one such project when the Public Works Administration (PWA) helped fund the construction of the two-hundred-thousand-dollar, five-story county courthouse.[14] The art deco–styled architecture made a big splash among residents upon its opening celebration the last week of November 1939. Later, this courthouse served as the place of employment for the mother of Janet McCain—better known now as the wife of Mike Huckabee. When Mike and Janet married, it was the county clerk who issued the marriage license. Janet's mother held that position during Janet's teen years. Small world. Small town.

The PWA also helped fund the 1939 construction of Hope's fire station. The newspaper account states: "One of the most modern fire station buildings in Arkansas is that of the City of Hope's new building at Second and Laurel streets, completed this past summer and now being occupied."[15] The building, costing $26,681 to construct, would factor into Mike Huckabee's life. His father worked from this location—just blocks away from the Huckabee home—and young Huckabee could walk over and see him most any time.[16]

If some aspects of the small-town picture being painted sound reminiscent of *The Andy Griffith Show*, it's because they are. When the show debuted in October 1960, child actor Ron Howard (Opie) was six years old and Mike Huckabee was five. Picture Opie running in to see "Pa" and Barney in the sheriff's office, and then imagine Huckabee running around the corner to see his father at the firehouse. Or picture the various episodes where Sheriff Andy and Deputy Fife break up a moonshine still. In fact, photos exist showing Hempstead County sheriffs doing the same thing, and they could easily pass for characters from the television show.[17]

Dorsey and Mae (Mike's parents) came of age during the Great Depression, and their economic worldviews were forever affected. They avoided debt and prided themselves on paying their own way through hard work and thrift. Mae was the first of seven children, so there were more mouths to feed at her table—*and* her father died when she was in her twenties. They were poor, but never destitute or in poverty.

Being frugal in areas where they could, families could save a few dollars here and there for extras. In April 1936, the *Hope Star* ran a full-page advertisement on behalf of *The Modern Encyclopedia*, a one-volume source of self-knowledge that could be bought for $1.25. The paper also ran a grocer's advertisement: roast beef for twelve cents per pound (making the encyclopedia worth ten pounds of roast beef) and sausage for ten cents per pound—those were the days.[18] The encyclopedia ad displayed a list containing the names of Hope's citizens who had purchased the volume. Virgil Huckabee is on the list, having bought the volume for thirteen-year-old Dorsey.

Six months later, the paper published a "Coming and Going" news item, stating, "Mr. and Mrs. Virgil Huckabee and son Dorsey and Mr. and Mrs. Irvin Huckabee have returned from the Texas Centennial at Dallas and Fort Worth."[19] The Coming and Going section would list travelers to and from Hope. These news items would be called in by the family or friends, presuming that their fellow citizens wanted to know such information. In reading these submissions today, one catches small glimpses into the life of the Huckabee family, revealing a modest lifestyle, yet one that still made it possible to take a road trip for a grand event. Two years later, in 1938, fifteen-year-old Dorsey helped his parents welcome home his only sibling, a sister named Alta Joyce, or "Aunt Joyce," as young Mike Huckabee would come to know her.

With the onset of World War II, Hope's citizens focused their efforts on securing victory for the nation and her allies. In 1941, the town raised $4,035 for the Red Cross, a record amount for Hope, and the paper lists Virgil Huckabee as a contributor to the cause.[20]

———

Dorsey Huckabee attended high school alongside Virginia Cassidy, the mother of Bill Clinton. Her name appears in the paper on a regular basis throughout the 1930s, as she earned honors in school or performed and worked in school plays. During Memorial Day weekend in 1941, she and seven friends in swimsuits made the front page of the paper. The headline above their large photograph read: "Summer Weather Brings Out the Bathers at Hope's Pines Pool on Opening Week of the Swim Season."[21] Five years later, the September 28, 1946, paper printed this birth announcement: "Births: William and Virginia Blythe, Hope, boy, William."[22] William, the father, had died in a car accident the previous May, even as he and Virginia were in the process of setting up a home in Hope.

In 1943, Dorsey was called on to report for induction into the military but did not make it past the physical: flat feet.[23] So, he did the next best thing and went down to Houston with his father, Virgil, and uncle Irvin to work in the shipyards. Uncle Irvin had been a fireman with the Hope fire department until 1941, and this may have been what led Dorsey into firefighting as a career. At some point, probably in 1953, Dorsey began working for the Hope fire department, though not yet on a full-time basis. In January 1954, the town council decided they needed another "regular" fireman, and Dorsey got the job. This promotion took place in between the births of Mike Huckabee and his older sister, Pat.

"Like a plate of spaghetti" is how current residents of Hope describe the fact that "everybody knew everybody" in the town. To trace anecdotes of the friends and family of Bill Clinton is to bump continually into the friends and family of Mike Huckabee.

One such "plate of spaghetti" comes by way of the November 8, 1948, Social and Personal section of the *Hope Star,* with a news item about a birthday party for a trio of two-year-olds, held at the First Methodist Church. Fifteen children are mentioned by name, including the Weisenberg children, Billy Blythe, and Phil McLarty. You are already familiar with the Blythe and McLarty names, but the "Mrs. Weisenberg" was the wife of Judge Royce Weisenberg, whose sister was married to Irvin Huckabee, Virgil's brother. Virgil was the father of Dorsey, who was the father of Mike Huckabee. Confused? In summary, a toddler Bill Clinton attended a birthday party hosted by the wife of the brother of Mike Huckabee's aunt. That's what people in Hope mean when they say that everybody is either related or best friends.

And just one week prior to this party, the Weisenbergs got all dressed up for a different occasion, also at a church. This time it was for the wedding ceremony of Dorsey and Mae:

Miss Mae Elder, daughter of Mrs. L. R. Garner and the late W. T. Elder, became the bride of Dorsey W. Huckabee, son of Mr. and Mrs. Virgil Huckabee, Saturday evening [October 30] at six o'clock in the Hope Gospel Tabernacle. . . . The bride was becomingly attired in a two piece suit of chocolate brown covert with winter white and green accessories. . . . Dale Hockett of this city was best man.[24]

So members of the Weisenberg family attended the wedding of Mike Huckabee's parents one weekend, then attended a birthday party for toddlers the next weekend, with Bill (Clinton) Blythe in attendance.

And the best man for Dorsey, Dale Hockett, not only stood alongside his friend that day, but he also later contributed the middle name to Dorsey's firstborn son: Michael Dale Huckabee.[25]

———

Everyone comes from somewhere. Whether or not they remain there for all their life, the "there" remains in them—a fixed point of biography, referring back to something that made and marks them. None of the living "famous people from Hope" mentioned in this chapter actually live in Hope now. Most, if not all of them, left Hope as soon as they became adults. The town gave each of them something important they needed, something that contributed to their success in life, but it couldn't hold them there.

CHAPTER 3

ONE DAY IN 1955

August 24, 1955

> None of us got to choose how we came into this
> world. We can't choose our parents, our hometown,
> or the physician who ushers us into this life.[1]

> —MIKE HUCKABEE

MICHAEL DALE HUCKABEE WAS BORN ON WEDNESDAY, August 24, 1955, at Julia Chester Hospital, the same hospital where Bill Clinton was born. The doctor who delivered Huckabee, Dr. George Wright, is the same doctor local residents of Hope suspect was the biological father of Bill Clinton. An entire chapter of the book *In Search of Bill Clinton* documents a factual case for this claim.[2] If true, it stands as one of the most fascinating overlaps between the lives of Huckabee and Clinton.

Had Huckabee waited just one more month to be born, he could have enjoyed the splendor of the brand-new Hempstead County Memorial Hospital, which opened just weeks after his birth. He may even have been held or kissed by then governor Orval Faubus, who came to Hope to dedicate the hospital upon its opening. As it was, Huckabee became the agent of change for health care in Hope, seeing how he was one of the last babies born in the old digs. The town converted the old hospital into a nursing home, and then eventually tore it down. A funeral home now sits on the site. Which is to say, people in Hope old enough to have been born in Chester might have the distinction of having their births and deaths commemorated on the exact same patch of ground.

Governor Faubus had just been elected to his first term of office that year, and he would go on to serve the state for twelve years. As Huckabee turned two, Faubus earned himself a place on the front cover of the September 1957 issue of *Time* magazine because of his defiance of court-ordered desegregation.[3] Three weeks earlier, Faubus had ordered units of the Arkansas National Guard into Little Rock to "maintain or restore order and protect the lives and property of the citizens."[4] Nine black students were to begin classes at the previously all-white Central High School in Little Rock, but segregationists determined to prevent this from happening. Faubus, acting on both racist and political impulses, argued that it wouldn't be possible to maintain law and order if forced integration were to take place. Therefore, he said, "the schools in Pulaski County, for the time being, must be operated on the same basis as they have been operated in the past."[5]

President Eisenhower devised a different strategy. On September 24, he ordered the 101st Airborne Division of the U.S. Army into Little Rock, and he federalized the Arkansas National Guard. The ten thousand members of the Guard would report to the president, not the governor. Faubus responded by shutting down Little Rock's high schools for the 1958–1959 school year.

———

Historians debate the meaning of the 1950s. Some describe the decade as a peaceful time of building highways, jobs, and families. Others paint a less rosy picture, describing the decade as ten years spent ignoring urgent social problems for the benefit of keeping the economic wheels turning. In 1975, Ronald Reagan commented on what he considered to be the strengths of Eisenhower's administration—and the 1950s in general. Challenging the prevailing view of Eisenhower, Reagan wrote:

> [Consider] the "Eisenhower years"—the era of the '50s when we are supposed to believe an entire college generation stagnated,—probably because they didn't burn down the library. Well, Ike ended a war in Korea that

had killed tens of thousands of our young men and for the rest of his eight years, no young Americans were being shot at anywhere in the world. He also halted dead in its tracks the advance of communism. Big government didn't get any bigger and a citizen could go for an evening stroll in the park without getting bopped over the head. Wages went up steadily but prices remained the same. Steak was 85 cents a lb. and a gallon of gas was only 28 cents. You could be well dressed in a $50 suit and $9 shoes. The work day & the work week grew shorter and our taxes were reduced. Suddenly more kids were going to college, more families were buying homes, never had a nation's wealth been so widely distributed and we were so strong that no one in the world even thought about challenging us.[6]

In closing, Reagan could not have been more clear about how the nation could find an "old path" on which to walk out of the moral morass of the late 1960s and first half of the 1970s: "Well as I say you can make up your own mind about the images versus the man but maybe we ought to go back and see what they did that we aren't doing."[7]

So what *did* the 1950s mean? For Mike Huckabee's parents and grand-parents, the 1950s represented stability, tranquility, and routine. By 1955, Mrs. Virgil Huckabee (Mike's grandmother Ernie Jo) began showing up in the newspaper on a monthly basis, thanks to her participation and leader-ship in various ladies groups: "The WMS [Women's Missionary Society] of Garrett Memorial met in the home of Mrs. Virgil Huckabee."[8] For Ernie Jo, who would be a major presence in Mike's life, weekly routines revolved around domestic responsibilities and church activities at Garrett Memorial Baptist Church. Now in her fifties, she had a teenage daughter, a son (Dorsey) and new daughter-in-law (Mae) approaching thirty, and a toddler grand-daughter (Pat). Soon, Mike would join the family. Life was good.

The fireman's pay was not Dorsey's only income, as he also worked on automobiles in his off hours. Mike remembers the family finances being modest but workable for a frugal family, and he learned from his parents to pay cash and avoid debt.[9]

An essential part of making ends meet meant practicing good home economics, skills handed down to both Dorsey and Mae. And since one could never stop learning new skills—or passing them down to younger women—the "Melrose Home Demonstration Club" became a regular event on Ernie Jo's calendar. On Valentine's Day 1955, the "HDC," as these clubs were known throughout the state, met for their monthly meeting. You don't have to wonder about the highlights of the meeting; they were promptly printed in the *Hope Star*. For example, "Mrs. C. J. Barnes gave an interesting demonstration on trends in furniture arrangements." And, "Trends in window treatment will be the demonstration given at the March meeting." One other Huckabee-historic point of business that month: "The club welcomed Mrs. Virgil Huckabee as a new member."[10] Then, in June, Ernie Jo hosted the club's meeting in her own home, as the ladies discussed "How to make a collar."[11] Over the next thirty years, the newspaper recorded the monthly involvement of "Mrs. Virgil Huckabee" in such meetings. The reported discussions maintained their domestic focus throughout the decades, and Ernie Jo enjoyed such pursuits.

And why shouldn't she? Sure, when Betty Friedan polled her former female Smith College classmates in 1957, she discovered many of them were unhappy with the limitations of domestic life. Friedan took her interviews and wrote *The Feminine Mystique* in 1963, ushering in second-wave feminism. The feminist trees of the 1960s were planted as seeds in the 1950s, but Smith College in Massachusetts is a long way removed from Hope, Arkansas.

Friedan's nascent critique of women's roles would shape the conversation about gender for the entire baby boomer generation, continuing today in the endless "How to Juggle Career and Home" magazine articles, or in words like, "I suppose I could have stayed home and baked cookies and had teas," stated by Hillary Clinton during Bill's 1992 campaign. "But what I decided to do was to fulfill my profession which I entered before my husband was in public life."[12]

Friedan, four years older than Mae Huckabee, enjoyed the intellectual open doors she had been given, knowing that most women, past and present, did not have such opportunities. Mae had longed to go to college, but the large family of younger siblings demanded a different course of life: work. But the people who knew her, as well as the record of her advancement in the workforce, testify to her strong intellect and giftings. It is fascinating to consider how, though Huckabee's grandmother filled a traditional domestic role, his mother was stuck rather in the middle. She was neither a traditional stay-at-home mother nor a college-educated professional. And Janet Huckabee's mother also missed out on the "Leave It to Beaver" experience of motherhood, having been abandoned by her husband to raise five children on her own. It would seem that Mike Huckabee has a unique background for bringing an empathetic eye to the economic and educational realities that face everyday women in America.

Compared to Elvis Presley, the name of rock-and-roll pioneer Carl Perkins would be less familiar to people today. But near the time of Huckabee's birth, Perkins was a star of the new rock-and-roll sound. In 1956, he sold a million copies of a song he wrote called "Blue Suede Shoes." Perkins found inspiration for the song one night at a gig when he looked down at a guy who should have been happy dancing with his beautiful date, except that he couldn't stop worrying about the gal stepping on his . . . blue suede shoes.

Perkins's "rockabilly" spanned the genres of country and the emerging rock and roll. The rockabilly style can be heard in the early recordings of Bill Haley, Elvis Presley, Johnny Cash, and Jerry Lee Lewis. Cash was raised in the Arkansas Delta, west of Memphis. Presley came from Tupelo, Mississippi, two hours from Memphis. Perkins resided in Jackson, Tennessee—halfway between Memphis and Nashville. All of these men would testify to the importance of their having grown up within earshot of the music of the African-American community, coming from the workers in the fields or from the congregants in the pews of segregated churches. That is to say, early rock and roll came about through the cross-racial mixing of blues, jazz, country, western, and gospel. And all of this happened just a few hours' drive from where Huckabee was born.

Another such gifted musician with Memphis-area roots was B. B. King, an African-American blues player who strummed a guitar he called "Lucille." God put B. B. King on this earth within the state of Mississippi— Leflore County, Mississippi, to be precise, south of Memphis. King was born in a tiny town with a funny name: Itta Bena. And just twenty miles to the north—but still in Leflore County—sat another little town with a funny name: Money.

On the very day that Mike Huckabee was born—August 24, 1955—Emmett Till, an African-American teen from Chicago, walked into a store in Money, Mississippi. His visit set off a chain of events that led both to his murder and to the expedited passage of the Civil Rights Acts by the United States Congress.

Till was visiting his cousins from Chicago, and together they headed to the store for some gum. What exactly happened next has been debated for sixty years, but the basic story goes like this. Till allegedly flirted with the cashier, a married Caucasian woman, before leaving the store and wolf-whistling at her. Two days later, the woman's husband came home and heard the story. He and another man rode over to where Till was staying, kidnapped the teen, and brutally killed him.

The men were arrested, tried, and acquitted. Newspapers throughout the nation ran the ongoing story, and regional bias determined the vocabulary of the headlines. California's *San Bernardino County Sun* stated the facts: "Body of Kidnapped Boy Found in River." But the Blytheville, Arkansas, *Courier News* printed: "Mississippi's 'Wolf-Whistle' Murder Trial Opens Today."[13] Too often, the Southern headlines were shorthand for: "The boy deserved what he got." The next year, one of the men bragged to *Look* magazine that they had, in fact, killed the teen.

Therein lies the struggle with wearing Mayberry-tinted glasses. Sheriff Taylor's fictional town aired for eight years (1960–1968), but it only gave speaking lines to one African-American during that entire span of time. There were a few other blacks in the background on occasion, but you have to look closely for them. Even if you argue that, in real life, some towns just didn't have any blacks living in them at all, does that justify the abdication of leadership for a popular national television program? In like manner, the *Hope Star* essentially ignored the Emmett Till story. Nevertheless, Jim Crow's days were numbered, hastened along by the national scandal of tragedies like Till's murder.

In August 1961, six years after the birth of Mike Huckabee and the murder of Emmett Till, Barack Obama was born. Forty-seven years later, he became the first African-American president of the United States. The Chicago residence of President Obama sits just two miles from the house where Emmett Till lived at the time of his death and the church where his body lay in state.[14]

Before Till's murder, the last major civil rights legislation passed into law came in 1875. But in the thirteen years following Till's death, five new, major civil rights acts became law. More important, they became enforceable by cultural pressure. To even consider the possibility of an African-American president in the United States, so very much had to change. In at least one Chicago home, that change came at the cost of deep, maternal sorrow. Mamie Till Bradley, Emmett's mother, insisted that her son's mangled body be laid in an open casket, with nothing but plate glass to separate eyes from viewing Jim Crow's carnage. Thousands of Chicagoans streamed through the Roberts Temple Church of God to mourn. They left with an energetic resolve to change their nation.

As America reflected on Till's murder, many began to form a fresh opinion about the entire nation's culpability in the crimes perpetrated mostly in one region. "All of us, even the most righteous, had a part in Emmett Till's death," wrote columnist Robert Smith in a small-town newspaper in western Massachusetts. "We endorse it every time we exchange shocked whispers when a colored girl and a white boy sit in church together, every time we openly despair that the presence of Negroes 'lowers property values,' whenever we preach that in educating the young people of the land, segregation is a 'secondary' matter, every time we connive to bar colored people from public inns and restaurants, anytime we try to wriggle out of hiring a colored person for a job he is obviously titled to do."[15]

———

Because nobody gets to determine the cultural context into which he or she is born, each person's active response to existing evil and injustice becomes the moral measure of who he or she really is as a person. When Mike Huckabee entered the world as a son of the South, his culture gave him a permission slip granting him the right to view African-Americans as being less worthy of human dignity and his respect. But he chose not to use his permission slip—or even to accept the reality of the permission slip. In the national march toward racial equality, Mike Huckabee walked ahead of even his own cultural inheritance.

CHAPTER 4

AMERICAN PIE

1959–1964

> We didn't lack. I didn't know I was poor until I got in high school.
> I mean, it never occurred to me that we were underprivileged.
>
> —MIKE HUCKABEE

IN AUGUST 1960, A YOUNG MIKE HUCKABEE ENTERED
"Miss Mary Purkins' School for Little Folks." Because public schools did not
yet offer kindergarten, families with working mothers had to look for such
alternatives. Purkins, a veteran teacher of said "little folks," had also taught
Bill Blythe (Clinton), making her one of the few people in American history
to have taught two presidential candidates as children. Miss Purkins understood the daily rhythms that made for happy five-year-olds. The *Hope Star*
published a photograph of Huckabee with his classmates. A similar photograph exists for Clinton.[1] In both pictures, these two future governors of
Arkansas posed with cherubic smiles, tempting us to imagine they were
already planning their campaigns. Huckabee describes his early childhood as
a time when he struggled with shyness. "I was a good kid, but shy," he said.[2]

Mae Huckabee took Mike and his older sister, Pat, to church and Sunday
school regularly, as all good folks in the Bible Belt knew to do. He admits
that the religion of his home was "nominal." To be sure, a *quantity* of religion existed for young Huckabee, in the form of the Garrett Memorial

Baptist Church. Huckabee would also attend additional religious meetings in the home, as both his mother and his grandmother hosted Bible studies and mission-support meetings. By necessity, Mike and Pat were often present at such meetings. The *Hope Star* recorded: "Mrs. Dorsey Huckabee was hostess to the Dorcas Sunday School Class of the Garrett Memorial Baptist Church. Mrs. Virgil Huckabee gave a most inspiring devotional on tithing." An inspiring devotional on tithing? For eight-year-old Mike, the highlight of the evening was probably this: "a delicious snack plate and punch was served."[3]

With all that religion being practiced by the women of the family, what role did the men play? The answer is that Dorsey Huckabee did not attend church at all. "Our dad never went," Mike's sister, Pat, recalled, "He always thought it was the woman's place to take the kids to church. I just thought that was the way things were. I guess there were families where both the mommy and daddy went and took the kids . . . but ours did not."[4]

Let that sink in. Mike Huckabee, arguably one of the best-known evangelicals in the world, grew up in a home led by a father who did not practice the Christian faith. Though Dorsey passed along a rich inheritance of general Judeo-Christian values, he was not a professing Christian during Mike's formative years. In fact, it wasn't until after Mike had started into ministry in his mid-teens that his father started to attend church regularly. Pat adds some detail to Dorsey's conversion: "My dad was never a bad man. He was a good man—excellent work ethic. He was the guy in the neighborhood that was always changing lightbulbs and fixing fences for no money—lots of elderly people lived in the neighborhood. 'Call Dorsey Huckabee; he'll come and help'—he was *that* guy. But about the time Mike was called to the ministry, our dad gave his life to the Lord and went and got baptized. After that, he didn't miss a day. So the last part of our growing-up years was pretty wonderful because our whole family was there at church. But that was when Mike was about sixteen."[5]

What Mike's father *did* pass down to him was family stability paid for through hard work and personal sacrifice. He desired to see Mike succeed and find all the happiness America offered to those who would strive for it. He considers himself to have grown up privileged, not poor: "Privilege is not about money. Privilege is about being loved. It's about having two parents who would sacrifice their very lives to give my sister and me all the things that they didn't have."[6]

Neither Huckabee nor Clinton grew up with wealth, but the stability of the Huckabee family stands in sharp contrast to the home life the former president experienced. "Even though we were born in the same town, we grew up in very different environments," Huckabee said. "The president has told the story of how he grew up with an abusive, alcoholic stepfather. I was fortunate to grow up without that sort of family tension."[7]

Huckabee comes by his "common folk" populist routine honestly—it's not a pretense. And yet, his family was at least stable and respectable. Their low economic status wasn't foisted on them because of drink, gambling, bad debts, profligacy, or divorce. Even so, when you don't earn much to begin with, when you're generous with what you do have, and when you invest so much in your children's futures, then there's not much left over in the bank. "I consider myself a conservative Republican, but I tell people I have a different point of view," Huckabee said. "[I] certainly didn't grow up with the silk stockings and . . . the country club crowd."[8]

Another intangible inheritance Dorsey gave to his children was a sense of humor. Mike Huckabee wrote years later that it was a gift he could appreciate only as an adult, when he realized that not every home was so happy: "It's not that his Irish temper didn't come through occasionally. But no matter how little we had, we always had a home filled with laughter."[9]

———

A point Huckabee often makes in describing these years is that they were good because society had not yet imploded on itself. Culture wars and moral revolutions had not yet splashed across the lingering calm of the Eisenhower waters. Huckabee calls himself "a child of the optimistic 1950s" who believed in the vision of a world where everyone "lived happily ever after." He wrote those words in the opening paragraphs of his 2000 book, *Living Beyond Your Lifetime*, in a section he titled, "A Legacy Lost." He wrote, "I dreamed that life might be something like that. No matter what obstacles, dangers, and perils might come my way, in the end we could all 'live happily ever after.'"[10]

A few years into the 1960s, portents of future trouble could be felt, even in

Hope. In the same month (May 1964) that twelve men publicly burned their draft cards in New York City—becoming the first public act of resistance to the war—the *Hope Star* printed the Home Demonstration Club's report for the month: "Mrs. Virgil [Ernie Jo] Huckabee gave the lesson: 'Food, Feed, and Water During Disaster.'"[11] That topic certainly sounded more ominous than "How to make a collar" or "Future trends in window treatments"—the topics discussed eight years earlier. With the Cuban Missile Crisis and JFK's assassination, the Soviet threat seemed imminent. Senator Barry Goldwater promised "a choice, not an echo" in that fall's election,[12] even as nine-year-old Huckabee was being looked after by a grandmother who was teaching ladies how to prepare their homes for disaster. One day, as governor of Arkansas, Mike would play a major role in responding to disaster—though from tornadoes and hurricanes, not Soviet missiles.

———

The real gem in the previous news clipping comes in the final sentence: "The meeting was closed with all repeating the club creed." The club creed? Did a home economics group have doctrine? Yes, in a way, it did. You see, the origins of groups like the Home Demonstration Club can be traced back to President Theodore Roosevelt, who, in the form of a Commission on Rural Life, promoted "life on the farm." At the turn of the century, people asked prophetic questions about the future of the farm and agriculture in America: "How can we expect intelligent, ambitious, young men and women to remain on farms and make farming their life's work if farmers and farm homes cannot be held up as an ideal to be attained?"[13]

World War I only exacerbated these concerns, as tens of thousands of farm boys, like the famous sergeant Alvin C. York, were shipped across the oceans and exposed to exciting and alluring things. Though York returned back home to his beloved Tennessee hills, others decided that a life on the farm seemed like a dull existence they could leave behind.

In the context of these concerns, organizations sprang up to promote and support the ideal of farm and rural life: 4-H (1902), the Arkansas chapter of the Home Demonstration Club (1912), the American Farm Bureau (1919), and Future Farmers of America (1928). Segregated until 1965, Arkansas membership in the HDC grew from 2,083 in 1917 to a peak of 64,863 in 1941.[14] Though the organization was created to help promote agrarian lifestyles, the end result was broader, with general instruction in self-sufficiency and sustainable homes. As a result, these ladies would help lead their communities through the hardships of two world wars, a worldwide outbreak of influenza, the Great Depression, and the horrific flooding of the Mississippi River. Because they were "prepared for anything," the HDC of Arkansas helped alleviate human suffering.

The text of that HDC creed remained the same in 1964 as it always had been. It stated:

> I believe in the open country, and the rural life in the country. I believe that through working together in a group we can enlarge the opportunities and enrich the life of rural people. I believe that the greatest force that molds character comes from the home and I pledge myself to create a home which is morally wholesome, spiritually satisfying, and physically healthful and convenient. I believe in my work as a home maker, and accept the responsibilities it offers to be helpful to others and to create a more contented family and community life so that in the end farm life will be most satisfying.[15]

How can you make them stay on the farm? That's a good question. But the ironic thing is that Hope's HDC clubs were meeting each month in homes that, for all intents and purposes, were not rural. They planted backyard gardens, but they weren't farmers. They cut grass lawns, but not fields of hay. They got their eggs from the grocery store at the end of the block, not out of the henhouse. So the original intent of the organization began morphing into something that better reflected the realities of postwar domesticity.

By 1960, as young Mike tagged along as a guest for some of these meetings, many of the ladies present were also full-time workers outside the home, like Mike's mother, Mae. Further, these ladies' husbands had left agrarian jobs behind to grab better-paying and more stable jobs in town. The world was changing.

Huckabee grew up just a few blocks off the downtown square in Hope, which was the seat of an agrarian-driven county. Farms and undeveloped land surrounded Hope on all sides, but Huckabee himself lived in town, on a block with other houses. He had neighborhood kids to play with and neighborhood adults to serve as surrogate parents when his own were not around. "A child could leave his house in the morning on a bicycle and not return until after dark, and it caused no one alarm," Huckabee said. "It was the kind of place where I could misbehave eight blocks from home, but by the time I pedaled back to 509 East Second Street, six people would have called my parents to report my behavior. I am not sure that it took a village to raise a child, but I am quite sure that an entire village did its part to help raise me!"[16]

Mike's sister, Pat, recalls one particular act of neighborhood transgression committed by her little brother. "We had an older lady next door to us, Mrs. Maggie Cole," Pat said, "and she had pecan trees which we knew not to pick up. They were her pecans, and everybody was supposed to harvest their own. But Mrs. Cole's always looked better. I remember one time when Mike got into some of Ms. Cole's pecans and stuffed them into his pocket—he was about four or five. Well, the pecans were full of ants. We joke that he was the original kid with ants in his pants, because he was hopping all over—and got ant bites on his legs and everything else. That was his first thieving event of his life—and I think that kind of turned a corner for him on that business."[17]

Friends recall Huckabee having a very tender heart—and an insatiable curiosity. These two characteristics collided when four-year-old Huckabee helped his sister bury their recently deceased pet parakeet in the backyard. "Cookie," the parakeet, had meant a lot to Huckabee. So, after a few days of mourning, he decided he needed just a bit more time with his beloved bird. He went out back and dug up the corpse, but he was shocked by the grossness of what "ashes to ashes" looks like in real life. The family loves to tell these kinds of stories on him, and they're all as angelic and innocent as these two. Ants in the pants and discovering how a body decomposes—that's about as sophisticated as his childhood foibles come.

At the public pool, Huckabee learned how to swim from David Watkins, an older teen whose father volunteered at the firehouse with Dorsey. Watkins later went on to work in the Clinton White House and became a key figure in one of the initial scandals of Clinton's first term. "Travelgate," as it became known, concerned Watkins's firing of a handful of staff in the White House travel office, allegedly at the vehement urging of Hillary Clinton. Then, in 1994, Watkins flew on a Marine helicopter at taxpayer expense to go play a round of golf. Watkins lost his job over the event and reimbursed the Treasury thirteen thousand dollars, but stated, "I'm not admitting I did anything wrong."[18] Watkins told reporters that he had been scouting out a golf course for the president.

Hope, Arkansas, has a country club and golf course, but Huckabee has never played the game in his life—not even once. He means it when he says that he's never been a country-club Republican.

On the other hand, when he wasn't yet four, his parents enrolled him in the upcoming summer baseball league. The *Hope Star* published notice of Huckabee's being drafted onto the "Giants."[19] If he was destined to play Major League baseball, his parents certainly gave him an early start down that path. For people growing up in Arkansas, the St. Louis Cardinals were the Major League team to root for. Cardinal Hall of Famers Dizzy Dean and Lou Brock came from Arkansas, along with numerous lesser players for the team. "Cardinal baseball is genetically embedded into the DNA of kids born in Arkansas during the baby boomer generation," Huckabee recalls. "I still remember my teacher at Brookwood Elementary School letting us sit on the playground on a beautiful October day so we could skip class and listen on a cheap AM transistor radio as the Cardinals beat the Yankees in the 1964 World Series. I was a nine-year-old kid, but the memory of that will live with me far more than any of the lessons we would have had."[20]

Be that as it may, it was academics (and ironically, calling play-by-play for local radio), *not* athletic competition, that became Huckabee's field of high achievement during his school years. In February 1964, he made it into the *Hope Star* for "Honor Roll"—a news item that would show up frequently throughout the next decade. And that very same week, something else caught his attention. Together with 45 percent of American households, young Huckabee tuned in to *The Ed Sullivan Show* and watched four flop-haired boys from Britain play their hit songs. The Beatles and the "British Invasion" had arrived, and Huckabee took notice. The only question was how to get his hands on a guitar. Rock and roll was making strong impressions on young people everywhere.

Five years earlier, in the darkness of a cold February night in 1959, a small Beechcraft airplane crashed into a snow-covered cornfield in northern Iowa. Though eight hundred miles north of Hope, Arkansas, the accident made the front page of the *Hope Star*:

> Three of the nation's top rock n' roll idols were killed during a light snow when their chartered plane crashed shortly after taking off from the airport here early today. The trio, Buddy Holly, 22 of Texas, Richie Valens, 21, Los Angeles, and J. P. Richardson, 24, of Louisiana known professionally as the "Big Bopper" had completed an engagement at the Surf Ballroom in nearby Clear Lake a short time before.[21]

A teen from New York state—a huge fan of Holly's music—remembers reading the shocking headlines as he made his deliveries of the local newspaper. Thirteen years later, he wrote a song inspired by the memory of that fateful day. The singer, Don McLean, released "American Pie" in November 1971. It climbed the charts and hit the number one spot in January 1972. "This idea for a big song about America had been on my mind for a long, long time," McLean said. "I wanted some sort of a song that summed up the world known as America . . .

"So all of a sudden this memory of Buddy's death had the dramatic power that I needed and started my mind operating on a different level. And I was able to see where this song had to go, how big it had to be, how long it had to be."[22]

In 2008, during a presidential campaign event, forty-eight years after Buddy Holly and his fellow troubadours played the Surf Ballroom in Clear Lake, Iowa, Mike Huckabee's band, Capitol Offense, had the honor of playing the Surf Ballroom. Hundreds of people came out, many driving several hours to hear the band cover 1950s songs and to show support to Huckabee. On that cold November day, both the music and Huckabee's underfunded campaign were on fire. Huckabee had just taken a slight edge over Mitt Romney in Iowa polling, and the caucuses were just two months away. Savoring every moment of the campaign trail, he joked about campaign finances—before his band lit into a cover of the Beatles' "Money."[23]

PART 2

FAITH, HOPE, LOVE, AND THE BEATLES

CHAPTER 5

GUITARS, HOBOS, AND KOOL-AID

1965–1967

> The guitar was hidden behind the couch. The other gift was just a decoy—the guitar was the surprise, and we were all in on it. We were so happy to be able to get that for Mike.
>
> **—PAT HUCKABEE HARRIS, MIKE HUCKABEE'S SISTER**

IF YOU LISTEN TO MIKE HUCKABEE OR HIS SISTER, PAT Harris, talk about their childhood, nearly every anecdote contains the common theme of gratitude for their parents. Dorsey and Mae, devoid of great wealth, poured their lives into their two children, hoping that the sacrifices they made would impact their future—and perhaps even the world.

It should come as no surprise, therefore, that even Huckabee's well-known passion for music finds its origins in Dorsey and Mae. First, they exposed him to a lot of music. Okay, so it was the music *they* enjoyed—Big Band and classical—but they kept songs pouring out of the old record player. "I think it would be unfair to say they played it for me. They played it for themselves," Huckabee said with a laugh on an NPR program where famous people talked about the music they remember hearing in their youth. "They knew that I would have preferred anything rock 'n' roll, but we had a little record player, and my mother particularly loved music even though she didn't play an instrument. And she was especially fond of Glenn Miller."[1]

Even when people today fail to recognize his name, Miller's "In the Mood" remains a familiar and favored dance number.

"To this day, one of the things that appeals to me is the signature sound of the Glenn Miller orchestra," Huckabee said. "He was the first to combine woodwinds as the primary instrument—in his case, a clarinet, the tenor saxophone playing the same melody line. The moment you hear it, you know exactly whose orchestra that is playing it because of that Miller sound."[2]

And classical music also rang out in Mae's living room. "I can distinguish between Rachmaninoff and Mozart and Bach," Harris said, "because Mom made us listen to all that stuff on those old records that she had."[3]

But Glenn Miller couldn't compete for Huckabee's attention once the Beatles came to American shores. "Like so many teenagers in that era, I disdained anything that wasn't filled with a back beat and pure rock 'n' roll," Huckabee said.[4] He dreamed of fronting his own rock band and playing shows around the world.[5]

The problem was, Huckabee didn't own a guitar. So, when he was eleven, he asked his parents to buy him the one he had seen in the J. C. Penney Christmas catalog. Ninety-nine dollars would purchase an electric guitar and accessories. But Dorsey and Mae didn't have that kind of money to spare. Instead, they purchased their son something else—some other present that he'd like.

On Christmas morning 1965, Huckabee opened up and saw the alternate present. He hugged his parents—the best in the world—and was grateful for them, guitar or no guitar. But then, a surprise awaited him. "The guitar was hidden behind the couch," Harris said. "The other gift was just a decoy—the guitar was the surprise, and we were all in on it. We were so happy to be able to get that for Mike."[6]

It was one of the happiest moments of his life.

As the wannabe Beatle began learning his chords, he received coaching from a local Assembly of God preacher. Harris remembers his fingers bleeding from his practice, but he stuck with it and soon began to perform worship songs with church groups. As he did, his earlier struggles with shyness began to melt away. With each performance young Huckabee undertook, standing in front of others became an event he enjoyed rather than feared.[7]

Visitors to Little Rock's Old State House can view that very guitar as part of a display of governors' memorabilia. "For many who come and see it, it probably represents little more than a kid's dream to be a musician," Huckabee wrote. "For me, though, it is a reminder that long before I ever played before an audience and heard the applause, I spent hours and hours in my room hearing only the complaints of a family whose members had to endure the throbbing sounds."[8]

In a speech to the 2008 Republican National Convention, Huckabee struck a populist tone when he said, "I really tire of hearing how the Democrats care about the working guy as if all Republicans grew up with silk stockings and silver spoons. In my little hometown of Hope, Arkansas, the three sacred heroes were Jesus, Elvis, and FDR. Not necessarily in that order." After the audience's laughter died down, Huckabee continued with a personal note of praise about his father: "My own father held down two jobs, barely affording the little rented house I grew up in. My dad worked hard, lifted heavy things, and got his hands dirty. The only soap we had at my house was Lava. Heck, I was in college before I found out it wasn't supposed to hurt to take a shower."[9]

———

Huckabee played Little League baseball and football, sponsored by the ever-generous Century Bible Class of the local Methodist church. His annual growth can be charted by scanning the archived summer newspapers. The published team photos show a steady progression of height and muscle as he progressed toward the teen years: an all-American boy lined up with his peers. Of course, in terms of sheer quantity of time spent playing ball, most of it wasn't of the organized variety. Neighborhood play, however, was an everyday, all-day event in the summer. "We had a neighborhood full of kids. We played all the time," he said.[10] Harris remembered how "he'd get all dirty and was always knocking the knees out of his jeans. These were the days of white denim. My poor mama. She would come home and scrub those knees and get so annoyed because of the grass stains and dirt."[11]

Part of the joy of living where they did in Hope was their proximity to downtown and all the excitement that brought. "Hope was little," Harris recalls. "We could walk down to the movie theater and back. We had a pretty good area where we could ride our bikes and go all through the neighbor-hood without any fears or anything."[12]

With Dorsey's firehouse being only a two-minute walk from home and his schedule being a twenty-four-hour on and twenty-four-hour off rotation, young Huckabee knew his dad was always around if he needed him. Friends remember Mr. Huckabee's crew coming to the school to demonstrate the ladders on the fire truck. To show how a fireman would rescue a child from the top of a building, they needed a child. Dorsey would grab his son, being close at hand and also kin (and to avoid liability issues), and up the ladder they would go. Dorsey also led training events for other firefighters or citizens in the community. A news clipping from 1966 reads: "Fire chief James Cobb reported today that Dorsey Huckabee, local fire department instructor, has returned from a three-day instructors conference in Little Rock. . . . Chief Cobb said this type of training is beneficial to local training classes which are held twice a month for both regular and volunteer firemen."[13] It's not hard to imagine the pride Mike Huckabee took in his dad being a fireman. "Most admired vocation" surveys may not have been taken in Hope in 1966, but recent national polls rank firefighting as the number one most-admired vocation across America. Newspaper clips about Dorsey would be hung up alongside the growing number of clips from his son's and daughter's achievements.

"Safe" best describes Huckabee's childhood neighborhood. That said, danger could be found if one went looking for it. "I remember one time he got into some real trouble," Harris said. "We lived close to the railroad track and he walked down to what they called 'Hobo Jungle'—I know that's not politically correct to say now, but that's just what they called it at the time. Trains pulled through Hope and these folks would jump off and meet up with one another. Well, our parents couldn't find Mike and they were just horrified. It turned out he had been down to Hobo Jungle just chatting with the hobos. Nothing bad happened that day, but I can remember our folks pretty well laid down the law."[14] Dorsey and Mae had good reason to be frightened. Every year the *Hope Star* ran news stories from across the nation about young people who had been murdered or kidnapped by tramps, hobos, and bums. Yes, there *is* a technical difference, but they'd all get lumped together when a crime at the railroad tracks took place. Little Huckabee's yukking it up with the hobos scared his parents good. To his credit, he was just honing his political campaign skills, drumming up support from any gathered crowd.

Marynell Branch, a classmate of Huckabee's beginning in fifth grade, said that he always had a great sense of humor and loved to laugh—"always positive and a people person. And he was always making a play on words."[15] There's not a boyhood picture around where his face does not display his trademark "aw shucks" look. His sister calls it his "most innocent look"—and said it usually came out in full force if he was trying to get away with some hijinks. "He used to sit by me in church and he'd 'frog' my leg—pulled up his middle knuckle then punched me in the leg, just to get a reaction out of me—knowing I couldn't do anything," Harris said.[16]

––––––––––––––

When Huckabee was ten, his grandma Ernie Jo took him to Garrett Memorial's summertime vacation Bible school program. He was enticed not by the opportunity for spiritual growth, but because his sister promised him that the leaders would give him all the cookies and Kool-Aid he wanted. "When I got there, I found out they didn't think I could eat more than two cookies or drink more than one cup of Kool-Aid, but by then, I was already there," he recalled.[17]

Whatever his motivation for going might have been, Huckabee found something more. When the pastor spoke about having a personal relationship with Jesus, Huckabee felt like the message was meant just for him, and he was moved to pray: "It doesn't matter whether you're ten years old and in a little town of Hope or whether you're . . . on the streets of Manhattan. It's an honest prayer that . . . says, 'God be merciful to me, a sinner.' And God hears that prayer."[18]

"His conversion came pretty early for a kid, but he never had doubts after that," Harris said. "He went there for cookies and Kool-Aid and got some Jesus too."[19]

CHAPTER 6 ──────────────────────────────

FORTUNATE SON

Fall 1967–Spring 1969 ──────────────────────

> Working hard was just instilled in us. Our parents
> worked hard, so we would work hard.
>
> **—PAT HUCKABEE HARRIS**

JOHN FOGERTY MUST NOT HAVE BEEN INVITED TO THE
wedding. The lead singer of Creedence Clearwater Revival found inspiration
for his 1969 hit "Fortunate Son" when he read news about the marriage of
former president Eisenhower's son to Richard Nixon's daughter. "You just
had the feeling that none of these people were going to be involved with the
war," Fogerty told *Rolling Stone*. "In 1968, the majority of the country thought
morale was great among the troops, and eighty percent of them were in favor
of the war. But to some of us who were watching closely, we just knew we
were headed for trouble."[1] After being drafted in 1966, Fogerty joined the
Army Reserves and served in a unit for six months. He was discharged in July
1967 and rejoined his band—though he changed the name. It wouldn't do to
sing protest songs with a band called "the Golliwogs."

That same fall, Bill Clinton headed back for his senior year at Georgetown
University. He worked for the U.S. Senate Foreign Relations Committee,
headed by Arkansas senator J. William Fulbright. "I admired him. I liked him,"
Clinton said in a 2002 speech honoring his former mentor. "On the occasions

when we disagreed, I loved arguing with him. . . . I'm quite sure I always lost, and yet he managed to make me think I might have won."[2] Fulbright served as U.S. senator for thirty years, from 1945 to 1974 and became best known for two things: he opposed American involvement in Vietnam, and he supported the establishment of a student exchange program—now known as the Fulbright Program. Young Clinton represented an intersection of those two interests.

At Christmas in 1967, the *Hope Star* printed a national AP news item they deemed of interest to local readers: "Arkansan Is Rhodes Scholar. William J. Clinton, a senior at Georgetown University, from Hot Springs, Ark., has been selected to receive a Rhodes Scholarship for a minimum of two years' study at Oxford University. Clinton, 21, son of Mrs. Virginia Clinton, was one of thirty-two Americans chosen. . . . Mrs. Clinton is the former Virginia Cassidy of Hope."[3] Bill's grandmother Edith, who had once sought to gain custody of young Bill after raising him for the first years of his life, still resided in Hope and would have taken great joy in her grandson's accomplishments. She died just one month later.

During his first year of study in England (1968–1969), Clinton received notice that he had been drafted. But with help from Senator Fulbright and Arkansas governor Winthrop Rockefeller, Clinton made arrangements to enter the ROTC program at the University of Arkansas Law School that fall, 1969. Instead, he returned to Oxford and held demonstrations against the Vietnam War. A profile piece of Clinton's protests was printed in various Arkansas newspapers, though not the *Hope Star*.[4]

———

As noted earlier, Dorsey Huckabee proudly answered the call of his country for World War II military service by reporting for induction in March 1943, but couldn't get in due to his flat feet—a Huckabee heritage he passed down the line to his son. "I was born with flat feet," Huckabee wrote in his 2005 weight loss book, *Quit Digging Your Grave with a Knife and Fork.* "Now when I say *flat feet*, I don't mean just nominally flat; I mean the bone structure in the arches of my feet is essentially inverted. My parents told me regularly that at birth my feet looked so hideously deformed, the doctors first warned them that I might never even walk."[5]

Huckabee told how his feet kept him from advancement in his college's ROTC program. All freshman males were required to take a semester of the program, but "when the army colonel saw my feet, he told me there was no point in my continuing because the army wouldn't have me anyway," Huckabee said. "My flat feet ended what I'm sure would have been a heralded military career in the post-Vietnam 1970s."[6]

Since Dorsey didn't make it into the Army, he signed up for service in the National Guard. He also headed down to Houston with his dad and uncle to build ships for the Navy. The one thing he didn't do, however, was finish high school. "Our dad was very smart, but he only had an eighth-grade education," Harris said.[7] In fact, no male in Huckabee's lineage had ever graduated from high school.

Not so for Mae. Huckabee's mom completed high school and desired to go to college too. The responsibilities attached to having so many younger siblings and the death of her father prevented her from doing so. She began working at a young age—even before the war's increasing demand for female workers—and she never stopped. "She wanted to go to college, but her chances were gone. She worked in an office as an administrative assistant for an oil company," Harris said. "That was at a time when most women were stay-at-home moms."[8]

For the two Huckabee children, their parents' story inspired them to work hard in school and to go to college. "Because neither of them had a college education, our going to school and college and doing our best—that was never an option," explained Harris. "I don't remember ever—and Mike doesn't remember either—our parents ever having to ask, 'Do you have your homework done?' We just knew that our privilege was to work really hard in school. Give it your best. And it wasn't based in fear—as if they were going to beat us for poor grades. Because of their own lack of secondary education, our parents really let us know you need to be lifelong learners."[9]

Harris remembers how, even as a boy, her brother read voraciously. "Sure, I used the *World Book Encyclopedia* when I'd have to do a report. But Mike was that kid who just read the World Books from A to Z. I thought that was a little creepy then. Actually, I still think that's creepy—but that's a true fact about Mike. Seriously though, Mike's always been big into reading—books, magazines, newspapers—all the time."[10]

Faith, Hope, Love, and the Beatles

Dorsey and Mae provided a living example of a strong work ethic, and their children caught it. "Working hard was just instilled in us. They worked hard, so we would work hard," said Harris. "I'm not trying to make it sound like we were superheroes—we're talking about simple stuff like taking the initiative to help out with supper or the laundry. That's just the way we were raised. Don't put yourself first—you're down on the list. Take care of your responsibilities first. We can give a hearty thanks to Mom and Dad for that."[11]

Harris also credits her parents for the way she and Mike relate to everyday people, regardless of where they are from or what their current station in life happens to be. "We treat everybody well, just like our parents trained us. It doesn't matter who the person is: treat them with respect. Remember people's names, call people by their name, look around at everybody when you're in a room, think before you speak, give back to others, and remember that no matter your situation, there's always somebody else worse off."[12]

One powerful example of Dorsey and Mae's selfless care for others came during the fall of 1967, as Mae invited her terminally ill bachelor brother Garvin into their home to die. Huckabee took an entire chapter of his book *A Simple Christmas* to relate the story of Uncle Garvin's four-month stay with them at the losing end of his fight with cancer. Of all the dozen or so books and thousands of speeches Huckabee has written, this chapter may be the most poignant. He wrote about caring for Garvin in the midst of vomit and feces, watching his robust, dignified, and fashionable uncle waste away before their eyes. As a bachelor, Garvin had limited options for where to go when he needed help. But as Robert Frost wrote, "Home is the place where, when you have to go there, they have to take you in."[13] Mae and Dorsey gladly took Garvin in, and then called on Mike and Pat to assist in the hospice care.

Huckabee wrote,

We did the most menial and at times unpleasant and degrading tasks to make sure he was comfortable. In so many ways, I became a man that year. I was forced to face the realities of death and the uncertainties of life. I saw life in its ugliest form when a disease robs a person of his strength, his pride, his privacy, and his ability to choose even the simplest things. More than being robbed of my youth, I was endowed with an extra dose of maturity and adulthood the very year I would become a teenager, 1968. Uncle

Garvin lived through Christmas and died on April 6, 1968, when in the early morning hours of that day, two days exactly after the assassination of Dr. Martin Luther King Jr., the voice of my dad woke me up as he climbed to the top of the attic stairs to tell me that Uncle Garvin had just died.[14]

On the campaign trail, Huckabee often says, "I grew up having a lot more in common with the people working in the kitchen instead of those sitting at the head table. . . . I had to learn how to sit at the head table."[15] Or, a favorite Huckabee metaphor is that he stands for "Wal-Mart Republicans, not Wall Street Republicans."[16] The truth is, his "working folk" language reflects his home life. Mike says that he has authentic respect for the working class because when he looks at them, he sees his own parents. Mike's higher educational and economic position has not stripped him of remembering who he is—Dorsey and Mae's son.

Gratitude for the gift of their parents is a recurring theme rolling from the lips of Dorsey and Mae's grown children. "There was nothing remarkable about our childhood or our family except that we had the most wonderful parents in the world," Harris said. "We were very fortunate."[17]

A September 1967 issue of the *Hope Star* reported news from Michigan: "Governor George Romney took his undeclared quest for the Republican presidential nomination into a Negro neighborhood Wednesday night, looking for answers—and got some hard questions." Romney didn't earn the nomination. But if you scan over just two inches to the right of the Romney news, you'll see the picture of a twelve-year-old Boy Scout named Mike Huckabee, who had just earned his "second class" award.[18]

The first Scout troop for Hope came in 1911 when F. R. Ethridge was commissioned as the original scoutmaster for the town. Ethridge's 1911 certificate lists "Theodore Roosevelt" and "William H. Taft" as honorary president and vice president of the Boy Scouts of America.[19] For several decades, the First Methodist Church had served as the sponsor of Huckabee's unit, Troop 62. A 1937 newspaper ad exhorted citizens to "Boost the Hope Boy Scout Movement."[20]

Today, the scouting movement continues on in Hope and Hempstead County. In fact, Huckabee's lifelong best friend, Lester Sitzes, serves as a scoutmaster for Troop 5—sponsored by the Century Bible Club of First Methodist Church. In the fall of 2013, Sitzes brought in the Huckabees to help dedicate a new building and grounds for Scouts, the Harlan Scouting Center.

"It is terrific to be back in Hope," Huckabee said at the dedication. "I grew up in Hope and I was both a Cub Scout and a Boy Scout here. Lester has been my best friend for about 50 years, since the third grade. We've been through a lot of good times and some bad. Hope has changed a lot since I was growing up."[21]

Looking with hindsight at the years 1967 to 1969, most people would agree that there was an unprecedented amount of turmoil and revolution. A loss of innocence. Huckabee, in numerous interviews and in his books, equates this time as the season when the wheels fell off the bike for our nation. He recalled how the events of the period—"the assassinations of Martin Luther King, Jr. and Robert Kennedy, the shooting of George Wallace . . . the Chicago Democratic Convention, the hippie movement . . . Vietnam"— upset the balance of everyday life: "The world was changing so rapidly . . . We go to church on Sunday, and we go to school and get our homework, and we behave, and we say yes sir and no sir. . . . All that was sort of going out the window, and suddenly we were listening to Jimmy Hendrix, and we were watching people burn buildings down in American cities, and throwing Molotov cocktails at police cars. And it was a shocking time. I think that maybe was the pivotal moment in American history in many ways. . . . It was a tough year."[22]

Huckabee recognizes that in the midst of the chaos, there were a few bright spots in Arkansas. For example, the assassination of Martin Luther King Jr. that year led to a public demonstration of solidarity between the governor of Arkansas and the civil rights movement. He recalled,

> I remember vividly the tragic and senseless murder of a man who both taught and lived the model of non-violent resistance. . . .
> The day after Dr. King was killed[,] Governor Rockefeller stood with

black leaders on the steps of the Arkansas State Capitol. He linked arms with them and he sang "We Shall Overcome" as a tribute to Dr. King.

It was a remarkable act of courage on the part of Governor Rockefeller...

Because of the vision and leadership of Dr. King ... things are much different today.

No longer are there separate water fountains, theater entrances, and restrooms for people of color. No longer do people who are black sit in separate waiting rooms in a doctor's office or a train station. No longer does a person of color receive a different wage than a white person for doing the same job.

And no longer is a black child forced to go to a separate and inferior school than the white child.[23]

The task of making sense out of difficult pages of history becomes easier when you've had three decades to analyze the events. In 1968, however, Hope's high school was not yet even integrated—fourteen years after the *Brown v. Board of Education* decision. But integration was set to come in the fall of 1969—Huckabee's freshman year of high school.

CHAPTER 7

BRIDGE OVER TROUBLED WATER

Fall 1969–Spring 1971

> If there was tension or a fight that broke out, my friend Donald
> Ogden and I would run to the middle of it. I would go talk to
> the white guys. He'd go talk to the black guys. We'd tell them to
> stop the nonsense. Pretty soon, classmates and parents stepped
> up and said, "We've got to make this work." And we did.
>
> **—MIKE HUCKABEE**

DORSEY AND MAE BECAME CONCERNED WHEN THEY HEARD about plans for a railroad bridge to be built a few blocks from their home. They had no complaint with God when it came to being poor, but if the Highway Commission thought their inane construction plans would pass without a murmur, they underestimated the Huckabees—and a hundred of their neighbors. The plan called for a bridge to be built over the railroad line that sat just north of the Huckabees' house. But the lead-up to the bridge would effectively "create a Berlin wall right here in Hope." So stated a full-page protest-advertisement in the *Hope Star*, paid for by the rankled citizens whose property values would take a hit because of the bridge. In large font, the ad asked, "East Second Street Blockade?"—and carefully laid out their reasons for opposing the plan.[1] With the ad's language of "blockade" and "Berlin Wall," the coalition of citizens understood the power of metaphor (with a touch of hyperbole). Winston Churchill and his "iron curtain" would have been proud. In the end, the Highway Commission changed the plans, shifted the routes, and killed the bridge idea.

———————

At the same time, a pair of songwriters from Queens entered a recording studio and created what became their signature song—"Bridge over Troubled Water." Simon and Garfunkel, arguably the most popular folk rock group from the sixties, released the song in January 1970. It hit the top of the charts and remained there for six weeks. There is an irony in the song's mood of serenity and peace, given that the duo would split and go separate ways after the release of the album.[2]

Cultural revolutions continued to create troubled waters, even as technological achievements brought a sense of awe and pride to the nation. The Huckabees joined in with 500 million others worldwide to watch Neil Armstrong and Buzz Aldrin step onto the surface of the moon: "That's one small step for man, one giant leap for mankind." On the baseball diamond, pitchers Nolan Ryan and Tom Seaver led the "Miracle Mets" to win the World Series, only one year after coming in ninth among ten National League teams.

But other big events that summer, like Woodstock, also flashed across the screen. Images of young people rolling in mud and smoking marijuana were printed on the covers of national newsmagazines; people in the proverbial heartland didn't understand, let alone approve. That feeling was mutual for many in the "Don't trust anyone over thirty" generation. As the Vietnam War continued to send American soldiers home injured or in coffins, the tension over the war continued to increase. The younger generation was turning its back on the conflict, but even older Americans wrestled with the competing desires of patriotism and wisdom.

On April 28, 1970, President Nixon announced the expansion of the war into neighboring Cambodia. Student protests escalated overnight. One week later, members of the Ohio National Guard fired on students who were protesting at Kent State University, killing four and wounding nine. Canadian rocker Neil Young gave an immediate response to Kent with his song "Ohio."

However, a high school teacher in Fort Smith, Arkansas, responded by writing Senator Fulbright, urging Congress to award Medal of Honor status to the Guardsmen who were "protecting their lives and tax property," adding, "If the students had been in the classroom where they should have been they wouldn't have been shot."[3] Obviously, the nation was divided on the war, and on the legitimacy of the student protests.

Nixon did not set foot on a university campus for another month after the tragedy. And when he did so, he chose one of the most conservative public universities in America, and also the largest in the South at the time—the University of Tennessee in Knoxville. On May 28, Billy Graham introduced Nixon to the podium at his Knoxville-area evangelistic crusade. Seventy-five thousand people crammed into Neyland Stadium, and another twenty-five thousand listened outside. Hundreds of protesters also attended, inside and outside the stadium, making sure the world knew that not everyone approved of Nixon's policies.

Before belting out "His Eye is on the Sparrow," world-famous gospel singer Ethel Waters responded directly from the stage to hecklers in the crowd: "Now you children over there listen to me. If I was over there close enough, I would smack you. But I love you, and I'd give you a big hug and kiss."[4]

Graham told reporters, "I love all those young people at the university—even the protesters. A few are being misled, using the wrong methods. Their methods lead to violence they pretend to disapprove. I am praying that some of them will find Christ."[5]

Nixon addressed the crowd: "Billy Graham, when he invited me to come here, said that this was to be Youth Night. He told me that there would be youth from the university, from other parts of the State, representing different points of view. I am just glad that there seems to be a rather solid majority on one side rather than the other side tonight."[6]

The *Hope Star* printed a front-page headline: "Nixon Booed at Graham Crusade Talk."[7] Arkansans were consummate Democrats, so Nixon being booed wasn't really a cause for concern. The fact that it happened at Graham's crusade, however, gave them a reason to pause. Of course, in an adjacent article, the U.S. senator from Arkansas reported that 95 percent of constituent letters he was receiving supported Nixon's Cambodian vision.[8]

Just over two years later, Nixon resigned the office of the president in

Watergate disgrace. Nixon's true character became known to the public through the release of White House transcriptions of Nixon in foul-mouthed conversation with others. Graham said he found the White House transcripts "profoundly disturbing and disappointing."[9] Nixon had betrayed the confidence of the entire nation, and of his close friend.

Years later, Jerry Falwell, pastor of Thomas Road Baptist Church and president of Liberty University in Lynchburg, Virginia—and a founder of the Moral Majority—offered his analysis of Nixon's attendance at the Graham crusade. "I saw him on television at the Knoxville, Tennessee, campaign. This was prior to the Moral Majority and political involvement, which is no big deal today. But it was a big deal then, and when I saw him there . . . it was obvious to me—he's not attending Billy's crusade to hear Billy preach. He's there because Billy invited him there. And anybody with any amount of moxie was aware that this was a tacit endorsement. I think if Billy was sitting here, he'd be the first to tell you, that was a major mistake in his ministry and life."[10] To this day, evangelicals continue to wrestle over the relationship between public church officials and politicians. Huckabee is one of the few who have served in both capacities on a national stage.

Huckabee, who had been a supporter of Nixon, found himself disappointed and perplexed at the president's actions. "The Nixon administration was vilified because back then we had an idealistic image of a president," Huckabee wrote. He continued:

> We wanted him to be the most honorable, most statesmanlike of all of us. He represented more than himself. He represented all that was good about our country. We wanted our political leaders to be statesmen, and we thought of them in those terms.
>
> But in the post-Watergate era, cynicism mushroomed. People started not only accepting the worst, but expecting the worst from their elected officials.[11]

The context of that quote, taken from his book *Character Makes a Difference*, is Huckabee's explanation for why American voters elected Bill Clinton into office in 1992, despite all the allegations swirling around him at the time. Huckabee said that voters couldn't relate to the patrician George

H. W. Bush. They wanted to elect someone who looked like themselves, and "they were more like that young, flawed, sincere man, Bill Clinton"[12]— Huckabee's point being that Watergate set the nation up for Bill Clinton's presidency.

———

Back in Hope, Arkansas, even the nonpolitical concerns of life seemed to be undergoing change and transition. The annual watermelon festival, long a staple of Hope culture and economy, wasn't working anymore. Hope was in danger of losing her place of distinction as a major destination point for watermelon tourism. So Hope businessman C. E. "Pod" Rogers began to travel the country and reclaim the brand. He went on *Let's Make a Deal* with Monty Hall and told the world about Hope's melons. Then, he talked up watermelons on *The Glen Campbell Goodtime Hour* alongside Tommy Smothers.[13]

That was the year CBS canceled *The Smothers Brothers Show*, citing complaints about the comedy routines involving criticism of the president, the Vietnam War, and prevailing racism in the country. The brothers used satire to make their point, but protestors and riots in the streets employed more physical means to get their message across. "There was a real definite choice . . . would we be a country of law and order or law of mayhem?" Huckabee said forty years later. "I believed in law and order, not mayhem. I believed that some things were right and some things were wrong, and when we went with the right, we had strength. And when we saw that there was no moral center and there was nothing that really ever could be defined a moral absolute, then we were lost and confused."[14]

How did young Huckabee decide on "law and order"—even as he refused to simply toe a political party line? How was he able to win teacher-nominated awards for being an outstanding student, while also getting sent to the principal's office for involvement in a mild student antiwar protest at Hope High School? How did he wind up being a conservative and a Republican from a county where, he jokes, there were "only seven Republicans"?[15] He needed a sage, a guide to help him through these "troubled waters." Huckabee found his mentor at the end of his forefinger—his broken forefinger, that is.

That story actually begins back in 1967 during a Little League game.

Coached by future Arkansas Supreme Court justice Jim Gunter, Huckabee played catcher, though reports vary as to the depth of his abilities. Huckabee says he enjoyed the competition but wasn't endowed with talent. To hear his older sister's report, however, he was on the verge of moving from junior high directly into the major leagues (that's what older sisters are for). The world may never know the real story, however, because about halfway through the season, Huckabee left his ungloved hand exposed to a foul tip. The ball broke his right index finger, ending his season and his baseball career, given the trajectory of his life which was to follow.

What does a Little Leaguer with a broken finger do next? Enter Haskell Jones, operator of the local radio station, KXAR. Either within a few seconds or a few months of breaking his finger (depending on who is telling the story), Jones invited Huckabee up to the broadcast booth to help out with the radio coverage of the Little League games. That's right: the radio station provided some live play-by-play of Little League games.

Then just twelve, Huckabee entertained listeners with his confident and lively banter, and Jones took notice. Soon, he offered Huckabee the opportunity to host a youth show during the Saturday afternoon time slot—once he was old enough to obtain his FCC license. He did just that when he turned fourteen, and thus launched a broadcast career now approaching fifty years in duration. "I look back and I think, what an incredible thing," Huckabee said. "Here's a guy that looked at a 14-year-old kid and saw something in him and said, 'I want you to work for me.'"[16]

KXAR played a little bit of everything, and Huckabee's duties similarly ran the gamut. In addition to his youth show, he did the news; at fourteen, he was named the sports director, with the responsibility for calling the high school football, basketball, and baseball games.[17]

Huckabee was still too young for a driver's license, and Harris recalls her parents driving him to the radio station every Saturday and Sunday morning. On Sundays, he'd arrive and open the station, and then get picked up for church before returning again during the afternoon. "He started getting a paycheck at twelve or thirteen years old, before he even had a car," Harris said.[18]

Haskell Jones arrived in Hope later in life—a transplant—and according to Huckabee, that fact explains everything about Mr. Jones:

It was sort of just inbred in us that we were all Democrats. Now, it wasn't because folks there were so much liberal, but there was just this sort of gravitation toward it. In fact, there were only seven Republicans that I knew of in my entire home county. Every one of them had moved in from either Kentucky, Indiana or Illinois. None of them were native to Hempstead County. There used to be a saying that "There are no Republicans here except the ones that either moved in or had been messed with." Jones was one of those seven Republicans who had moved in from somewhere, and I was one of those guys that got messed with.[19]

Jones is clearly the chief cause for Huckabee's entrance into conservatism and the Republican Party—a decade ahead of even the Reagan Revolution that brought in Southern Democrats. Huckabee contrasted Jones with his own parents' traditional leanings toward the Democratic Party. "[Jones] loved this country. He was a great patriot. He understood the blessings of America," Huckabee said. "And even though I had not grown up in a Republican household, I understood something about the blessings of America. I was raised to love this country. I was not allowed to be unkind toward it."[20]

Jones said that when he first moved to town, some people predicted that his Republican leanings would hurt his business. But Jones said, "If it has hurt my business, I certainly can't tell it. When people realized I was a Republican and that I was going to stand by what I said, they accepted me."[21] And accepted him the town did, honoring him with "Haskell Jones Day" in 1975, just before he moved on to another town and radio station.

Jones's mentorship of Huckabee also included steering him intellectually by giving him a copy of Phyllis Schlafly's 1964 bestseller, *A Choice Not an Echo*. "That book had a tremendous impact on me as a teenager," Huckabee said. "It reminded me that in all of our lives, we should not simply be echoing the sentiments of others, but making deep personal choices about what we believe and, most importantly, why we believe it."[22] Huckabee's own record of governance shows that he refused to walk anyone's party line, a direct influence of Jones and Schlafly.

Huckabee completely lights up when he speaks about his first boss. "Jones began to help me crystallize what I understood was part of a greater movement." He describes Jones as a "remarkable human being" and a "communitarian." "He instilled into me that when you live in a community and you're blessed, that you owe something back, so you must be involved in civic endeavors," Huckabee said.[23] Indeed, Jones was known for saying, "I regard politics as part of my civic duty."[24]

A quick perusal of newspaper archives from those years reveals the accuracy of Huckabee's statement about Jones's community involvement. Republican governor Winthrop Rockefeller appointed Jones to the Arkansas Publicity and Parks Commission in January 1969.[25] That same month, the Citizens for Good Government group formed to "promote Governor Rockefeller's tax package" and named Jones the chairman for Hempstead County.[26] He also served as the "Blood Program Chairman" for the Hempstead County Red Cross bloodmobile drive.[27] Huckabee took note of all this and patterned his own civic involvement in like manner. The job training wasn't just learning how to work the radio equipment; it was learning to give back and serve others. It was an education that laid the foundation for his future.

By the fall of 1969, KXAR included Huckabee's name on their quarter-page newspaper ads for broadcasts of Hope High School football: "Follow the Bobcats by Attending the Games. If You Can't Go, Ralph Routon and Mike Huckabee Will Describe Them For You."[28] Routon, now the editor of an award-winning newspaper in Colorado, was a senior that year and remembers well that football season, first because he was "helped by a skinny ninth-grader named Mike Huckabee." But even more memorable was how this was the first year that Hope fielded an integrated football team. "Yerger High School, after nearly a century of educating generations of blacks in the community, turned into a junior high for everyone," Routon recalls. "And nearly 400 teenagers came from one end of Walker Street to the other in the late summer of 1969, creating an enrollment of about 800 at Hope High."[29]

"I always thought those pep rallies were what really pulled Hope High School together," Routon wrote. "Many of us wondered how hard it had to be for the Yerger kids, losing the identity of what had been their school. But at those pep rallies, everyone was united. We all knew something else. Hope wasn't winning championships before full integration, and neither was

Yerger. But together, they could win. And together, they could make Hope a role model for other schools and communities making so many difficult adjustments."[30]

Huckabee remembers working hard with other students, black and white, to get to know one another in the summer before integration. "We introduced each other to the other kids and within the student council," he said. "We worked toward having a real plan for creating a friendly and cordial environment and building trust. And so if there was tension or a fight that broke out, my friend Donald Ogden and I would run to the middle of it. I would go talk to the white guys. He'd go talk to the black guys. We'd tell them to stop the nonsense. Pretty soon, classmates and parents stepped up and said, 'We've got to make this work.' And we did."[31]

Following the lead of Haskell Jones, Huckabee became active in public service and leadership. At the close of his junior high career, the local chapter of the Daughters of the American Revolution awarded him with their Good Citizenship Medal for 1969. "Mike, an eighth grader, was chosen because of his high grades in history and his good citizenship. He is a member of the junior high student council, science club and is a junior fire marshal."[32]

Taking a full measure of leadership in public high school would require Huckabee to earn a spot on the student council, which he promptly did for the freshman year. His classmates, the first desegregated freshman class in the history of Hempstead County, voted for him to be their class president for the coming year.[33]

All this news was duly reported in the local paper. And directly adjacent to the news announcing Mike's election to the student council, the *Hope Star* reported on Judge Harry A. Blackmun's 94–0 confirmation to the Supreme Court by the U.S. Senate: "Blackmun Likely Bends U.S. Court a Little More to the Right." The article said that Nixon and chief justice Warren Burger wanted to find a justice who would "slow down the court's drive for social reform." Burger stated, "The law is not geared for giant leaps forward" and added that the high court is "hardly the body to be entrusted with the destinies of a free people. . . . Judges should not confuse their jobs with those of legislators." During his confirmation, Blackmun assured the senators he would try to keep his personal ideas and philosophies out of his decisions. The story closed with this bit of prophecy: "Unless Blackmun changes radically, however, this adds up, overall, to a hesitant, but decided conservatism."[34]

Of course, nothing could be further from the truth of what actually happened. Fewer than a thousand days later, Blackmun wrote the majority opinion in *Roe v. Wade*. He would go on to become one of the most liberal and activist judges on the bench—and intensified his support for abortion rights with every decision he made throughout his twenty-four years on the Court. Given Huckabee's public disdain for judicial activism, it is ironic that he and Blackmun shared newspaper space announcing their arrivals on the scene.

———

Two examples of Huckabee's activity on the student council during this time period will serve to illustrate the manner and mission of his leadership.

First, he created, planned, and executed "Operation Goodwill"—a Christmas event that benefited needy children by supplying them with presents and personal attention. Around eighty-five children participated in the event, held two days before Christmas. Each child received toys and a stocking stuffed with fruit and candy. A member of the student council handmade the stockings, and the Hope Lions Club donated four hundred dollars to the cause.

To read Huckabee's quotes in the newspaper regarding the event is to catch a glimpse of the style and substance of the future governor: "This unprecedented project was a huge success and reached its goal of spreading happiness to as many deserving children as possible."[35] That language— "unprecedented project"—is at the same time both true to the events of that day, but also attention grabbing. In other words, Mike already knew how to both tell the truth *and* captivate the imagination.

When asked whether the event had the potential to become an annual event, Huckabee responded, "Yes, I'm sure it will. The involvement and morale of the many students was almost enough to carry out the project again next year, but the thing that really decided its future was the satisfied grins on the small children's faces as they received their gifts from Santa himself. That alone was worth every bit of work and effort put into this project."[36] In now-typical Huckabee fashion, he spoke with polish and exuberance, but, more important, he painted a picture of the humanity of the event (note the "satisfied grins on the small children's faces"), which answered the cost-benefit question.

Looking back years later, he said, "That project was one of the things I think I was most proud of. The way we got all the students involved, each class in competition with one another to raise money—car washes, bake sales, mowing lawns. We had scores of kids in every class actually participating to help do something for underprivileged kids. It was remarkable."[37] Lester Sitzes added, "Operation Goodwill was his baby—all the way."[38]

In response to Huckabee's leadership of the event, high school principal Bobby Whitmarsh awarded him the "Joe Amour Award," given out quarterly to the student who "has done the most to serve his school." Huckabee's principal took note of his age: "Mike is one of the very few underclassmen to receive this high award. . . . He is also a sports announcer for KXAR this year, following the football and basketball teams. His dad is his constant companion on these trips since Mike is not yet a qualified driver."[39]

Second, pulling off the logistics for the Christmas event was a small affair compared to the "May Day Festival in Fair Park," which Huckabee helped coordinate. Though this event had dozens more people helping, his responsibility was substantial, as he was to "acquire the music and the preparation of the fairgrounds." This community-wide event, described as "the most unique, new, and original project to be undertaken by a local group," would offer food, music, and a slate of big-name speakers who would take part in a forum on drug abuse.[40] In organizing the music, Huckabee sought to please fans of both country and rock. He pulled in groups from six cities and intermingled the styles back and forth to keep everyone on the fairgrounds until that evening's events.

Twenty-two-year-old Pittsburgh Steelers quarterback Terry Bradshaw served as the main attraction that night. Bradshaw grew up just one hundred miles away and had played close by at Louisiana Tech before heading to the Pittsburgh Steelers the year before as the first overall draft pick. What is amazing about Bradshaw's story is that he was the second-string quarterback for a time, behind *Duck Dynasty* patriarch Phil Robertson. It was only after Robertson gave up a final year of eligibility and left school in order to get back to his first love—duck hunting—that Bradshaw began starting. "The quarterback playing ahead of me, Phil Robertson, loved hunting more than he loved football," Bradshaw wrote in his autobiography, *It's Only a Game*. "He'd come to practice directly from the woods, squirrel tails hanging out of his pockets, duck feathers on his clothes."[41] Robertson later clarified the story about the contents of his pockets—it was squirrel *guts*, not tails.[42] In 2013, Huckabee would come to Robertson's defense after he was benched from his own reality TV show because of comments he'd made in an interview with *GQ*.

The point here is that Huckabee, even as a young man, knew how to pull off the logistics for big events and worked hard to do so in service to the public. The people of Hope had a good time together; they experienced community and civic pride, and money was raised for charity. It took a lot of brains and legs, and Huckabee led the way in getting the job done.

The final "bridge over troubled water" for young Mike Huckabee—and arguably the one with the greatest long-term impact—came in the form of Bible studies he attended in the home of some everyday folks. Here he found a deeper and more internalized spirituality, impacting his vision of Christianity and providing him with a deep spiritual foundation for the civic activism to which he was becoming committed.

As we saw earlier, Huckabee had a Christian conversion experience as a ten-year-old. That basic commitment never wavered, but five years more of intellectual maturing had made him ask questions. He poked at the foundations of the external moralisms prevalent in his community of faith, and he refused to accept "Because I said so" as an answer. "I grew up in a culture where everybody went to church, but nobody took it that seriously," Huckabee said. "People would say boys and girls shouldn't go to R-rated movies, or that they shouldn't swim together."[43]

Moralism pricked at Huckabee. It's one thing to avoid the bad, but that still left a desire for putting your life to work doing something positive. And the idea of simply chasing material prosperity didn't appeal to him any more than the "sex and drugs" culture did. He wanted his life to have significance, to do something that was going to have an impact on other people.[44]

This vision for a "purpose driven life"[45] took a distinctively Christian focus through the Wednesday night Bible studies offered by Burgess and Loretta Garrett. The couple opened their home to a group of teenagers, Huckabee among them, and talked to them about the practical matters of faith. He was impressed that their belief didn't start and end on Sundays; they were believers full-time.[46]

"For them, Christianity was not a cultural expression—it was a personal relationship with God," Huckabee said. This encounter in the Garrett home helped shift Huckabee's vision of Christianity away from fundamentalism, which focuses on God's judgment, and more in line with evangelicalism, which focuses on grace—"We're all sinners, we're all screwed up, we all need help, that's why we keep Jesus." With all the competing voices in the culture fighting for Huckabee's attention, the Garretts' Christian hospitality and discipleship came at just the right time. "Before some of these moments in my faith really took root, I think I could have gone a totally different way," he said. "I think I could have become the hedonist because I had rejected what I had grown to believe was a completely superficial and inauthentic approach to life. I did not want to be a sheep."[47]

Because so many people had invested in Huckabee—his parents, Haskell Jones, his teachers, and now the Garretts, just to name a few—he determined to turn these investments back around for the benefit of others. "To him who has been given much, much will be expected"—a paraphrase of Luke 12:48—became a theme verse, not in a legalistic fashion, but as an overflow of a heart of gratitude for what God had done in his life.

It was in this context that Huckabee went out and preached his first sermon. This is the South, after all, and if a young man expresses a desire to please Jesus *and* he is good with words, then preaching a sermon just seems like the thing to do. "I heard his very first sermon," remembers Marynell Branch. "When we were in ninth grade, I went with him to hear him preach. He used props, and he just did a great job. He had a good command of speech and people and how to connect with an audience."[48]

In addition to all the activities mentioned earlier, Huckabee also started the Christian Student Union. Modeling the on-campus discipleship group after what he saw in the Garretts' home, he wanted to "encourage Christian behavior," he said. "It was an 'anything goes' world at that time. And this was to offer an alternative to the alternative."[49] Even as Huckabee had been given adult friends who served as a "bridge over troubled waters," he chose to become a bridge himself to his classmates.

CHAPTER 8

ROCKET MAN

Summer 1971

> I'm a child of the Space Age and remember well, as a small child,
> John F. Kennedy's vision to get us to the Moon. I remember sitting
> on my living room floor in July of 1969 when Neil Armstrong put
> his foot on the Moon. I believe that the space program has brought
> about far more benefits than simply the exploration of space.
>
> —MIKE HUCKABEE

THERE'S A TRUISM THAT FLOATS AROUND IN VARIOUS FORMS, but this is the basic gist: "Five years from now, you'll be the same person you are today, except for the books you read, the people you meet, and the places you go." Beginning in the summer of 1971, Mike Huckabee had the good fortune of taking four trips, three of them outside of Arkansas, that would impact the trajectory of his life.

The first of these trips came when Huckabee applied and won the right to be Arkansas's representative at the Hugh O'Brian Youth Leadership Foundation (HOBY). Though a younger generation of readers may not recognize the O'Brian name, from 1955 to 1961 he starred as the ruggedly handsome lead in the ABC Western series *The Life and Legend of Wyatt Earp*. In 1958, O'Brian spent nine days in Africa alongside Christian theologian Albert Schweitzer, then came home and established HOBY to provide a vital leadership development opportunity for a select group of youth about to enter their junior year of high school. "The great majority of our youth are positive, but we only hear about the negative minority," O'Brian said. "I figured it was time to pat the good guys and gals on the back and show them that there are rewards for being responsible members of the community."[1]

As told in the last chapter, Huckabee filled his freshman and sophomore days with leadership characterized by service and creativity. Even as Operation Goodwill, his charity program, brought joy to needy children in Hope, it also brought recognition to him. The scripture "Whoever can be trusted with very little can also be trusted with much" (Luke 16:10) took on new meaning as the adults in his life began to nominate him for unique experiences and opportunities for growth. With Haskell Jones and other leading men of Hope writing letters of recommendation on his behalf, Huckabee soon felt the "pat on the back" from O'Brian's foundation.

Huckabee became one of the seventy-one delegates to attend a space seminar in June, at Cape Kennedy Space Center in Florida, one boy from each state plus ten international delegates and eleven special guests. All the expenses were paid by the foundation, including his airfare from Little Rock to Orlando. This would be the first time he had ever flown on a plane, and his first time out of the region. He quickly discovered that not everyone shared his particular religious background or worldview. "I was shocked by how many of them had no belief in God at all," Huckabee recalled to a journalist decades later.[2] He remembers being labeled a "Jesus freak" by one of the participants, but rather than making him defensive, the comment caused him to take stock of how to engage with those who didn't see the world the same as he did.

Patrick Air Force Base, near Cocoa Beach, Florida, housed the delegates. Each day began at 5:30 a.m.—reinforcing his early-morning habits—and lasted well into the night. The teens took part in space simulations and drills, and they heard from a panoply of speakers—including Hugh O'Brian himself.

The boys went up on the launchpads for the towering rockets, those man-made marvels of engineering standing two or three times as tall as any building Mike had ever seen in Hope, Arkansas. This trip came during the height of the Apollo program, which landed twelve men on the moon from 1969 to 1971. In fact, it was only the previous April when the failed-yet-famous Apollo 13 mission took place—now well-known because of the 1995 movie depicting the aborted mission. Huckabee soaked up the vision of this magnificent federal program, and he heard astronauts, engineers, and politicians explain how such big projects came together. The federal government could tackle problems that lone individuals, corporations, or even states would not have been able to achieve on their own.

From Haskell Jones, Huckabee had come to understand that with such power and purse came great responsibility—even, perhaps, the responsibility to refrain from using the power and purse altogether. How does one decide on the legitimate use of government funding and the promotion of a particular vision for the future? Such are the questions that leaders must answer. The space program itself would not have existed in its 1971 form had it not been for President Kennedy's incredible vision of putting a man on the moon by the end of the 1960s. Though he did not live to see the reality of his dreams, the space center bears Kennedy's name because of his forward-thinking leadership.

After Huckabee returned home, he received numerous invitations to speak about the trip. He told the Rotary club "the things he experienced made him proud to be an American."[3] He told the Lions Club how the NASA program led to technological advances impacting their everyday lives—electronics, food processing, propulsion, and weather study. "Last year's cost of 3.3 billion dollars for space study and exploration has long been a topic of discussion as to its worth," the *Hope Star* reported. "But Mike pointed out that this sum was only a part of the cost of the food stamp program and that only time would bring the answer and that the march of progress would have to be balanced against the cost."[4] Huckabee probably picked up that particular comparison to food stamps during his time at NASA, but this type of argument by metaphor and analogy is now a staple of Huckabee's political rhetoric.

Decades later, while on the campaign trail in 2007, the topic of NASA came up. Someone asked Huckabee whether the space program should be reinvigorated by planning a fresh trip to the moon. After joking about sending Hillary Clinton, then the front-runner for the Democratic nomination, Huckabee answered the question nearly word for word as he had in 1971 when he spoke to citizens of Hope. He said:

I'm a child of the Space Age and remember well, as a small child, John F. Kennedy's vision to get us to the Moon. I remember sitting on my living room floor in July of 1969, when Neil Armstrong put his foot on the Moon. I believe that the space program has brought about far more benefits than simply the exploration of space. The side benefits of medical technology, navigation technology, digital technology, audiovisual, you know, it's endless. And largely it was launched from the scientific research that was done in order to help us in the space race. So I think there are tremendous benefits that we would gain from an accelerated space exploration program. I certainly would be in strong favor of increasing our efforts in space exploration and technology.[5]

Hugh O'Brian encapsulated his vision of leadership and youth development in a speech he often gave, titled "The Freedom to Choose." President Ronald Reagan and Pastor Robert Schuller, both friends of O'Brian, used similar themes in their own speeches and sermons. So does Huckabee. O'Brian's words serve to explain Huckabee's own vision of himself and the importance of helping others envision their God-given potential:

I do NOT believe we are all born equal—CREATED equal in the eyes of God, YES—but physical and emotional differences, parental guidelines, varying environments, being in the right place at the right time, all play a role in enhancing or limiting an individual's development. But I DO believe every man and woman, if given the opportunity and encouragement to recognize his or her potential, regardless of background, has the freedom to choose in our world. Will an individual be a taker or a giver in life? Will that person be satisfied merely to exist or seek a meaningful purpose? Will he or she dare to dream the impossible dream?

I believe every person is created as the steward of his or her own destiny with great power for a specific purpose: to share with others, through service, a reverence for life in a spirit of love.[6]

CHAPTER 9

(NO) TEENAGE WASTELAND

1971–1972

> How many towns could you grow up in where as a seventh
> grade kid you've got the keys to the radio station—and
> you're in charge? You've got to be in the right place at the
> right time for that to happen—and Hope was special.
>
> **—LESTER SITZES, LIFELONG FRIEND OF MIKE HUCKABEE**

THE WHO? YES, OUTSIDE OF THE BEATLES, ONE OF MIKE
Huckabee's favorite bands was the Who. "I had most of their albums, and my
favorite was *Tommy*, their rock opera," he said.[1] The band's November 1971
release of "Baba O'Riley"—better known by the lyrics of its chorus, "teenage wasteland," kicked off introspection about the excesses of the late 1960s.
"'Baba O'Riley' is about the absolute desolation of teenagers at Woodstock,
where everybody was smacked out on acid and 20 people, or whatever, had
brain damage," lead singer Pete Townshend explained decades later. "The
contradiction was that it became a celebration: *'Teenage Wasteland, yes!* We're
all wasted!'"[2]

The introspection continued as *Rolling Stone* that same month published a
two-part series of articles by Hunter S. Thompson, titled "Fear and Loathing
in Las Vegas." Thompson expanded the articles into a book with the same
title, which has now become a classic work from the decade, and a movie,

with Johnny Depp playing the lead character. "[The book] perfectly captured the zeitgeist of the post–'60s era," stated *Billboard* magazine.[3] *Rolling Stone* said Thompson gave "voice to the mindset of a generation that had held high ideals and was now crashing hard against the walls of American reality."[4] Of course, both of those reviews of Thompson's work came much later. In 1971, most Americans were not yet ready to process the 1960s. To embrace or not to embrace the previous decade, that was the question—and still is.

No town is without its problems, but Hope, Arkansas, was no "teenage wasteland," not even among the youth who loved playing rock music. Huckabee had joined his friends to form a variety of bands that played in churches and at youth functions. One of these groups, which came together around this period, was his Bois d'Arc Boogie Band, named after the lake just south of Hope on which he and his friends had spent many days together over the years. The group covered songs from all their favorite bands, but they also played the new "Christian rock" music they were hearing. One historian has noted, "By 1977, approximately one thousand 'Jesus rock' bands were performing in churches, outdoor concerts, and alcohol-free 'Jesus nightclubs.'"[5] Larry Norman, the father of Christian rock, asked (and wrote a song with the title), "Why should the devil have all the good music?"[6] Huckabee, a fan of Norman, responded by picking up his bass guitar.

Huckabee prefers action to ideology, movement over motionless theories. He knows that taking a stand involves both the mind and the feet. He doesn't devalue the intellectual side of a problem, but he doesn't want to get stuck in the proverbial ivory tower, discussing but never doing. Two of Huckabee's favorite Bible verses exemplify this dual focus: "Come now, let us reason together" (Isaiah 1:18 ESV), and "I can do all things through Christ who strengthens me" (Philippians 4:13 NKJV). Thinking and doing—that became Huckabee's strategy for making an impact in the world.

For example, the journalism department sponsored a forum on the topic of pollution. Once again, the yearbook shows Huckabee at the center, sitting on the stage, leading the discussion.[7] Though the environment did not register as a major concern with most adults in 1973, by the time Huckabee became governor two decades later, he would lead his state to make such issues a high priority.

He served as the vice president of the student council his junior year, organizing the annual events of high school life, along with another round of his Operation Goodwill. The executive members of the council went to a convention held that year in Huntsville, Alabama. Part of the fun involved a tour of the space and rocket museum, rather ironic since Huckabee had just spent the previous summer at the Kennedy Space Center. Drawing on his recent experiences in Florida, he gave a speech to his peers on the "benefits of the space program."[8]

Accompanying Huckabee on the trip was his friend and fellow council member Bud McLarty, the younger brother of Mack McLarty—President Clinton's friend and the White House chief of staff during his first administration. During his own journey through high school, Mack had also taken part in student council. This is where you find one strong connection between the success of Mack McLarty and that of Mike Huckabee: Mrs. Anna E. Williams, a Spanish teacher and the faculty sponsor of the council, strongly influenced both of these men.

Mrs. Williams, who wore pearls around her neck and her hair neatly up in a bun, made disciples—that is, she saw certain students as having strong potential for leadership if only they could be chiseled a bit and refined. She was a very proper woman, with dignity and Southern refinement. She practiced and taught good manners and etiquette. Most important, she commanded the respect of all her students, but especially those serving on the council.

Once you became an executive member of the student council, Mrs. Williams expected you to arrive at school early and be prepared to show her your list. What list? The daily "to do" list that you had written out the night before in preparation for an efficient day—not simply a day of getting a lot of things done, but of making sure you were getting the *right* things accomplished. To be on the good side of Mrs. Williams meant that you weren't going to be sleeping in, hitting the snooze button, and showing up disorganized for school. That wasn't the way leaders were built, and, over the years, Mrs. Williams had built a lot of them.

Huckabee stays up late *and* gets up early, and when he rises, he already knows what his day holds in store for him—because of those lists. He readily credits Mrs. Williams's pivotal influence in his life as having shaped him.

Though nearly a decade older than Huckabee, Mack McLarty has also publicly said the same thing about Mrs. Williams. Like Huckabee, McLarty's family and colleagues know about the list making and discipline. Not every family member is fond of the list-making trait, especially when on vacation, but the leadership successes of both these men attest to the powerful influence this one particular woman had in both their lives.[9]

———

Huckabee continued his broadcasting work alongside Haskell Jones at KXAR as the radio station celebrated its twenty-fifth anniversary that spring. From the photograph of the packed banquet hall of people gathered for the celebration, you get an idea of the positive influence this station had on its community. Of course, much of that influence came by way of Jones's personal investment in the town he had adopted as his own.[10]

Huckabee called many of the high school sporting events for KXAR, including the girls basketball games. When you take a look at the box scores from these games and see who was doing most of the scoring, you can imagine that the name "Janet McCain" must have rolled off his tongue and over the airwaves hundreds of times each season. Janet, of course, later became Mrs. Huckabee. How many people can say that even before they dated their future wife, they talked about her on the radio? With all the scoring Janet did on the court, Huckabee certainly couldn't have forgotten her name. And speaking of forgetting names, Lester Sitzes recalled the explanation for Huckabee's ability to call football games without stumbling over names—especially the names of the visiting team's players. "If he forgot a name in the middle of an active play, he'd just make one up. Mike told me, 'It's radio. The important thing is to keep rolling along. You can't really mess up if you're quick on your toes.'"[11]

When pressed for an explanation for why so many successful people came from Hope—and how they all seemed to start so young in their accomplishments, Sitzes answered, "How many towns could you grow up in where as a seventh grade kid you've got the keys to the radio station— and you're in charge? You've got to be in the right place at the right time for that to happen—and Hope was special."[12] Haskell Jones let students run the airwaves. Alex Washburn, the owner of the newspaper, had high school kids write up news and sports articles. To be sure, he got the news cheaper that way. But he also did it because he believed in giving the next generation a chance to shine. Ralph Routon, who ended up as the editor of an award-winning newspaper in Colorado, got his start writing for the *Hope Star*. Where else could young teenagers get so much experience?

———

In 1963, Mack McLarty joined up with a thousand other high school juniors from across the state, including his childhood playmate Bill Clinton, for a week of Boys State. This nationwide program—both in the "Boys State" and "Girls State" versions, is an American Legion–sponsored program designed to promote leadership, patriotism, and knowledge of how civil government operates. Community leaders would sponsor a vanload of high-caliber students and send them off to make their hometowns proud by competing for "elected office." McLarty did not disappoint, returning home victorious with the top prize of governor. Clinton was also recognized, having been marked as one of the two most outstanding delegates from Arkansas that year. Clinton's win set him up for a historic trip to the White House in 1963, where he shook hands with President Kennedy.

In July 1972, Huckabee loaded up with a group of classmates and friends and headed to Camp Robinson in North Little Rock for their turn at Boys State. Janet McCain earned a spot as a delegate that year, too; Girls State took place at the same location, but on a different week. In retrospect, Boys State was the second of four life-altering trips Huckabee would take during high school (the first being his NASA adventure).

The students stayed in rustic military barracks. "Those days it was run like boot camp with calisthenics and exercises every morning," Huckabee recalled. "Reveille, assembly, marching everywhere we went, marching in time—very militaristic."

The weather was hot, the drills were grueling, and the boys loved every minute of it. Huckabee said, "It was a 'misery loves company' sort of experience. The deprivation of all your favorite things, having to sit through long assemblies, junior counselors who would pop you upside the head if you went to sleep during a speech."

"It was very patriotic," Janet Huckabee added.[13]

The highlight of the week was when the delegates began campaigning for the elected offices. When Huckabee arrived at Boys State, did he have a plan to win? Did McLarty's legendary win nine years earlier inspire Huckabee to think he too had a chance? "I knew there would be a governor elected at Boys State," Huckabee recalled. "I figured I would check it out when I got there. When I arrived, I discovered a lot of guys—like my future friend Rick Caldwell—had been thinking and preparing for it beforehand. They brought printed posters and cards. They had a whole organization set up. I thought, *Well, gosh, I can't compete in this.* I had nothing. Nothing."[14]

Apparently, the underfunded, underdog political campaigns Huckabee is now well known for had their origins at Boys State.

"I had a second thought," Huckabee said. "I figured, since I didn't spend any money, so I had nothing to lose. The campaign would come down to whether or not you can make the speech and win your party's nomination and then the overall elections. So, I threw my name in the hat and made my speeches. And, not to be immodest, but I blew everybody out."

To be more precise, Huckabee beat Dexter Reed 778 to 153. Reed, one of the best basketball players to ever lace up shoes in Arkansas, would go on to become an all-time leading scorer for Memphis State. He had come to Boys State that week with nearly universal name recognition and still lost to Huckabee in a landslide. Huckabee also ended Caldwell's campaign in a crushing manner.

How? Huckabee says it was the speeches. Sure, he made his way around the camp, meeting the other delegates and shaking hands like everybody else. "But I have people to this day who come up and tell me, 'I was at Boys State with you. I couldn't believe your speech, I couldn't believe somebody our age could speak like that,'" Huckabee said.

When asked exactly what he spoke on, or how much preparation he had made, Huckabee didn't remember the topic or having had any genuine opportunity to prepare. "It was extemporaneous," he said. He did recall making the strategic decision to focus his words on differentiating himself: "There's a pack you have to break out from—don't ever do what everyone out there is already doing: 'Vote for me! Here's my card! Here's my poster!' Instead, I got up in front of everyone and said, 'I didn't come here this week with a bunch of cards. I didn't come here with a bunch of posters. I came here with a love of this country and a desire to stand up and represent our generation. The governor of Boys State is going to be asked to speak for our class, for our group, for our generation. So, what matters is not that you can go into the bathroom and shake everybody's hand. What matters is—can you articulate what matters to us and explain why America needs us to lead this country?"

The point was simply that with so many candidates running around with a mind-set that "shaking a hand or slapping a back leads to a vote," it was hard to get a moment's peace—even in the bathroom. He poked fun at something everyone knew to be true—the glad-handing was too much and came across as manipulative. Drawing on Malcolm Gladwell's concept of an "outlier,"[15] Huckabee analyzed his victory at Boys State: "It's always the risk. Will the outlier be the trendsetter or will he be the guy who looks like an eccentric idiot? You never know which way it's going to go, but you can't innovate and do great things simply by copying what a dozen other people are doing."

At this point in the conversation about Boys State, Huckabee drew a sketch of his philosophy for leadership. "Why is Apple Computer so successful? Because Steve Jobs was a weirdo, an outlier. He didn't think like people thought. And nobody thought Steven Spielberg had any future when he was such a weird little kid playing with his 8-millimeter camera all the time. But nobody is laughing at Steven Spielberg now. Just look at all these stories of people who have done significant things, and they did it because they didn't do what everyone else did."[16]

In addition to hanging with his hometown friends, Huckabee also met dozens of young guys with whom he would remain friends for life. Rick Caldwell said, "As a result of getting acquainted with Mike and humbled by him through that election process, we became fast friends. He defeated me so decisively and I was so humiliated, I never since that day sought an elected office, which is one of the nicest things he's ever done for me."[17]

When asked whether he saw something in Huckabee that made him think his friend would go on to be the leader of Arkansas, or even a U.S. presidential candidate, Caldwell answered, "I saw his charisma, his leadership, his ability to connect with all kinds of people and hear them and make them feel like they would be listened to when he was a seventeen-year-old kid. That was all there, even back then. I knew that the gifts and abilities he had went beyond anybody else in our age group. He was just in a different league."[18]

Caldwell is quick to point out that Huckabee's greatest strengths are found in his character and principles, not simply in his gifting as a speaker. "Mike had a real concern for issues. I remember when he was in high school, he heard an African-American war hero [USAF general Daniel "Chappie" James] deliver a great address at the Hugh O'Brian Space Seminar. So Mike invited him to speak to the Arkansas State Student Council. It [inviting an African-American] became a political hot potato, but after the speaker came and was well received, everybody celebrated. But that was a stretch in 1972 in southern parts of Arkansas. In 1972, Mike was ahead of his time with his peers. He was very color-blind. He truly saw the value of people of all races, of all creeds, of all colors."[19]

At the end of the week, Huckabee returned to Hope victorious as the "governor." Hope celebrated his success with a parade and great fanfare, taking pictures and writing up a story for the newspaper. "Several area Hope citizens were responsible for organizing the committee which met and formed a caravan in Emmet to escort the 'governor' into Hope."[20] As you read the text and look at the photo of Huckabee standing there with his 1970s-style

Boys State T-shirt and a mop of hair, you have to wonder if even he realized just how historic that week would become in his life. In the span of five days, he had gone from being a nameless face in a crowd of one thousand high-achievers, to being one of the best-known young men in the state. Even as Huckabee rolled back into Hope, influential men across the state, including then governor Dale Bumpers, were dictating congratulatory letters to be sent to Huckabee—encouraging him to pursue a vocation where his talents would best be used: law and politics, of course.

In a bit of historical irony, on that very same page of the *Hope Star*, directly butting up against the photograph of Huckabee, ran a story about the death of Saul Alinsky, a political activist who pioneered the role of the community organizer. His *Hope Star* obituary reads: "'Life is too short not to be full of passion and conviction.' The words are those of Saul David Alinsky of Chicago who spent more than a quarter of a century practicing what he preached as one of the nation's leading organizers of community-action groups."[21] Alinsky's death came only two years after he published his now-famous *Rules for Radicals*. And it had only been four years since Hillary Rodham wrote her senior thesis at Wellesley College: "There Is Only the Fight . . . : An Analysis of the Alinsky Model."

From where does Mike Huckabee's optimistic outlook come? In response to overwhelming evil and brokenness in the world, why isn't he a cynic, a pessimist, or at least an Alinsky-style Machiavellian, ready to jettison principle in order to establish and maintain power?

Why does Huckabee choose to care at all? After all, many in his "late boomer" generation simply checked out altogether, opting to drown out the messiness of the world through physical pleasures.

By contrast, Huckabee seems to chew on an Everlasting Gobstopper of hope. Many people find his optimism inspiring. An equal number find it nauseating. Either way, those are value statements about his optimism, but we're asking a question about origins. From where does Huckabee's optimism originate? Part of the answer to *that* question is found in the next road trip Huckabee undertook, two days after he got home from Boys State.

PART 3

THE CITY OF GOD

CHAPTER 10

THE CHRISTIAN WOODSTOCK

Summer 1972

> You can experience this revolution. In fact,
> you can help bring it to pass.
>
> —BILL BRIGHT, FOUNDER OF CAMPUS CRUSADE FOR CHRIST

MIKE HUCKABEE ARRIVED BACK HOME FROM BOYS STATE
on a Saturday. He had just experienced a life-transforming week and had
flown across the radar of important Arkansas leaders. He was only sixteen,
but his future trajectory now seemed to have more definition to it than did
those of the vast majority of young men walking around in 1972. But Boys
State was only the first of two life-changing trips he experienced that summer, and the second came right on the heels of the first.

The following Monday, Huckabee and Lester Sitzes loaded up into a car
and drove three hours south to Dallas, Texas, where Billy Graham and Bill
Bright were hosting an event several years in the making. Tens of thousands
of Christian teens and college students were all arriving for the International
Student Congress on Evangelism, also known as Explo '72. Indeed, eighty
thousand would show up for the week's culminating event, a worship service
in the Cotton Bowl on Saturday, June 17.

Bright had founded Campus Crusade for Christ in 1951 on the UCLA
campus as an organization for Christian evangelism and discipleship. In 1952,

he wrote an evangelistic tract called *Have You Heard of the Four Spiritual Laws?*, which aided Christians in their communication of simple gospel truths. Bright knew that tracts could help strip away the fear Christians expressed when thinking about sharing their faith with others.

The student protests and drug culture of the 1960s concerned Bright. Church leaders with a heart for the students—Bright, Graham, and Francis Schaeffer, to name just a few—recognized that the younger generation were calling for an answer to the existentialist question: Does my life have meaning or purpose?

Bright had heard expressions of spiritual longing from students all across the United States. He began to formulate a new approach, which did not go without controversy in the established church, to refrain from focusing on the morally neutral expressions of the rock-and-roll culture. Instead, he would focus on giving students Jesus. In 1969, Bright published a book titled *Revolution Now!* as a challenge for students to ground their desire for a purposeful life in the person and work of Jesus Christ. He wrote:

> We live in the most revolutionary period of human history. Campus disorders have assumed epidemic proportions! . . . What does the future hold? Is there a hope for a solution? . . . Social band-aids and reform antiseptics give little hope for a cure or even an improvement. A revolution is needed. I have seen men and women from all walks of life commit themselves to this Revolutionary. The result? A complete transformation, resulting in true freedom, happiness and purpose. The greatest Revolutionary gives release from the guilt and frustrations of the past. He offers a challenge and a cause worth living for. He provides the only hope for the mortal ills of our society.
>
> The world needs a revolution—the right kind of a revolution. One that will build, not destroy. One that will propagate love, not hatred. A revolution that will bring equality, not suppression. One that will restore man to God's image, rather than debase him to a bestial level.
>
> You can experience this revolution. In fact, you can help bring it to pass.[1]

Bright recognized that genuine revival needed to take place within the church, but that the youth culture, with its longer hair and rock music, was not finding a home within the institutional church. As historian John Turner explains, "Mr. Bright's son Zachary remembers telling his father: 'You can have a conservative view of music and keep what worked for you, or you can win [young people to Christ].' 'I'd rather win,' Campus Crusade's president responded."[2] Bright chose to risk, and he began showing the youth of America that Christianity had a future, not just a past—and that the youth themselves could be a vital force of energy for revival and renewal of the church. And for teens like Huckabee, Bright also gave off an aroma of positive, forward-looking Christianity that was discontent to focus on petty issues.

Bright knew that many of the teens needed to respond in faith to Jesus Christ for the first time. But he also understood that, more than a pep rally alone, the long-term effects of a crusade-style event would be most felt if the youth were taught to *be* disciples and to *make* disciples.

Bright had written another paperback in 1970, titled *Come Help Change the World*.[3] With all those action verbs, Bright's vision appealed to Huckabee. "Suddenly, I'm one of nearly 100,000 very young evangelical Christian believers who had a very fervent faith and wanted to change the world," Huckabee said in describing his week in Dallas. "Suddenly, I was confronted with a feeling of 'Wow! There are a lot of people like me, too.'"[4]

And he was not alone. That week, many of the students at Explo '72 were born again—that is, they responded to the work of God in their souls, leading them to an expression of faith, repentance, and commitment to Jesus Christ.

And the impetus for action-oriented spirituality came with an outward focus: the world in need of the gospel. Because the students found little hope or home in the institutional church of the day, their feet turned instead toward taking Christ outward. A decade later, as this generation began to find itself in the leadership of existing churches, new forms of church life would bring fresh approaches and life to the church. The impact of the "Jesus generation," or "Jesus freaks," on the church continues to this day. It is no coincidence that pastor Rick Warren, born one year earlier than Huckabee, wrote best-selling books titled *The Purpose Driven Church* and *The Purpose Driven Life*.[5] Christianity that seeks to impact the world was the desire.

Space does not permit a full recounting of all the events of Explo '72, but there is an abundance of published material chronicling that fascinating week. Paul Eshleman, the director of the Explo's events, penned an instant-history recap aptly titled *The Explo Story: A Plan to Change the World*.[6] Again, you hear that language of revolution, that "Christians can change the world" vision, that permanently impacted so many of the attendees. Eshleman himself went on to lead the world-altering JESUS Film Project, sending the gospel throughout the world through the medium of a film that many estimate has been seen by more people than any other film—upwards of two billion.[7] Revolution indeed.

You will look in vain for any historian, whether a Christian or not, who fails to attest to the long-term significance of this one, singular event. People now in their early sixties who took part in Explo '72 as students still recall that week as being a spiritual turning point in their lives. The six days in Dallas offered them a chance for intense Bible study, prayer, and training in disciple-making. And there was music—good music their own generation enjoyed. Mainstream artists, like Johnny Cash and Kris Kristofferson, sang alongside Randy Matthews, Larry Norman, and a number of groups who would go on to pioneer the genre known as "contemporary Christian music." Cash performed his song "I See Men as Trees Walkin'"—a reference to the biblical story of Jesus healing a blind man (Mark 8:22–26).

Billy Graham served as the honorary chairman and also spoke six times during the week. As he was already a household name by this point in his ministry, Graham elevated the press coverage and credibility of the event beyond what would have been possible without his involvement.

The Saturday night worship event took place in the Cotton Bowl. At the conclusion of the service, Graham lit a candle. Then he used his candle to light the candles of the people standing next to him onstage. They repeated the action to others, who did likewise. In short order, the entire stadium was glimmering with candlelight. Years later, Mike related the experience to a reporter:

> Two things made an impression. Even though I was extremely far away, that tiny flickering of the one candle penetrated the darkness, and I saw it. That told me that even a little bit of light in the midst of darkness is worth

something. . . . The second thing that happened was, as those candles began to accelerate—because obviously it happens pretty quickly through the principle of multiplication—this light just starts expanding around the stadium, faster and faster, until the stadium is aglow. It had a big impact on me—the rapidity with which something can spread, good or bad, and the impact that one life, and one light, can make. That's when it really sunk into me that one person can make a difference.[8]

Earlier in the year, President Richard Nixon's administration had courted an invitation to address the students. The Explo leadership declined to offer such an invitation, not wanting to disrupt the evangelistic goals by politicizing the event. However, a telegram from Nixon was read to the attendees on that Saturday night, June 17, 1972. The president reminded them, "The way to change the world for the better is to change ourselves for the better."[9]

That very same night, in Washington, DC, local police arrested five men within the Democratic National Committee offices located in the Watergate building.

Coming off the thrill of his victory at Boys State, Huckabee could have gone home and laid out a road map for a life of public service and political activity. Given his Republican Party inclinations, he would have joined right on in with the GOP. Had he done so, Huckabee may have spent the remainder of the 1970s in a political wilderness brought on by Nixon's transgressions.

Instead, on the very same night as the Watergate break-in, Huckabee felt a stirring to make a more direct impact on the kingdom of God—more direct than the lawyer or political careers being pitched to him because of his Boys State victory. Coming off the thrill of Explo '72, Huckabee turned his eyes away from the political world and toward a much different vocational path.

CHAPTER 11

LIVE AND LET LIVE

1972–1973

> I say what I mean and I mean what I say.
>
> —MIKE HUCKABEE

MIKE HUCKABEE'S SENIOR YEARBOOK DEPICTS HIS BOIS d'Arc Boogie Band performing at a school event, with the guys dressed in the fashion of the hit movie from that year—*American Graffiti*. Huckabee resembled "the Fonz" from *Happy Days*, the hit show that had piloted a few years earlier but now shot to fame as nostalgia for the early 1960s ran high.

A decade earlier, in the spring of Bill Clinton's senior year, the Beatles sang for Ed Sullivan a ballad about wanting to hold a girl's hand—etching a shared cultural memory of saccharine, teen innocence. "I remember being an 8-year-old kid in a little town in south Arkansas that no one had ever heard of," Huckabee wrote on his Facebook page the day of the fiftieth anniversary of the Beatles playing on Sullivan. "I watched the Beatles with my family on our black and white TV that got its signal off our housetop antenna, all the way from Shreveport, Louisiana. As our parents screamed, 'Turn that noise down,' we turned it up. Who would've thought that 50 years later, we'd be telling our grandchildren, 'Turn that music UP! It's the Beatles!'"[1]

But by the time Huckabee graduated high school, the Beatles had already been dissolved for three years, and John Lennon and Yoko Ono were fighting deportation charges. Paul McCartney's new band, Wings, released "Live and Let Die" that spring, written as the theme song for the new James Bond movie of the same name. This would be the first 007 film starring Roger Moore, and the villain was a narcotics dealer who dabbled in voodoo, not an almost-comical megalomaniac attempting to conquer the world. The times were changing.

You don't have to be a cultural Luddite to recognize the shift that had occurred in the space of ten years. In the early 1960s, "the music was as innocent as the time," wrote film critic Roger Ebert. "Songs like 'Sixteen Candles' and 'Gonna Find Her' and 'The Book of Love' sound touchingly naive today; nothing prepared us for the decadence and the aggression of rock only a handful of years later. The Rolling Stones of 1972 would have blown WLS [the radio station of Ebert's youth] off the air in 1962." Ebert, born in 1942, penned those lines in a 1973 review of *American Graffiti*. He thought the film captured the essence of his generation: "When I went to see George Lucas's 'American Graffiti' that whole world—a world that now seems incomparably distant and innocent—was brought back with a rush of feeling that wasn't so much nostalgia as culture shock. Remembering my high school generation, I can only wonder at how unprepared we were for the loss of innocence that took place in America with the series of hammer blows beginning with the assassination of President Kennedy."[2]

Even in the midst of vast cultural upheavals, the final year of Huckabee's living at home continued to provide the same reliable stability and lack of drama it always had. Dorsey celebrated his twentieth year of employment as a fireman for Hope, though he did make the newspaper in October when his fire truck flipped over after being clipped by a cement truck. Tough as nails, Dorsey walked away from the accident unhurt.[3] Mae, now promoted to supervisor, continued her work at the Louisiana-Nevada Transit Company, a natural gas supplier. Huckabee's sister was beginning her second year at Ouachita Baptist, studying to be a teacher. He would join her the following year, making them the first two Huckabees in their father's lineage to attend college. And Huckabee's two grandmothers and one grandfather still plugged along, alive and active in Hope. So not only did Huckabee's parents *not* divorce, separate, or die young, but they also maintained the same employment and employer throughout his entire time in their home. An immense amount of family stability surrounded him. Again, though he can't take credit for the home life into which he was born, he *does* speak with firsthand knowledge when he talks about the benefits of such intactness.

Huckabee's senior year capped off an accomplished high school career with a flourish of activity: he was in the Quill and Scroll Society (journalism), the Beta Club (academics and community service), the National Honor Society (scholarship and academics), the French club, Future Teachers of America, the Key Club (Kiwanis), and the Student Christian Union, and he was the president of the Hope High School student council. Of course, one should never "join a club just to say you are in it but join to actually do something positive," he later wrote. "And at all times, keep in mind your spiritual heritage, and be the different one in the group that doesn't always conform to everyone else's ideas. Because Christ has saved you, you are different from those who aren't. And you should be different enough (not weird, though) to where your peers could see a definite difference."[4]

As leader of the student council, Huckabee oversaw the big annual events, like homecoming and the powder puff football game. He also led the school to continue a third year of his Operation Goodwill program of Christmas charity for needy children. And when the Hope student council officers attended the meeting of the Southern Association of Student Councils, his peers from across fifteen states elected him as their vice president.

Huckabee was no athlete. And his grade point average, though good, was not the highest in the class. "We had a good time in high school, then buckled down in college," lifelong friend Lester Sitzes said. "Mike spent a lot of time and energy in positions of leadership, speech, debate, and drama—not just in the library with a pile of books."[5]

According to his high school classmates and teachers, the things that set Huckabee apart were his abilities in leadership and communications. Sitzes remembers how in drama class they were required to get up once a week and give an animated summary of an article from the newspaper, pushing the students to individualize the content and overcome stage shyness. The joke among the students, however, was that every time Huckabee got up, he used the same newspaper. Why? "Because he was just making up news off the top of his head anyway," Sitzes recalled. "He was so creative and had such a quick mind and speaking abilities that he could 'read the news' better, without the crutch of the newspaper, than the rest of us could do so with it."[6]

Alex Strawn, drama and speech teacher and the coach of the extra-curricular debate team, said Huckabee was already gifted before he arrived in the class. "I helped him with the format of the debate itself, but he was already so good at using logic and reasoning." When Strawn watched the 2008 presidential debates, he noted how often the moderators would ask Huckabee the first question. "But he was always on his game and had a good reply. I was proud of him during all those public appearances."[7]

Strawn taught his students the difference between having genuine content in a speech or debate versus sophistry and empty rhetoric. "A lot of people are good at rhetoric, and people fall for that instead of actually looking at what the issues are and discussing them on their merits. It's just, 'Take my word for it.' Mike had a good delivery, but there was also meat behind the delivery. He wouldn't speak on an issue unless he understood the facts. And he's honest enough—if he doesn't know, he'll tell you he doesn't know."[8] Friends recall Huckabee only losing one debate ever, and nobody seemed to think he actually lost that one either.

Huckabee also excelled in drama. The class would put on productions for the elementary school. Strawn said Huckabee contributed ideas for making things more entertaining—never just sitting back and putting in the bare minimum of effort. He instinctively knew about what went into good staging and performance, and what kinds of approaches would lead an audience in a desired direction of thought and feeling.

Huckabee moved audiences to tears of laughter with his portrayal of Dr. Seuss in the drama club's production of *Horton Hatches the Egg*. His performance also gave them a reason to reflect on the deeper message: keeping one's word no matter the cost. "Mike playing Dr. Seuss was like Johnny Depp as Jack Sparrow," recalled Sitzes to a reporter three decades later. "He was so good we won a state championship on the strength of that performance. If you're around Mike now, you'll hear him say, 'I say what I mean and I mean what I say.' Well, I hear that and think, *That's Horton!*"[9]

Huckabee had a knack for thinking of new ways to bond groups and teams together. When the speech team prepared to head out for the state-wide competition, he figured out an easy way to create identity and cohesion. "Mike talked the school principal into letting the speech team wear the football team's 'traveling jackets' emblazoned with school colors and insignia," Strawn said. "The team walked in the door looking real sharp and ready to unite for the win—something so simple, yet effective."[10] And they won.

Strawn also served as a faculty sponsor of the student council and remembers Huckabee's kindness driven leadership. "Mike always exhibited a care and concern, especially if someone was having difficulties or problems. He wanted to know if there was some way he could help. He led by bringing individuals together for the common good."[11]

On the twenty-ninth of May, approximately two hundred seniors lined up in the Jones Field House of Hope High School to receive their diplomas. They were Hope's first graduating class to have gone all four years in an integrated high school, and Huckabee had played a key role of student leadership in uniting the class. Accordingly, he received the Beryl Henry Award, given by vote of the school faculty to the "most outstanding senior."[12] "Any task that we set for him, he did 100 percent," Strawn said. "He had an enthusiasm for what he did, and that made all the difference."[13]

Graduation accolades served to remind Huckabee that graduation night was not the end of the race, but only the sound of the starting gun. He later wrote about the dangers of resting on one's laurels and becoming too self-satisfied with compliments from others: "I've watched sadly as gifted young people froze their talents at age nineteen because they believed they were as good as their admirers claimed."[14] Huckabee had no intention of doing that.

———

The summer after graduation, Huckabee continued accelerating his entrance into adulthood by leading "youth revival services" at local churches.[15] He was still only seventeen, but church members had no second thoughts about putting him in charge of preaching and leading special activities for the teens, though he was barely older than the youth. He carried himself with maturity beyond his years and was especially noted for his absolute dependability—character inherited from Dorsey and Mae.

Also that summer, the editors of the *Trumpet*, the state newspaper for the Baptist Missionary Association (the Baptist denomination of which Huckabee was a member), asked him to contribute an ongoing opinion piece. Huckabee accepted the task and called his column "The RAPture Express"—a reference to the Christian doctrine of the Rapture, wherein Jesus returns to lead his followers (both alive and deceased) into eternity. From the title alone, he used the column to remind readers that Jesus' return was imminent and that personal preparation in godliness was the best course of action to take. He wrote about an assortment of issues he felt Christian young people "under the age of 25" would find compelling: dating, dancing, smoking, evangelism, the "Jesus People," soap operas, and driving beyond the speed limit.

He acknowledged up front that not everybody would agree with him on everything, and in trademark Huckabee style, he used self-deprecation to soften his voice and gain a hearing: "Since I'm not the least bit spectacular as a writer, RAPture Express will probably be written in a very simple way. I hope that it will be conversational, instead of mere printed words about youth."[16]

He continually asked for and received letters of response, providing him with immediate feedback, both positive and negative. One of the sharpest critics responded after he quoted from the Living Bible, a modern translation recently published in 1971. Sitzes recalled that the woman admonished, "Don't you ever quote from that paraffin-coated tongue of the devil. If it's not King James, it's not fit to print." Sitzes was pretty sure Huckabee never used the Living Bible for that newspaper again, though he added that "nobody was exactly sure what a 'paraffin-coated tongue' meant."[17]

In 2015, the website BuzzFeed.com rediscovered the RAPture Express and published a dozen or so examples of the column. They pointed out what they considered to be damning evidence of Huckabee's lifelong goofiness. Of course, the columns had already been available online to anyone who dug into his background, but they had not been of any notice before this. Had Huckabee never talked about running for president again, this type of material would be of little interest to anyone. Such is the nature of being deeply vetted for the office of president.

Critics tweeted endless barbs about Huckabee's 1973 opinions. On dancing, he had written: "I strongly recommend that Christian teens stay away from dancing, mainly because some people would just not be able to respect a person who dances."[18] On smoking: It could "ruin your witness."[19] On picking a date: "If physical beauty is the quality you look for first in a date, then you have no business dating in the first place. The beauty of a person lies in their character and personality, not their body."[20]

A fair reading of the columns shows Huckabee could hardly be characterized as a legalistic prig. Even though he had the denomination's support for laying down the law—straightforward and strident—he'd go to great lengths to admit the merits of both sides of each argument. In other words, he didn't write to persuade only those who were already persuaded. Further, he admitted that many of these issues were best left to the individual conscience. For example, with dancing: "Most of the articles that I have read on dancing are written by people who know very little, if anything about what really goes on at a dance. Several years ago, I thought it to be perfectly all right to attend dances in high school, and I went. Since then, my beliefs have shifted somewhat, but at least I know the actual truth about some of the things that go on. Let's clear something up. Everyone does not go to dances to get drunk, or to get his date sexually aroused, or to participate in wild activities." So what *was* Huckabee's directive for Christians regarding dancing? "I personally don't see that much wrong with dances, but at the same time, I can't find a whole lot of good with them either. I strongly recommend that Christian teens stay away from dancing, mainly because some people would just not be able to respect a person who attended dances."[21]

If that answer sounds like fence straddling, that is precisely the charge laid against him in letters to the editor. His response to the critics: "I felt as though I approached this subject head-on. I admit that I tried to look at both sides of the coin, but you won't get an apology for that." And to clarify his earlier point, Huckabee wrote, "I don't want other young people to stay away from dances just because I do."[22]

The truth is, moral guidance in the particulars of life does change over the span of forty-two years. What may have been a topic of interest to teens in 1931 (or 1973) would sound archaic and old-fashioned in 1973 (or 2015). But this is true even for the "Dear Abby" columns of the world. The remarkable thing, given his regimented, religious upbringing, isn't that Huckabee would warn about dancing and drinking, but that he would frame his exhortation within the language of "live and let live." Even Southern Baptist pastors of the

95

time, considered to be namby-pamby by his Baptist Missionary Association denomination, would preach Moses lines like "A dancing foot and a praying knee don't belong on the same leg."

After BuzzFeed had published the columns, Huckabee responded with incredulity that they were newsworthy. "I read this and I laughed out loud. While other candidates are being outed for their teenage drug use, their teenage alcohol use, their teenage partying hard, doing all sorts of destructive things like painting graffiti on bridges—the scandal with me is that I wrote a column at age seventeen telling Christian young people to live a godly life. So, I mean, I just have to say—'Is this really controversial?'"[23]

As Huckabee prepared to enter his final semester of high school, two historic events happened within a week of each other.

First, beginning with the news item that had the most immediate impact, on January 27, 1973, the Nixon administration and the Selective Service of the United States ended the draft. The war would be over, and the young men of the country would no longer be subject to forced military service. Therefore, the vast majority of candidates for the 2016 presidential election never could have been drafted—beginning with Huckabee himself, if only by a few months. Of course, one could argue that Huckabee would *not* have been drafted anyway, given his extremely flat feet. But that's an entirely different discussion. Vietnam would still have been an issue for him, as his classmates would have been sent, and maybe have even died.

Thus far, Barack Obama, born in 1961, is the only post-draft president our nation has had. The "draft-dodging" issue has been a part of presidential campaigns since at least 1988 (Dan Quayle), but that may end with the 2016 election. A political pundit summed up the 2016 "presidential age game" like this: "In a very real way American voters may ultimately decide whether they want to move again to a younger leader or give the Vietnam Era Baby Boom generation one last chance in the White House."[24] The question remains, however: If a candidate could not have been drafted, is he really part of the "Vietnam Era Baby Boom generation" in terms of all the reaction and counterreaction involved in that era?

Second, on January 22, 1973, the United States Supreme Court handed down the infamous *Roe v. Wade* decision, announcing that abortion was a fundamental right under the Constitution. Since that decision, more than 50 million abortions have been performed in the United States.[25] Though abortion is always more than a political issue, it goes without saying that there is an immense political element to the battle. By 1980, candidates were aligning themselves one way or the other, and by the end of the eighties, the polarization of the parties was nearly complete. Newly minted eighteen-year-old voters in 2016 will have lived their entire lives in a world where, for all intents and purposes, there is no valid option for being a "pro-life Democrat" or "pro-choice Republican"—notwithstanding tiny groups that attempt such projects.

Historians debate about how active the antiabortion movement was among religious conservatives from 1973 to 1980. Was it a leading cause of the formation of the religious Christian right? Some say yes, while others give compelling evidence that it was the religious liberty and school segregation issue that brought Christian conservatives into the political realm. This biography cannot answer that question. Suffice it to say, without the issue of abortion, it is possible that Ronald Reagan would not have been elected president in 1980, and the Moral Majority may never have existed.

Every national election from the 1980s onward has been at least partially shaped by that fateful decision in January 1973. While most of the student protest politics existing during Huckabee's childhood centered on Vietnam, much of the politics for the next forty years—including every national election from the 1980s onward—was shaped by the issue of abortion. Unlike he had done in his columns for the *Trumpet*, on this issue Huckabee would have to take a definitive stand.

CHAPTER 12

I WISH WE'D ALL BEEN READY

1973

> Prior to [college], I didn't even have a passport. Why
> get one? I never thought I'd leave the country.
>
> **—MIKE HUCKABEE**

ESCHATOLOGY, THE CHRISTIAN DOCTRINES ABOUT THE
end times, went viral during the 1970s—and not just within the church, but
throughout all of American culture. The particular elements of these doctrines differed among groups, but most Baptists in the 1970s held that an
event called the Rapture would occur in conjunction with the second coming
of Christ. All non-Christians would be left on the earth during the calami-
tous days that would follow.

These teachings were popularized through books, movies, and song. Hal
Lindsey's 1970 book, *The Late Great Planet Earth*, became one of the bestselling
volumes of the decade—and Huckabee had a copy of his own.[1] Lindsey, a
graduate of Dallas Theological Seminary and a staffer for Campus Crusade
until the 1960s, would influence much of the evangelical world into which
young Huckabee was entering.

Eschatology came to the big screen in 1972 with the release of *A Thief
in the Night*. The plot revolves around a woman who considered herself a
Christian but who awoke one day to find millions of people had disappeared,

even her husband. The Rapture had taken place and she had been left behind. The success of this film helped inaugurate the current era of evangelical film production. Some estimate *A Thief in the Night* has been seen by more than 300 million people—including a young moviegoer named Huckabee.[2]

Of course, any good movie needed a memorable sound track. Enter Larry Norman, who wrote and sang "I Wish We'd All Been Ready" for his 1969 album *Upon This Rock*, which is considered "the first full-blown Christian rock album."[3] Huckabee vividly remembers listening to Norman on vinyl *and* live at Explo '72. "He was a big influence on me," he said. "I still have some of his stuff on my iPod."[4]

NASA, Explo '72, and Boys State: all three of these trips impacted the life trajectory of Mike Huckabee. But whereas each of these was a onetime experience, in the summer between high school and college, Huckabee went to Israel—the first of what has now become more than forty such trips to the Holy Land during his lifetime.

Rick Caldwell, his friend from Boys State and future OBU roommate, called and asked Huckabee if he wanted to go on an all-expenses-paid trip to see Israel. Caldwell's father, Harley, was an oilman and a cattle rancher in Arkansas and a generous Christian gentleman. Rick wanted to go see the land of the Bible with his own eyes and asked his dad for permission. "Son, I'm not going to let you go there by yourself," his father responded. "'I'll tell you what—if Mike Huckabee will go with you, then I'll pay his way. If he goes with you, I'll let you go.' And that is how I went on this incredible, life-changing trip," said Huckabee. "Prior to that, I didn't even have a passport. Why get one? I never thought I'd leave the country."[5]

The boys spent two weeks on the trip. They took some of the official tourist jaunts, but that industry was not yet as developed in Israel as it is now. "We were on a ship each night, and we got off each day at a different spot: Jordan, Lebanon, Israel, Turkey, Greece, the Island of Patmos. And this was just two months before the Yom Kippur War. Looking back now . . . that trip was nuts."[6]

Indeed, given the situation in the Middle East, this trip *was* nuts.

In May 1973, the Egyptian Army rattled her saber by conducting military exercises close to the Israeli border. Israel responded by mobilizing her army for war, but there was no conflict at that time. Egypt repeated the action in August; once more, Israel mobilized, but again there was no war. Egypt was attempting to trick Israel into ignoring the genuine war preparations being made.

In spite of all the secrecy and subterfuge, Egyptian president Anwar Sadat had threatened war in an April interview published in *Newsweek*.[7] Perhaps he calculated that if he so openly stated his ideological commitment to destroy Israel, nobody would believe that he was making real-world plans to do that very thing. For her part, Israel felt confident that if there were to be another conflict, the Israeli Air Force would repel the enemy in the same crushing manner she had used during the Six-Day War of 1967.

Egypt began the attack on October 6, which was the Jewish holy day Yom Kippur—hence the name of the war. This time, the conflict lasted a few weeks, but Egypt lost again. The Cold War between the United States and the Soviet Union had added extra intrigue to the conflict, as each side was the major supplier of arms for opposite sides.

Israel has had no greater friend than the United States, and at least some of that support during the 1970s came from Protestant Christians motivated by an eschatological vision of Israel. Theologians argued, and still do, over the specifics, but most of the popular treatments in the 1970s—and certainly those read within Huckabee's circles—viewed the 1948 formation of Israel as the fulfillment of events the Bible predicted would usher in the season of the end times. As historian Thomas Borstelmann wrote, "[F]undamentalist Christians began overcoming their historic anti-Semitism, in an era of rapidly diminishing discrimination against Jewish Americans, to identify increasingly with Israel as a pro-American and anticommunist society. The New Christian Right believed that Israel had a role of ultimate eschatological significance to play: it would be the site of God's final battle and victory at Armageddon, the precursor to the Second Coming of Christ."[8]

Fresh off his trip to the Middle East, Huckabee began his freshman year of college. His first semester overlapped with the Yom Kippur War. Given the eschatological fervor present within evangelicalism, it was no surprise that the war seemed to be evidence that the world was in its last days. But whatever influence the eschatology may have had on Mike's thinking as a teenager—and he does still believe the Rapture will come—his support for Israel grew to rest on a broader foundation than particular dates, charts, and timelines coming out of the popular dispensationalist point of view.

Huckabee remembers what Israel was like back then as compared to now. "The nation was only twenty-five years old in 1973, a relatively new and struggling country. I saw a lot of communal living, where people lived on farms and shared everything together. The economy was primitive—a combination of tourism and agriculture—but nothing spectacular. Since that was pre–Yom Kippur War, many of the areas of Judea and Samaria were still under the control of the Arab countries and Israel itself was not as thoroughly defined," he said. "But when you go back now, it's truly the biblical fulfillment that 'the desert has bloomed.' Areas that were very barren—nothing but rock and sand—are now lush in vegetation. Their economy is one of the strongest in the world. Nobel Prize winners in science come from Israel. High tech comes and advanced medical technologies come from Israel. The dry bones have come to life, and the desert has bloomed—Israel is a miracle. Before my very eyes, I have seen it happen in the last forty-two years."[9]

Huckabee, along with most evangelicals, are often accused of an end-game anti-Semitism because of their belief in the exclusivity of Jesus Christ for eternal salvation. Huckabee deflects the criticism by pointing out that he worships a Jew, and without a Jewish faith, Christianity wouldn't exist. In a speech to the Jewish Knesset, Huckabee said, "I promise you, you do not have a better friend on earth than Christians around the world, who know where we have come from and know who we must remain allies and friends with."[10]

Related to the general support for Israel during the 1970s, groups in America and across the globe also worked for an increase of attention given to the memory and meaning of the Holocaust of World War II. In 1980, Congress chartered the United States Holocaust Memorial Museum in Washington, DC.[11] Huckabee leads tour groups there, as well as to the memorials and museums in Israel and at the Auschwitz death camps near Krakow, Poland.

When Huckabee's daughter was eleven, he took her to Yad Vashem,

Israel's Holocaust memorial in Jerusalem. He wondered how much of what she saw could even be processed by her young mind—what would be her response? "Why didn't somebody do something?" she wrote in the museum's guest book. Huckabee uses this anecdote in speeches: "Let it never be that some day in this wonderful country . . . that some father has to look over his daughter's shoulder and watch her write words like that." He exhorts his listeners to be "Somebodies," and to commit to doing something to preserve this great American heritage.[12]

CHAPTER 13

OUACHITA

Fall 1973–December 1975

> I've always been pretty intense. I'm not a person who sleeps
> eight hours a night. I sleep four or five and I'm good to go.
>
> **—MIKE HUCKABEE**

IN THE 2007 RUN-UP TO THE GOP PRIMARIES, DAN BARTLETT,
former counselor to President Bush, said that Huckabee was the "best candidate" and "the most articulate, visionary candidate of anybody in the field."
But when asked, "Can Huckabee win?" Bartlett responded, "He's got the
obvious problems—being from Hope, Arkansas, and, quite frankly, having
the last name 'Huckabee.' I hate to be so light about it, but it is, it's an issue.
Politics can be fickle like that. I mean, you're trying to get somebody's attention for the first time. . . . 'Huckabee? You've got to be kidding me! Hope,
Arkansas? Here we go again.'"[1]

Yet when it comes to talented men from the South with a native drawl,
Huckabee is in good company.

The 1973 World Series opened at Oakland's Alameda County Coliseum
on the thirteenth of October, featuring the hometown Athletics versus the
New York Mets. Willie Mays, who had played twenty-one seasons for the San
Francisco Giants just across the bridge, suited up for the Mets for his final
two seasons. This Series would be his swan song.

As game one prepared to get under way, the players walked onto the field one at a time. Long, bushy hair and mustaches were everywhere. By contemporary standards, the television announcers spoke with a mellow cadence, and the screen did not overstimulate viewers with a constant rotation of graphics. This was 1973, and Americans had not yet become concerned about baseball's soporific qualities. On the other hand, batters mostly remained in the box between pitches, so a typical game was shorter than *The Godfather* (three hours), the hit movie from the previous year—and one of Huckabee's personal favorites.

Someone needed to sing the national anthem. Nowadays, Major League Baseball (MLB) invites popular groups to sing the anthem, to pull youngsters into watching the national pastime. In 1973, MLB might have chosen Bay-area favorites the Steve Miller Band to play their current hit, "The Joker." Instead, they chose Jim Nabors (aka "Gomer Pyle" from *The Andy Griffith Show*) to do the honors. Most people recognize Nabors's higher-pitched voice and Southern twang, all of which served to emphasize his character's role as the naive hillbilly. However, Nabors was actually an accomplished singer with a rich baritone voice and operatic style. People often mock Huckabee by calling him "Gomer Pyle." But in real life, both Nabors and Huckabee are more sophisticated than their "aw shucks" friendliness conveys.

———

Huckabee entered Ouachita Baptist University (OBU) in the fall of 1973 and graduated magna cum laude five semesters later at the Christmas break in 1975. Between those two dates, he also pastored a church, DJ'd for a local radio station, worked as a custodian, got engaged, got married, and helped his newlywed wife defeat spinal cancer. And he also had a lot of fun pulling pranks and making lifelong friends—a real joker, as friends recall.

OBU sits in the small city of Arkadelphia, fifty miles north of Hope and sixty-five miles southwest of Little Rock. Both cities serve as the seat for their respective counties and were settled in the 1800s; Arkadelphia incorporated about twenty years earlier than Hope, in 1857. Arkadelphia differed from Hope chiefly in terms of higher education and geography. In contrast to Hempstead County, which had no opportunities for higher education in 1973,

Arkadelphia served as the home for two universities: OBU and Henderson State, sitting adjacent to one another.

Geographically, the town is situated in the foothills of the Ouachita Mountains and intersects with the waters of the Ouachita River. The eighty-five-acre campus sits on the banks of the rivers, a "very beautiful campus," Huckabee recalls.[2] The name "Ouachita" means something like "good hunting grounds" and is named after the Native American tribe who formerly lived in that region.

The Arkansas Baptist State Convention (ABSC) founded Ouachita Baptist College in 1886 (changed to "University" in 1965). Ouachita remains affiliated with the ABSC, along with Williams Baptist College. There have been other Baptist colleges in the state, but Ouachita has always held the place of prominence: a central location within the state, strong academics, a small teacher-student ratio, and the fact that one-fourth of Arkansas citizens claimed "Southern Baptist" as their denominational preference.

That's not to imply that Huckabee matriculated into OBU as a member of a Southern Baptist church. He didn't. Garrett Memorial Baptist Church belonged to a different family of Baptists altogether.

Beginning in the late 1800s, Baptists throughout the South began disputing and separating over differences in the doctrine of the nature of the church. The ever-increasing presence of the Southern Baptist denomination seemed to call out a response among those who had never been very keen on the idea of denominations in the first place. Local Baptist congregations took pride in their autonomous nature, even though they also had a connection on the associational level (county), as well as the state and national conventions. Of course, all these conventions cost money to operate, and the Southern Baptist Convention had not yet devised its "Cooperative Program" mechanism for collecting and distributing money from the churches.

A theological answer to the perceived threat of denominationalism came in the form of Landmarkism—an ecclesiology (church doctrine) holding to the belief that Baptists could trace their lineage and legitimacy all the way back to the apostles. Therefore, as a corollary belief of Landmarkism, all non-Baptist churches lacked full validity. And practically speaking, Landmarkists railed against the "cooperative" efforts of denominations in the funding of missions. Men like James M. Pendleton and James R. Graves gave the

107

movement much of its doctrinal shaping earlier in the 1800s, but the actual formation of a new group of Baptists came in Little Rock, Arkansas, under the leadership of Ben M. Bogard.

In 1973, if you asked a journalist from a national newspaper to provide a taxonomy of "Christianity in America," he or she would probably state two groups: "Roman Catholic" and "Protestant." Depending on the reporter's background, "Protestant" may have been subdivided into "mainline" and "fundamentalist" (or "evangelical"). But the fact that dozens of variant forms of "Baptist" exist would not be of interest—or maybe even known—to a journalist.

The point of this exercise in Arkansas Baptist church history is that Mike Huckabee wasn't a Southern Baptist until he entered the seminary in January 1976. He grew up at Garrett and then pastored a similar church while at Ouachita. He grew up in a church and a network of churches that held even tighter lines of orthodoxy and orthopraxy than the Southern Baptists did at the time, and do even now. In the battles for control of the Southern Baptist Convention, fought from the 1960s through the 1990s, it is safe to say that neither faction held to the rigid, sectarian lines of exclusivity characterized by the churches Huckabee was birthed into—and then leapt out of.

———————

Sexual liberation and the drug culture may have been causing a cultural revolution on university campuses throughout America, but not so much among the Ouachita student body—and not in the dormitories (which were definitely not coed). But in areas where neither the campus rule book nor the Bible drew a moral line, hijinks soon followed. "All of us on that whole first floor had such camaraderie together," Randy Sims said. "We all still keep up with one another to this day." He remembers late-night talks and late-night adventures. For example, "I got sick once—swelled up from eating some kind of nut—they had to rush me to the hospital." Or as another example of "crazy stuff" they got into, Sims recalled, "staying up late" and "fighting over the last piece of ham for a sandwich."[3] Obviously, this wasn't UC–Berkeley.

Rick Caldwell roomed with Huckabee their freshman year. Now that their own children are through college, he is amazed at just how different the dorms are today. Caldwell said, "We had no microwave. We had no telephones, except a hall telephone. No toaster ovens. The only appliance you could have was a popcorn popper." A hungry eighteen-year-old belly is the mother of invention, so these dorm mates learned how to make their own "donuts"—in a popcorn popper. "We'd put Wesson oil in there and get it hot," he said, "then take a canned biscuit and pill bottles . . . make a hole in the biscuit. Deep-fry it. Put some powdered sugar and milk on top. We'd have our own Krispy Kreme delights right there with our popcorn popper."[4]

Caldwell enjoys telling these stories of high cuisine ingenuity. "We were all sitting around eating donuts late one night. Then a dorm mate brought in a squirrel that he'd killed. So we battered it, deep-fried it, and ate it too. Fried squirrel from our popcorn popper." When Huckabee ran in 2007 and reporters started hitting up his old college pals, looking for the "wild-side" skeletons in the closet, all they came away with was this anecdote about Arkansas boys frying squirrel meat. Some of the stories even made it sound as though they threw an entire live squirrel into a vat of hot grease. "We didn't think anything about it," Caldwell said. "In Arkansas that was something we'd heard of when we were young. Today it sounds pretty ridiculous."

Caldwell had met Huckabee at Boys State and had hung out together during their senior year, and when they both decided on Ouachita, it only made sense to room together. "We were the original Felix and Oscar of the Odd Couple. He was very serious—get up early, stay up late and study, work hard. I didn't quite have that kind of an attitude toward college. We endured each other. After our freshman year we jokingly decided we were so incompatible, it was time to get married."

And so they did. They both got married to their girlfriends and have each been married for more than forty years. "We drove each other to it," Caldwell joked. "After living with each other, we could handle any adjustment that marriage offered."

According to Caldwell, Huckabee was an "overachiever" who consistently was the "smartest guy in the room." Caldwell said that it wasn't a show for Huckabee; he "wasn't arrogant about it, but he just knew a lot about everything." And his work ethic was incredible. Caldwell said that, by comparison, he barely made it to class.

Huckabee deflects his friend's remembrances of his being a whiz kid, setting his achievements more in a context of focus and determination. "I've always been pretty intense," he said. "I'm not a person who sleeps eight hours a night. I sleep four or five and I'm good to go. I do have the ability to analyze things quickly. Give me a bunch of materials and I'll digest it quickly and figure out what's the basic core of it."[5]

Being the first Huckabee male in his line ever to go to college, he didn't want to disappoint those who had invested in him. "I worked hard, but I worked very efficiently. I didn't have time to waste, running my motor without getting anywhere. I had filled up my dance card; there was no time to piddle. Plus, I was a cheapskate and wanted to make sure I was getting my money's worth."[6]

Huckabee focused more on the books than he had in high school, but he still found time to give student leadership. He served as a senator for his freshman class as chairman for SELF—the Student Entertainment and Lecture Fund. In that role, he brought Victor Marchetti to campus for a free lecture. Marchetti, a former CIA agent and author of the bestselling book *The CIA and the Cult of Intelligence*, said, "I cannot help wondering if my government is more concerned with defending our democratic system or more intent on imitating the methods of totalitarian regimes in order to maintain its already inordinate power over the American people."[7] Huckabee, deflecting potential criticism SELF might receive for inviting the controversial author, said matter-of-factly, "With the CIA in the news the best way to form personal opinions is to hear an expert discuss the facts from his first-hand experience. That's why SELF is bringing Marchetti to Ouachita."[8]

———

Randy Sims does remember one strange thing about his dorm mate. Huckabee subscribed to not just one, but both of the daily newspapers—the *Arkansas Gazette* and the *Arkansas Democrat*. "He had them delivered to his room! I mean, nobody took the papers. We were interested in girls and intramurals and just passing our classes. But he took the papers and read them every morning—every day. He'd read them and then stack them around the walls of his room. All the way up to the ceiling; then he'd start another stack."[9] He had them organized and in a system so he could go back and look something up. In a day before instant online access to information, Huckabee created his own method for information retrieval. Everybody else just thought, *What in the world is going on with this guy? Is he really that serious or what?*

During the spring 1974 semester, all the Arkansas newspapers were running articles about Bill Clinton, the young law professor in Fayetteville who was seeking to unseat incumbent Republican John Paul Hammerschmidt in the Third District—the one area of Arkansas where Republicans could be found in concentration.

Clinton ran a spirited race, especially once Hillary Rodham moved to Arkansas and began assisting his campaign. One news piece noted, "Clinton, strongly backed by the Democratic Party state organization and the state AFL-CIO, came up with surprisingly plentiful financing for a first-time candidate."[10] Another article noted that Clinton "outspent Hammerschmidt by better than three-to-one."[11] In the end, Clinton lost a close race, 51.8 to 48.2 percent.

When Hammerschmidt died in the spring of 2015, Huckabee took to Facebook for a eulogy:

[He was] one of the true pioneers of the Arkansas Republican Party. All of us who have ever been elected in Arkansas as Republicans owe this statesman our deepest respect. But John Paul Hammerschmidt was far more than a Republican leader. He was the purest of public servants, who created the template for serving his constituents and living his life with impeccable integrity and honor. He was the most unselfish and self-effacing person I've ever known in politics. If he had an ego, it was the best-kept secret in Washington where there are no secrets. In my first race, I was a delegate to the Republican National Convention in Houston, the year that John Paul Hammerschmidt was retiring. Reporters came to him and asked his opinion of the news of the day. Knowing that I could use the publicity since I was a newcomer, he turned to me seated behind him and told the reporters they should ask me. Not before or since have I ever known of a political figure who would take himself off the stage to make room for someone else. When I was Governor, I called upon him many times for advice and counsel and he was the creator of the mechanism of our highway construction program. Arkansas has lost one of its most treasured senior statesmen. Janet and I will forever be grateful for the kindnesses that he and Ginny extended to us.[12]

At the end of the semester, Huckabee's newspapers played a prop for his prankster side. Sims and his roommate both went home for the weekend, and when they came back, there was a surprise for them in their dorm room. Huckabee had gotten everyone else in the hallway to take his precious stack of newspapers and make an endless pile of newspaper balls to fill Sims's room—one sheet of newspaper at a time. "Little wads of newspaper all fell out. The entire dorm room. I mean, under the bed, in the bathroom—everywhere," Sims remembered. "Floor to ceiling was nothing but little balls of paper. It was stuffed full. Everyone came out and was just dying laughing."

It got better. "We made everyone help us clean it up," Sims recalled. "Everyone grabbed the balls of papers and headed outside where a huge Dumpster sat. We loaded the whole Dumpster up—full." It wouldn't all fit, so someone decided they'd have to burn the paper. Then somebody else threw gasoline on the pile. "The next thing we know," Sims said, "flames three stories high were rolling up into the air. It wasn't an explosion, but it was the biggest bonfire you ever saw." The fire department came out—sirens going off everywhere—and Huckabee was nowhere to be found. "It took every bit of fast-talking to get out of trouble," Sims said. "We just played dumb. Of course, everybody knew who did it."[13]

Huckabee majored in religion and minored in speech. The "religion" name was a Baptist university's way of dressing up their Bible degree in more sophisticated garb: Greek, Hebrew, preaching, evangelism, pastoral ministry, and so on. During the 1990s, many Baptist universities on the conservative side of the denomination changed their "religion" degree to "Christian Studies" or some other more forthright nomenclature.

OBU had a partnership with its neighboring university, Henderson, allowing students to take courses interchangeably. Huckabee picked up courses like criminology there, and studied broadcasting with the latest equipment available, rather than being limited to the lesser-funded OBU media labs. He clearly had his nose pointed down the vocational path of Christian broadcasting and soaked up every opportunity to hone his craft. "Nobody in the early 1970s saw Christian broadcasting becoming what it did," Huckabee said. "I didn't. I was sort of on the trailing edge of the Jesus movement, trying to figure out a better way to reach people. Instead, I thought the future impact would come through radios and TV sets—very media-focused. And, of course, we saw Christian rock being important too. But the days were gone when a church could just say, 'Here's a nice brick church building, so come down here on Sunday.'"[14]

Mike began pastoring a church his freshman year. He was eighteen. He preached to the tiny congregation—just forty members—on Sundays, and he also made hospital visits and performed other pastoring duties as necessary. He was in Arkadelphia, just ten minutes from the dorms, so it fit well into his schedule. When he thinks back and reflects on just how young he was, Huckabee said that he is amazed anyone would have turned anything over to him.[15]

It all worked out though, and the church experienced a sudden sense of interest from OBU students. Sims remembers going with Huckabee, especially on Sunday nights. "Ladies in the church would fix food for college kids. It was 'college night'—every Sunday night." The dorm mates couldn't have forgotten to go because "Huckabee would go up and down that hallway and make us all go. He'd say 'Come on! Y'all are going to church! Let's go, let's go, let's go.' And so we went. We'd all be at church on a Sunday night, to hear our hall mate preach and get a free supper too."[16]

"He snookered me into attending his church," Caldwell said. "Here I am, my freshman year of college, when most guys experience a time of rebellion." There'd be no wild weekend partying for Caldwell though. "My roommate was my pastor. I couldn't even backslide. I had to behave all the time," he said with a smile.[17]

Many students would show up at the church. "It was kind of a novelty for them to be able to go to a real church and see one of their peers actually in charge," Caldwell remembers. The thing is, they'd also hear him during afternoons as the disc jockey for the local radio station. "You had to have real political capability when, at the same time, you could be a rock-and-roll disc jockey and pastor a Baptist church—on the same day even! To get away with that, you've got some real diplomacy skills."[18]

Caldwell, who also went into the pastoral ministry, remembers well one late-night conversation he and Huckabee had that year. "We were sitting on the floor, talking about what we wanted to do when we grew up. And I remember him saying, 'You know, I just don't feel like I'm cut out to be a normal pastor. You know, I like helping people and I like teaching and I like communicating. But I see me somehow getting involved in a movement—to help good people step up and make government and our nation better.' He said those words more than forty years ago. It was very prophetic."[19]

CHAPTER 14

I WALK THE LINE

1973–1975

> If Mike was ever going to leave me, that
> was his prime opportunity.
>
> —JANET HUCKABEE

WINSTON CHURCHILL ONCE SAID, "MY MOST BRILLIANT
achievement was to persuade my wife to marry me."[1] Even a scant knowledge
of Churchill's biography reveals just how much he was telling the truth. The
stability and joy that Clementine "Clemmie" Hozier brought to the private
life of her husband made it possible for Winston to lead his nation to victory
in World War II. Though more than ten years apart in age, the couple formed
a union of loyalty and love, remaining together for fifty-six years.

When Winston Churchill died in 1965, Mike Huckabee and Janet
McCain were attending elementary school in Hope. Then they shared junior
high and high school classes—always friends but never more. But halfway
through their senior year, mutual participation in basketball brought them
together. Was he a star player and Janet a cheerleader? Hardly. Janet was the
famous athlete, an all-time leading scorer on the girls varsity team, while
Huckabee called the radio play-by-play of the games for his beloved KXAR.
The girls team played the half-court style of three on three, where you played

either offense or defense exclusively. When a defensive rebound was made, the player would run the ball out to the half-court line and pass it off to her teammates on offense. McCain was a scoring machine.

On January 29, 1973, the Hope Ladycats won their game against Ashdown High School, 64 to 51. After the game, Mike and Janet looked for somewhere to go to get something to eat, but there weren't a lot of late-night options in Hope. So they headed over to the Fulton Truck Stop to eat at the Red Oak Café, a late-night diner. This was their first date. The next day's *Hope Star* put a large picture of Janet McCain on the front page, not because she went on a date with Huckabee, but because of her basketball prowess the night before. Still, how many couples can say that the morning after their first date, one of them had made the front page?

"After several postgame trips to the eatery, you could tell Mike and Janet were becoming more than friends," Sitzes recalled. "The truth is, they always had been really good friends with one another, so romance made perfect sense. Janet won his mind and heart—he really enjoyed being with her."[2]

When asked if she remembers when they were "steady," Janet said matter-of-factly, "I don't know that we ever went steady. We just dated. We got engaged. And now we're here."[3]

———

Sitzes and McCain went to church together at the First Baptist Church of Hope, a prominent congregation with impressive facilities and a faith-building youth program. Sitzes remembers mission trips, choir tours, and a strong discipleship program. He also remembers getting jabbed by the kind of Baptists Huckabee went to church with: "Southern Baptists aren't true Baptists!" In contrast, FBC offered a less strident version of Christianity.

Though Huckabee grew up poor, the McCains were poorer still. Janet's father abandoned the family when she was a young girl, leaving her mom to raise and support the five children. They were too poor to travel or go on vacations, but Janet does remember a time when they got to go to Six Flags down in Arlington, Texas. "At the grocery store, every time you bought something, you could get entered to win tickets. Someone—we don't know who—entered my family in the hat. Somehow or other we won, so my mother took all of us. But my mom was so afraid the whole way down, thinking that maybe Six Flags wouldn't honor the coupons."[4]

For much of Janet's childhood, her mom served as the clerk of Hempstead County, an elected position. So not only did her mom oversee the results of county elections; she also campaigned—though the clerk's position did not warrant the full-scale electioneering hoopla of other public offices. "As a result of her mom's job," Huckabee said, "Janet has always had this real sense that people ought to run for office and they ought to vote. That's just part of life."[5]

He and Janet dated solidly through the spring and summer before college, and then entered Ouachita Baptist College together. "Dating is one more blast," Huckabee wrote in his RAPture Express article that fall. "And when you find a Christian dating partner that loves Jesus as much as you do, then you've really got something. I'm saying it because I know the difference that Christ can make in a dating relationship, and I want you to experience the same happiness that I've found in a Jesus-loving mate."[6]

Though they were not engaged yet, they were definitely committed. No other guy at OBU had a chance with Janet, because "on campus, you always saw Mike with Janet, hand in hand," Caldwell said. He remembers Janet initially being "kind of shy in college," but "she sure broke out of that right away."[7] Janet enrolled in a full load of courses while also playing basketball for her college. Even with all her high school accolades on the basketball court, however, she was not on a scholarship. "They gave out only a few scholarships for the girls program, and I wasn't on that list." Her academic plan was to become a physical education teacher, combining her giftedness in athletics with her desire to impact the next generation. "No one knows for sure what I might have done," she said, "but it's fun to think about."[8]

———

The couple announced their engagement during Christmas break, intending to marry in May, when school let out for the summer. They were not quite nineteen. Why get married so young? Well, hormones and the affections of the heart will lead any young couple to desire intimacy, but Christian sexual ethics will direct them into lifelong marital commitment—*before* partaking of the pleasures of marriage. Because of their desire to obey the scripture's teaching that "your bodies are members of Christ" (1 Cor. 6:15) and the command to "honor God with your bodies" (1 Cor. 6:20), Mike and Janet never considered cohabitation. Once, when asked by a reporter to describe his best friend's marriage, Sitzes offered this golden quote: "Those two folks were virgins when they got married, I can tell you that."[9]

For Janet and Mike, it also just made more financial sense to get married. Instead of paying for two dorm rooms, they'd just be paying rent on one apartment. Besides, they were in love, so why wait anyway?

Their wedding ceremony did not take elaborate planning or vast reserves of money; they married in the basement of Janet's home on May 25, 1974. "I actually officiated the wedding," Caldwell said. "'Wow, what an honor you were given,' people say, but I tell them, 'No, you just don't know how frugal Mike was. He knew he could get his roommate to do it for free.'"[10] Sitzes served as best man. Vocal and guitar music came from a friend, Garry Hamvey, and Janet's sister Patty House. According to the *Hope Star*, "The bride carried an old fashioned bouquet of white glamellia atop a silver-bound Bible from the Holy Land, a gift of the groom."[11]

Years later, Huckabee wrote about how couples invest so much time and money into preparing for a wedding that lasts only minutes but spend next to no time preparing for the lifetime commitment of marriage.[12] Nobody can accuse Huckabee of preaching one thing after doing something different himself. In addition to the ring, the most expensive cost for Huckabee was the tuxedo. Sitzes remembers going with Huckabee to pick out the suit. "That was his doing—that baby blue thing," Sitzes said. "I had nothing to do with that suit. But, I'm sentimental enough that I still have the bow tie I wore. Maybe I'll sell it on eBay if Mike becomes the president."[13]

The newlyweds returned to Arkadelphia for Huckabee's sophomore year of college, setting up house in an off-campus apartment. "When we got married we were flat broke," he recalled. "Our first place we lived in was a forty-dollar-a-month duplex that was grossly overpriced at forty dollars per month."[14] Janet ceased her own studies in order to work, though two decades later she finished her degree at age forty-seven, completing it while raising a family and running for secretary of state of Arkansas. But in 1974, the newly-weds focused on frugality and living on love.

Meanwhile, a few hundred miles to the north, two Yale Law School graduates—Bill Clinton and Hillary Rodham—moved in together and became faculty members at the University of Arkansas–Fayetteville. They wedded the following year, though not before Rodham struggled to decide whether marrying Clinton would enhance or destroy her own career potential. "I chose to follow my heart instead of my head," she would later explain.[15]

In the Huckabees' first year of marriage, Janet underwent medical tests for a slipped disk in her back—or so they thought. The diagnosis shocked them: cancer. Worse, the location of the malignant tumor, on her spine, meant that its surgical removal ran the risk of leaving Janet permanently paralyzed. And the postoperative radiation therapy could render her infertile.[16] Finally, the bills for all these procedures would most likely weigh the young couple down under a mountain of debt.

"If we are a member of the human family, we will face extraordinary trials and testing," Huckabee later wrote. "The only way a boat can be tested is to be placed in the water. The only way a rope can be tested is to be pulled."[17] The Huckabees were being tested early.

Friends and family gave support. Also, Huckabee recalled the ministry of "a bivocational pastor who had never even completed high school who put his arm on my shoulder and offered an understanding and comfort that sur-passed any superficial platitudes or 'preacherisms.' He wept with me. He hurt with me. He didn't explain anything and he didn't try to interpret anything. His unconditional love didn't earn him any 'hours' of credit, but if it had, the grade would have been A+."[18]

In October 1975, doctors in Little Rock removed the tumor without injuring Janet's spine. Next it was time for radiation. Huckabee got up early in the mornings to drive Janet to Little Rock for her treatments before returning to Arkadelphia for classes and work—and *still* managed to shave three semesters off his baccalaureate degree, while graduating with highest honors, pastoring a church, and working as a DJ. And they were both just twenty.

Janet will joke and say, "If Mike was ever going to leave me, that was his prime opportunity."[19] But there was no chance of that. As Dorsey used to tell his son, "A poor man doesn't have much, but at least he has his word." Janet's father may have abandoned his family, but after those early days together, Janet knew that she and Mike could make it through anything.

"They kept their faith and marriage, and found victory through all those trials," Caldwell said. "They maintained their character and their winsome attitude toward life. Mike and Janet just kept moving."[20]

CHAPTER 15

BORN TO RUN

January 1975–May 1976

> When I finished college, it didn't occur to me to do anything
> else. I thought, *I'm out of school; let's go. Let's get to seminary.*
>
> **—MIKE HUCKABEE**

IN OCTOBER 1975, BRUCE SPRINGSTEEN APPEARED ON THE covers of both *Newsweek* and *Time*—the "Boss" had arrived. It was Elvis Presley's 1957 appearance on *The Ed Sullivan Show* that had launched the musical ambitions of Springsteen, then seven years old. By the late 1960s, he played at clubs and throughout his native New Jersey. A couple of albums in the early 1970s established his critical acclaim, although the commercial appeal was not yet there. In the spring of 1974, a reviewer wrote, "I saw rock and roll's future, and its name is Bruce Springsteen. And on a night when I needed to feel young, he made me feel like I was hearing music for the very first time."[1]

Springsteen entered the music studio once again, determined to produce a breakout album that lived up to his full potential. Feeling the pressure of the money invested in the project and the expectations of critics and fans, Springsteen spent fourteen months on the album, *Born to Run*. He worked on the title track alone for six months. The album's optimism centered on the narrative of the title track, wherein a young man with big dreams and a

121

muscular determination to succeed beckons his girlfriend, "Wendy," to run the journey together with him. He tells her that, though he didn't know how long it would take, they would get to where they wanted to go.

Springsteen released *Born to Run* the day after Huckabee turned twenty. You would be hard-pressed to find a song that better illustrates how the young couple were living out their newly married life together. Janet had lived through cancer, surgery, and chemotherapy that fall. And at the same time, Mike had plowed through his fifth and final semester of college.

But life passes you by if you slow down to catch your breath. So even as he finished up his OBU coursework, the Huckabees packed their belongings and prepared to move to Fort Worth, Texas, for graduate school. Entering Southwestern Baptist Theological Seminary (SWBTS) meant breaking with his Baptist Missionary Association once and for all. They had their own seminaries, so choosing one of the six SBC graduate schools marked a point of no return. Despite his friends' warnings that he wouldn't be able to pastor a Southern Baptist church, he knew that he was making the right decision.[2]

SWBTS was, and still is, one of the largest seminaries in the world, with several thousand students enrolled in its programs. At that time, the average seminary student was in his or her midthirties. Many were coming to ministry and to graduate school as a second profession. That statistic has changed much since then, as the average age of an MDiv student has dropped ten years, making it a degree program full of recent college graduates. Huckabee fit that description when he arrived from OBU, except that he was even younger. "When I finished college, it didn't occur to me to do anything else," he said. "I thought, *I'm out of school; let's go. Let's get to seminary.* So we packed up and went. I got to class and, my gosh, I thought, *I am a child. I'm twenty, and I look seventeen.* It was just bizarre because the youngest people in my class were twenty-five, but most of them were in their thirties. These people were so much older than I was, and with kids. My own friends started showing up at seminary two years later, but by that time I was already gone."[3]

Some of those friends also came from OBU, like Dwight McKissic and Rick Caldwell. Another student he walked the halls with was Rick Warren, pastor of Saddleback Community Church and bestselling author. Like Warren, Huckabee is not an ivory-tower theologian, splitting hairs on small issues. Huckabee sometimes makes theological statements that please nobody—not the secularist, the liberal, or the conservative. One side argues that his theology says too much; the other side takes issue with his lack of precision, finding an offense because he doesn't say more.

Though he did not complete the MDiv, Huckabee did not lack a strong program of religious studies. In addition to his undergraduate major in religion, Huckabee took 48 hours at SWBTS: systematic theology, church history, Greek, evangelism, archaeology, and counseling—to name just a few. And the "academics were challenging and academically stimulating," he said. "'These were highly skilled and theologically advanced professors with PhDs, ThDs—all the professors had terminal degrees. It's just that they also had a fervor. Professors like Dr. Robert Estep—he made everything come alive. He would talk about the Anabaptists, which normally would put people to sleep, but he'd have you just on the edge of your seat. He got it into you why it all mattered—there was always an application. There always was a sense of why we were studying this stuff."[4]

In 1976, the denomination was not yet under the control of the "conservative resurgence." The seminaries were not equal in terms of tolerance for liberal teaching and leadership. Even now, each has its own unique flavor and some doctrinal differences. But when Huckabee entered SWBTS, it was considered by many to be the most conservative of the six. During the 1970s, the issues became clarified and the factions became polarized. Robert Naylor served as president while Huckabee attended the seminary. Naylor was "a really great man," Huckabee said. "He would get up in chapel every day and quote these really long passages of Scripture from memory, with this deep, resonant voice. It was just wonderful to listen to him."[5] Russell Dilday followed Naylor as president in 1978, though Huckabee had already left for full-time ministry by that time. By 1989, conservatives held the majority position on the boards of trustees for most of the SBC entities. In 1994, the SWBTS board fired Dilday, changing the locks on his office within hours of their vote.

Was there liberalism at SWBTS during Huckabee's time there? "No, it was a hotbed of conservatism," Huckabee said. "It never had a theological left turn, even at the time when Southern and Southeastern were apostate. There really was not any liberalism that I ever encountered. Not in the classroom, not on the campus. The professors were phenomenal. I never had a bad professor. I never had a professor that I thought, *Wow! I can't believe the Baptists are paying this guy's salary.*

"Folks made fun of Southwestern," Huckabee said. "They called it a three-year camp meeting, like a revival. And when they called it that, we said, 'Dang straight.' We considered it a badge of honor to be at Southwestern.

"Of course, most students had to work," Huckabee continued. "There were very few people just sitting around contemplating their theological navels. These were people that worked selling shoes at J. C. Penney, taking classes at night, and trying to raise a family. Some were taking a little part-time pastorate job, driving off two hundred miles on Sundays."

The Huckabees were no different from the rest in that regard. Janet worked as a dental assistant for the first year. Then, in November 1976, their firstborn son arrived, and she left work to stay home with the baby, John Mark. Down to one income, the Huckabees found their already tight finances stretched even thinner. "For almost six months, our daily meals consisted of peanut butter and jelly sandwiches and alternating flavors of canned soup," he later wrote.[6]

On Sundays, the Huckabees commuted to church with another couple to save on gas. Then they'd pull out their loose change and "scrape together enough money to go get ourselves a treat—twenty-five-cent tacos—that was a big deal for us."[7]

During this period Huckabee sold his guitars in order to pay the bills. And a random and unexpected refund for an overpayment on a previous year's utility bill gave the Huckabees exactly the money needed for a week's worth of baby formula. Janet tried her hand selling Tupperware. She also baked cakes for friends and sold them (though he says she always just gave the delicious cakes away in the end).

The biggest windfall of unexpected money came when Huckabee was involved in a five-car pileup out on the interstate. While at OBU, a friend's family had sold them an extra car they owned, a four-door, baby blue Ford LTD. The price: one dollar.

The Huckabees drove that LTD during college and then down to seminary. But one day, as Mike tells the story, "My car was turned into an accordion. A car hit a car in front of me, so I was stopped. And as I looked in my rearview and I saw a tractor-trailer coming. I thought, *He can't stop*. And he didn't. He plowed into me, and that threw me into the other car. Then another eighteen-wheeler came behind him. It was a mess."

So how did that create a financial windfall? Well, they owned the car outright, obviously, and carried insurance on it too. The insurance company took one look at the back end all crumpled down (though the taillights somehow still worked) and declared it "totaled" in the insurance sense of the word. They paid Huckabee the salvage value of the car and walked away. "But miraculously, the car was still drivable it still ran," he said, "though there were a few cosmetic issues. Like, we had to get somebody to rig a crowbar where we could get in on the driver's side. And you couldn't get in on the backseat at all. Or on the back of the passenger side. And, of course, the back end was all rumpled up. But other than that, it was great. I drove that car around for another two years!

"We kind of called it God's car," he said, "because it was a blessing to our finances."

"It was huge," Janet declared.

"We could still use the car, and we had money in my pocket. Of course, I didn't want to make money that way very often. I didn't want to earn income being in a wreck. There had to be a better way to finance the family."

The couple has many of these anecdotes about living on the edge of poverty during this season. Huckabee worked hard, but the bills add up fast when you're in graduate school. That is when his part-time job in radio led to a full-time job offering. Should he embrace the promotion, an incredible position to be offered to a twenty-one-year-old? he wondered. Doing so would relieve his economic problems, but it would also end his educational pursuits.

"Fairly early in 1976 I was just starting to do some freelance radio spots for James Robison's evangelistic organization," Huckabee explained. "I was helping to make the promotional commercials for his crusades. Then they promoted me to be the part-time media buyer. I had an advertising budget for an upcoming event. It was up to me to figure out what the ratings on the station were and to calculate which stations would serve our needs the best." That's when Robison offered him a full-time job as his director of communications.

"Robison was highly respected at Southwestern overall," Huckabee said. "Sure, some professors might have thought, *Oh, an evangelist. He didn't go to seminary.* But most people would have been respectful of his effectiveness. At Southwestern, your effectiveness was more important than simply that you were an academic."

So he went to one of his professors, Oscar Thompson, looking for counsel as to what he should do. "I knew that he was going to tell me, 'You stay in school, son.'" Instead, the professor asked him what his plans were for ministry—what did he hope to do after seminary? Huckabee said he wanted to go into broadcasting. Thompson asked him what kind of work Robison was offering him. "Advertising and running a national television ministry," Huckabee responded. Thompson replied, "Okay, so what's your question?"[8]

Thompson reminded Huckabee that the seminary wasn't going anywhere. It would still be sitting in the same spot if the Robison opportunity didn't work out for Huckabee, not yet twenty-one. "Dr. Thompson oddly enough persuaded me that the opportunity was one that I really couldn't pass up, and it was the beginning of a whole chain of events in my life that eventually led me to the governor's office of Arkansas," Huckabee said. "I will forever cherish the fact that he didn't tell me what I expected to hear, nor tell me what I think he was probably expected to say as a seminary professor."[9]

In the fall of 1976, one year after Bruce Springsteen got double billing on *Newsweek* and *Time*, "born again" evangelicalism also received the same treatment. Jimmy Carter, a Southern Baptist layman Sunday school teacher who read his Bible and prayed daily, seemed to offer the nation an opportunity to vote for a man with a church life they could relate to and an ethical core they could trust. Carter contrasted sharply with the rottenness of the Nixon administration, or even President Ford, who had pardoned Nixon. Southern Baptist leaders talked about the nation being saved by "J. C."—a play on the initials of Jesus Christ and Jimmy Carter. Evangelicals gave Carter 40 percent of their votes, the highest percent that conservative Christians had given to a Democrat in over a decade.[10]

Huckabee voted for Carter. He said, "In '76 I was still very angry with Gerald Ford for the pardon of Nixon. I had been a Nixon coordinator in '72, and had been a Nixon fan, but felt really let down and disillusioned. In retrospect,

I thought that Ford did the right thing to pardon him; saved the country from a lot of grief. But it was hard not to be angry about it."[11]

On his way to prison, Chuck Colson, former chief counsel to President Nixon, converted to Christianity and wrote a bestselling book, *Born Again*, to testify of his changed life.[12] And on his way to defeating President Gerald Ford in the fall of 1976, Democratic governor Jimmy Carter expressed his Christian faith in a way that few, if any, presidential candidates had ever done before. "I serve Christ. I also serve America," Carter said. "And I have never found any incompatibility between those two responsibilities for service."[13] In a similar way, Huckabee was entering broadcasting with the same motto.

"Carter was campaigning as, 'Hey, I'm a born-again believer' and I thought it would be cool to have a Southern Baptist," Huckabee said. "I didn't have the attitude of 'We don't want one of ours.' I said, 'We *do* want one of ours.' Now, it turned out he was not really one of us, although Carter's testimony is pure as pure can be. I've actually been in church with him—I've preached in Plains when he's given the Sunday school lesson. His presentation of the gospel was the clearest plan of salvation."[14]

Janet Huckabee knows the former president even better, having served on the board for his Habitat for Humanity for over a decade. "She's done work projects alongside Jimmy Carter in Thailand, Nepal—all over the world," Huckabee said. "But that's a story for another book."[15] In 1976, the "born again" and "born to run" Huckabees were in Texas, not Thailand. But they were running fast and running deliberately, getting closer to where they really wanted to go.

CHAPTER 16

SON OF A PREACHER MAN

1976–1979

> I'd never even heard of prime rib before, and didn't even know
> how to order steak. Going out to eat in my home meant my dad
> picked up a sack of "six for a dollar" hamburgers with some fries
> on the side. Robison gave me a lot of invaluable experience.
>
> **—MIKE HUCKABEE**

WHEN CONSERVATIVE CHRISTIANS ENTERED THE VOTING booth in 1980 with a chance to reelect Jimmy Carter to a second term, they shifted their votes over to Ronald Reagan. From 1976 to 1980, the public leadership of conservative Christianity awoke to the very idea of being politically active. The evangelical/fundamentalist component of Nixon's "silent majority" gave life to the Moral Majority—to name just one of the groups birthed by the new "Religious Right" during these years. And Huckabee stood right in the midst of the labor and delivery.

Several issues of cultural and moral concern had percolated throughout the late 1960s and early 1970s. Many were local issues that had garnered national press coverage and led to a coalescing of the conservative movement as national figures intervened in support or opposition. In the late 1960s, parents in Anaheim, California, protested new materials for sexual education that began to reflect the changing mores of the time. In 1974, parents in Kanawha County, West Virginia, battled—in word and with fists—their school board over the issue of textbooks deemed unfit for their children. "If we don't protect our children we'll have to account for it on the Day of Judgment," one protestor said at a rally of eight thousand.[1]

In 1977, singer Anita Bryant began a campaign in Miami, Florida, called "Save Our Children," designed to overturn a recently passed ordinance that prohibited discrimination based on sexual orientation. In other words, she didn't want the parochial school her children attended to be forced to hire a homosexual teacher. President Carter expressed his opposition to Bryant's campaign and his support of the ordinance. An independent Baptist preacher from Lynchburg, Virginia—Jerry Falwell—came to Miami to help in the cause, and the repeal passed by a two-to-one vote. The victory, however, ignited grassroots homosexual activists across the nation.

Huckabee recalled those years. "A lot of people have forgotten how much public sympathy there was for homosexuality in 1980—not as much for same-sex marriage, but for accepting homosexuality as normal. There were parades, Anita Bryant was fired for her views from the Florida Orange Juice Association, and the movement was gaining traction."[2]

During the late 1960s, a great number of Christian schools and colleges opened their doors to parents who wanted something better for their children. For some parents, the "something better" meant a school where prayer was allowed; others were motivated by the controversies surrounding the textbooks or sex ed. Still others simply wanted their children shielded from the growing licentiousness and immorality of the day. Finally, forced desegregation also played a role—some parents did not want their children to attend a mixed-race school. Into all this, state and federal court decisions began to work on rooting out institutionalized racism, threatening to take away the tax-exempt status of religious educational organizations; Bob Jones University was the most public example. In 1976, during the Ford administration, the IRS revoked the university's tax-exempt status because of their policy forbidding interracial dating.

It was also during this same time that conservative pastors and laymen in the Southern Baptist Convention developed and implemented a political strategy to reverse what they saw as the liberal shift in their denomination. The discussion that had begun in the late 1950s led to a famous 1967 planning session by theologian Paige Patterson and Houston judge Paul Pressler. It would take twelve years for the conservatives to win their first election.

On June 12, 1979, Southern Baptists elected Pastor Adrian Rogers of Memphis to the presidency of the Convention. During the Pastors Conference, which comes just before the annual convention, one speaker after another had urged the election of Rogers, including Huckabee's mentor, evangelist James Robison. He said that if Southern Baptists tolerated the liberalism of the convention, they would "be guilty of the death" of the convention: "We must elect a president not only dedicated to the inerrancy of the word of God, but who will stand to remove any seminary professor who doesn't believe in the inerrant word of God."[3]

———

Robison's own biography makes a fascinating story. He was born in 1943 as the product of "forced sexual experience" to an impoverished and unwed forty-one-year-old mother. His mother then placed an ad in the Houston paper, asking for help in raising her son. A local pastor, H. D. Hale, and his wife raised him for the first five years—even as his biological mother continued to see him. Then, she took James back and moved to Austin, where he was "loved, but living in extreme poverty" for the next ten years.[4]

As a teen, James visited the Hales, made a profession of faith in Christ, and then finished his last two years of high school while living with them. Robison met his future wife while in high school, and they married at age twenty.

Robison began preaching and was quickly recognized for his gifts and passion behind the pulpit. In 1967, he founded the James Robison Evangelistic Association, and wealthy Christians took an interest in underwriting his ministry.[5] "Robison is the most effective communicator I have ever heard," Texas billionaire H. L. Hunt proclaimed.[6] Christian television stations broadcast Robison's sermons throughout the South, including in Hope, Arkansas.

As many as a half million viewers watched Robison each week on the television as he delivered fiery sermons denouncing immorality and declaring a simple gospel message of faith and repentance in Jesus Christ. One newspaper article in 1979 called him "God's Angry Man"—a title he has worked hard to lose over the years, even as he retained his core beliefs.[7] The "angry man" label might have seemed appropriate at one time, but the totality of Robison's ministry can hardly be painted with such broad brushstrokes.

———

As the Huckabees continued to struggle to pay their bills, a position for full-time work opened and Robison asked Huckabee to consider taking the job. "He believed in me and turned over the whole agency to me," Huckabee said. "As a twenty-one-year-old kid, I suddenly had twelve people that worked for me. A multimillion-dollar budget. Two titles in front of my name: executive director of focus advertising and director of communications for the James Robison Evangelistic Association."[8]

"I made $12,000 a year, which was phenomenally good money in 1977—especially for the two of us and our baby son, John Mark," Huckabee said.

Beyond just giving Huckabee a job, however, Robison also began mentoring him. "When I went to work for him, I only owned two suits," Huckabee said. "I might have paid five dollars for one and ten dollars for the other. They were cheap, pathetic, and double-knit. That was all I could afford. And I had just one pair of shoes. People made fun of me at school about the holes in my shoes, and the bottom was coming apart. They were uncomfortable too, but again, that's what I could afford.

"My first day at work," he continued, "I got word that James wanted to see me in his office. He grabbed his keys and said, 'Come with me. We're going shopping.' So we drove down to Waxman's department store in Hurst, Texas. Robison bought me three brand-new suits, shirts, and ties. He said, 'If you're going to work for me, you're going to have to look good. I'm going to take care of you and make you look good.'"

Through the experience working with Robison, Huckabee also gained practical skills he could never have learned in Hope. He flew on planes constantly, rented cars, booked hotel rooms, and ordered steak at a restaurant—for the first time. "I know it sounds silly, but I'd never even heard of prime rib before, and didn't know how to order steak," he said. "Going out to eat in my home meant my dad picked up a sack of 'six for a dollar' hamburgers with some fries on the side. Robison gave me a lot of invaluable experience."

In return, Huckabee gave Robison an honest evaluation when he needed a critique. "That was my value to him," Huckabee recalled. "When he would have a press conference which had gone awful, I figured that one of my jobs was to shoot straight with him. So, when I could get him alone, I'd let him know how he had botched things up in a given situation, especially with the press."

Robison valued Huckabee's youthful energy and his skillful hand in communications. And Huckabee benefited from having this "preacher man" in his life, a supplemental father figure who mentored him in many areas of benefit to his future pastoral ministry, his career in broadcasting, and his public service in government.

So Huckabee didn't leave seminary to work for just any revivalist-evangelist— and in 1976 there were plenty from which to choose. No, he went to work for a young (early thirties) and prominent preacher with a fast-growing television-broadcasting platform. This aligned perfectly with his own vision of his vocation—to combine his love for Jesus and the Great Commission with his skills in media and communications. And in Huckabee, Robison found a young man with relentless energy and an amazing résumé in communications, considering his age—twenty-one at the time of his being hired.

Any accounting of Huckabee's life must place him in the context of the rise (though not the fall) of television broadcasting—the "electronic church," as some called it. Or, as it is best known, *televangelism*—with all the pejorative connotations that word now conveys. But the negative impression came much later, at the end of the 1980s. In the mid-to-late 1970s, the fact that Bible preachers had come out of the proverbial backwoods and were standing in front of television cameras sending their images across space and into millions of homes by means of satellites—all of which took astronomical amounts of money to operate—what more could signal that Christianity was yet ascending in America? The idea that religious broadcasting could counter the counterculture was appealing.

Of course, conservative preaching had been a potent force for decades. The National Association of Evangelicals formed the National Religious Broadcasters in 1944 as a response to the mainline Federal Council of Churches' demand that broadcasters stop selling airtime to the more popular conservative-fundamentalist programming. The idea was to limit religious broadcasting only to the free time that networks had to provide as a service to the community.

Then, in the 1970s, the decision was made to allow television networks to fulfill their community service time slots through *paid* religious broadcasting. The new technique of using sophisticated mailing lists for mass fund-raising efforts allowed preachers who had the organizational means to purchase the "dead zone" time slots on Sunday mornings.

Estimates vary, but most historians put the 1970 viewership of religious programming at about ten million; by 1980, viewership had hit twenty to thirty million. The amount of money spent by broadcasters escalated from $50 million in the early 1970s to over $1 billion in the 1980s.[9] Behind every dollar was a viewer with a mailing address and a set of moral convictions that could be considered "conservative." In the minds of New Right political operatives like Howard Phillips (at the time, Jewish) and Paul Weyrich (Roman Catholic) and direct-mail pioneer Paul Viguerie (who once worked for anticommunist radio evangelist Billy James Hargis), the only question was whether or not the preachers behind the television camera could become politically active and convince their viewers to do so as well. Further, would the "megachurch" (a relatively new term at the time) pastors join in too?

No matter how reluctant these figures may have been in the 1960s to bring politics into the world of their religious media empires, the moral confusion of the 1970s provoked them into a new mind-set about the mixture. Television preachers led directly to the birth of nearly all the new political-religious organizations of the 1970s: Jerry Falwell's Moral Majority, Pat Robertson's Christian Voice, and James Robison's leadership with Ed McAteer's Religious Roundtable. To be sure, there were men behind the men—operatives and organizers who figured out how to make it all work. But the men who stood before the camera drove the publicity and the funding. It took only a spark of opposition to get fiery preachers aflame in the political realm.

That spark came in the spring of 1979 in Dallas, when a local television station, WFAA, removed James Robison from the airwaves after a February sermon aired in which he denounced homosexuality. Under the provisions of the Federal Communications Commission's Fairness Doctrine, members of the gay rights community demanded equal access to time—similar to other groups that had taken umbrage at Robison's attacks. WFAA management decided they had heard enough and took his program off the air. What happened in the ensuing one hundred days was "a pivotal moment in the formation of the New Christian Right."[10]

In the influential documentary *With God on Our Side: The Rise of the Religious Right in America*, Robison recalled that event: "It hurt me deeply when they did that. I went to them and said, 'This won't be accepted. I wish you hadn't done it.' It became a rallying point. Catholics, Church of Christ, Jews, every religious segment said, 'This is wrong. This man has spoken on a moral issue he feels strongly about, and you've taken him off the air.' I designed a bumper sticker that said 'Freedom of Speech, the Right to Preach,' and it just went everywhere."[11]

However, Robison needed more than a bumper sticker to get back on the air, so he began reaching out to friends. Local pastors did materialize in support of him—even some who disagreed with his theological understanding of homosexuality as being a sin. They agreed with Robison that this was a First Amendment issue and came to his defense. Even more support came from outside Dallas as the word spread among broadcast ministries across the nation. Instead of this being a localized issue pitting citizens against a city government ordinance, the Robison case threatened the freedom of the pulpit throughout the entire land. As Jerry Falwell said, "When it comes to preaching the Bible, we will not back up, we will die for our right to preach."[12]

Robison reached out to Paul Weyrich for help: "You are very familiar with the battle that I find myself now engaged [in]. I am convinced that we will be of much help to one another, as we join forces and strength together in the battle for the conservation of a free America."[13]

Robison hired a lawyer—the famous Texas trial lawyer Richard "Racehorse" Haynes—to work with the FCC in getting his program back on the air. A legal fund was established to pay for these services, as noted in the *Irving Daily News* on March 22: "Robison Association spokesman Mike Huckabee said today that donations should be mailed directly to . . . 'It will be separate from funds for the ministry,' he said."[14]

A "Freedom Rally" was planned for the first week in June. Huckabee went to work immediately, planning the logistics, crafting communications and publicity, making phone calls and invitations—just as one would in a political campaign. Though many historians—and even a few of the participants—have erroneously stated that the rally happened at Reunion Arena, that facility did not even open until the following year. The confusion is simple to understand when you realize that yet another historic event for the Religious Right *did* take place in Reunion Arena only one year later (see next chapter). The Freedom Rally actually occurred at the Dallas Convention Center Arena, mere blocks from the WFAA station.

The rally was held on the evening of Tuesday, June 5 (yes, exactly one week before the election in Houston of Adrian Rogers as president of the SBC). Between eight and eleven thousand people turned out—representing five hundred churches. Jerry Falwell called Robison "the prophet of God for our day" and declared, "I think this is the first time a television station has blatantly attempted to tell a gospel broadcaster what he can't say."[15]

Weyrich, a Roman Catholic, also spoke at the rally, with Robison making the introduction—and heading off at the pass any anti-Catholic sentiment. Weyrich observed that the barrier between evangelicals and Catholics was finally starting to fall.[16]

When it came time for Robison to speak, he said, "It is my prayer WFAA will rescind their horrendous, tragic decision and put us back on the air. I ask you to pray we might have in this community someone humble and honest enough to admit they made a mistake and reverse it. Just say, 'We made a mistake and wanted to correct it in the name of freedom, liberty and justice, and we don't care who doesn't like it.' That is my prayer."[17]

Huckabee remembers the event well: "There was this amazing energy coming up from these evangelical Christians . . . I remember almost being frightened by it. If someone had gotten to the microphone and said, 'Let's go four blocks from here and take Channel 8 apart,' that audience would've taken the last brick off the building."[18]

W. A. Criswell, a prominent local pastor and former SBC president, looked straight into the camera and told WFAA to reinstate Robison.[19]

They did.

══════════

Robison explained to reporters that the rally had been designed to mobilize people "around the Word of God and the Constitution. We want to let people hear from the Christians—the moral majority."[20] These words, printed in the Fort Worth newspaper on June 6, mark one of the first public uses of that phrase—the "moral majority"—since its being coined just one month earlier at a private Lynchburg meeting, attended by Weyrich, Phillips, Viguerie, McAteer, and Falwell.[21]

The close proximity on the calendar between the May meeting in Lynchburg and the Freedom Rally in June, combined with the common leaders at both meetings, led Huckabee to view the latter event as the bona fide origin of the Moral Majority. "In April of 1979," he wrote, "I had been one of the organizers of the 'Freedom Rally' that was held in Dallas Reunion Arena that was the actual birth of the Moral Majority and which gave the framework for the National Affairs Briefing."[22] The official entity known as the "Moral Majority" was chartered in June, so Huckabee's main point—"I was there at the beginning"—is duly noted.

The true long-term impact of the rally came as the result of a brief strategy session the leaders of the rally conducted that very night. They sensed they were being compelled by the circumstances of the moment to become more involved in the political realm. But the question remained—did their constituencies feel the same way? Paul Weyrich suggested they conduct a poll of their people in order to find out. Standing just outside the door of this historic strategy session, Mike Huckabee soaked up all that he had seen and heard that night.

In the months that followed, Ed McAteer, a retired businessman and member of Adrian Rogers's church, formed a political caucus called the "Religious Roundtable." He persuaded Pat Robertson, Charles Stanley, Jerry Falwell, and D. James Kennedy to serve on the organization's board of directors, and he made James Robison the vice president.[23] McAteer saw the

Roundtable as having the ability to pull in congregations and leaders from evangelical and mainline groups, not just the independents.[24]

The Roundtable met in December 1979 to discuss the results of Weyrich's survey. Present at the meeting were Falwell, Howard Phillips, Robison, Beverly LaHaye, and Phyllis Schlafly. Weyrich reported that church members were not against being politically active. In fact, his survey showed that they were emphatically in favor of it—"off the charts." "That was life-changing when these guys saw that," Weyrich said. "They fell over themselves to start some activity or to involve themselves."[25]

One of the first things that McAteer and Robison began planning was another rally in Dallas—a "National Affairs Briefing" to be held in August 1980. They figured it was time for a revolution. Robison was grateful to Huckabee for his organizational leadership in the 1979 rally, and he would once again lean on his young protégé for help in pulling together the 1980 event.

CHAPTER 17

REVOLUTION

1980

> All the complex questions facing us at home and abroad
> have their answer in that single book [the Bible].
>
> **—RONALD REAGAN**

DALLAS HAD RECENTLY OPENED THE DOORS ON ITS NEW Reunion Arena in the spring of 1980, providing an air-conditioned venue for entertainment: sporting events, conventions, and concerts. The NBA Mavericks and the NHL Stars would play in the arena, along with a panoply of other leagues, teams, and professional wrestling. Foghat was one of the first musical acts to play in the arena on June 25, followed by a three-act concert the next night: Ted Nugent, the Scorpions, and Def Leppard. The Who came in July.

Outside, it was hot. Freak atmospheric conditions kept much of the United States locked into a record-breaking grip of heat. Arkansas and Texas baked. In Dallas, the thermometer ran above 100 degrees for forty-two consecutive days and a total of sixty-nine times altogether. Twenty-eight of those days the heat rose above 105; five times it went above 110.[1] Across the nation, over a thousand people died and $20 billion (in 1980 dollars) worth of crops withered and turned to dust in the field.[2]

Queen, a pioneer in the art of music videos, filmed "Another One Bites the Dust" while at Reunion Arena during the first part of August. The song's disco beat exemplified the decade that had just passed, but the fact that the song had a video hinted at the decade to come, as MTV launched the following year.

In a similar fashion, Ronald Reagan's 1980 campaign offered a return to something stable, even as he was leading America to have a renewal of hope and optimism about the future. One week after Queen's concert, Reagan also arrived at Reunion Arena, at the invitation of Mike Huckabee's boss, to speak to more than fifteen thousand evangelicals gathered for the Religious Roundtable, including nearly every single leader of what became known as the "Religious Right." The sheer fact that Reagan came to the event, combined with the subtle force of what he actually said to the crowd, won their hearts and their votes and helped move him into the White House.

If evangelicals felt any reluctance to abandon Carter, the 1980 White House Conference on Families settled the question. Carter had announced the conference back in January 1978 and was determined not to break a promise, no matter how much his advisors told him that it wouldn't please anyone on either side of the cultural battle.[3]

Carter tapped an Arkansas lawyer and former congressman, James Guy Tucker, to chair the conference. *People* magazine profiled Tucker and remarked that his own blended family situation (he married a divorced woman with two children) was reflective of the nontraditional marriages that were just beginning to characterize America.[4] True as that may have been statistically, many Americans still desired to reverse those trends, not to accept them as normative. Tucker would later become the governor of Arkansas whose resignation opened the door for Huckabee's own term as governor. A long-term by-product of the conference was James Dobson's creation of the Family Research Council, a political action group with special emphasis on the kinds of issues addressed at Carter's conference.

Evangelicals united for a series of public rallies known as "Washington for Jesus" in late April. Around 125,000 attended the rally, essentially sponsored by Pentecostal leaders—friends of Pat Robertson.[5] The event aimed at being nonpolitical, but invariably speakers would mention Supreme Court cases and moral issues with obvious political ramifications. Huckabee, who longed to follow in Robertson's path in Christian broadcasting, took note of the broadcaster's back-and forth involvement with politics. Robertson later would run for president in 1988, providing Huckabee with the best example to date of a minister choosing to enter into elected politics.[6]

———

Building on the success of the 1979 Freedom Rally in Dallas and the positive results of the survey Weyrich conducted, McAteer and Robison planned for another political-religious rally in Dallas. Robison asked several political candidates to attend what he was calling the "National Affairs Briefing." Carter declined but Reagan accepted.[7] Though Huckabee had moved back to Arkansas by this time, he continued to provide communications support to Robison's efforts with the Roundtable.

In the research for his excellent biography of Jimmy Carter, Randall Balmer put his hands on Robison's letter of invitation to Reagan. Balmer wrote: "Robison had assured the candidate that the National Affairs Briefing would be 'the largest, most significant, political and spiritual gathering' in the South. 'I am thrilled with the progress you are making toward the Presidency of the United States,' Robison wrote. 'As one seeking to know and do the will of God, I stand firmly convinced that you are the best candidate to lead us during these crisis days in American history. I will do everything possible within the limits of my ministry to be of help to you.'"[8]

The letter of invitation to attendees was signed by McAteer, Robison, and local hero Tom Landry, the head coach of the Dallas Cowboys. It spoke about "'the domestic crisis which is morally enslaving our country' and promised to give attendees strategies 'to inform and mobilize your church and community in this non-partisan effort to do something that can determine the moral character of America.'"[9]

———

When the two-day event opened, attendees and countless journalists showed up at Reunion Arena. Flags and patriotic bunting were draped all around. Reagan would speak last, and Robison planned for his own sermon to come just before that—to set up Reagan.

Members of Reagan's team understood the particular nuances of the evangelical dictionary and prompted him of their importance—though Reagan needed no prompting when it came to his understanding of Christian redemption. He ignored the counsel from one of his advisors for him to stay off the stage during the lead-up to his own speech.

Robison recalls how he leaned into Reagan with counsel for a specific opening line he thought would go over well. "I suggested to Mr. Reagan that because it was a bipartisan [event] that it would be in his best interest since we could not and would not endorse him as a body. But it would probably be wise if his opening comment would be 'I know this is nonpartisan so you can't endorse me. But I want you to know . . . I endorse you and what you're doing.'"[10]

Reagan followed the Robison script, nailing it with perfect cadence and warmth. Then he went on to speak about all the things the folks came to hear—keeping the government in its place and restoring order and moral sanity. He had to stop repeatedly because of the applause and shouts of affirmation for what he was saying.

Reagan ended with a folksy hypothetical picture—if trapped on an island with only one book, he'd take the Bible. "All the complex questions facing us at home and abroad," he added, "have their answer in that single book."[11]

"We gave him a ten-minute standing ovation," Weyrich recalled. "I've never seen anything like it. The whole movement was snowballing by then."[12]

Historian Steven P. Miller, author of *The Age of Evangelicalism: America's Born-Again Years*, called Reagan's words here "the most famous lines of the Age of Evangelicalism."[13]

It was the first time Huckabee had met Reagan, and he was duly impressed. "No one had ever given so much attention to or paid respect for the evangelicals. It was magic and a major force in Reagan winning."[14]

Judge Paul Pressler, one of the architects of the conservative movement within the Southern Baptist Convention, recalled this about the event: "At the urging of some friends, I decided to go. I did not expect much, but when I arrived, I found a packed arena, full of enthusiastic individuals hearing great speakers. I went to the phone after the first few hours, called [my wife] Nancy, and said, 'Get a baby-sitter for the children. You must come up here and hear what is going on.' She flew to Dallas, and we had the opportunity to attend together. This was the first time either of us had met Ronald Reagan."[15]

Robison remembers a closing word he had for the candidate: "I looked at Mr. Reagan. I said, 'We really like you; we really like you. We like the principles that you espouse. But you need to understand something about the nature of this group that you'll speak to tonight and those of us in this room. We're not partisan; we're not pro-party; we're not pro-personality. We're pro-principle. If you stand by the principles that you say you believe, we'll be the greatest friends you'll ever have.' But I said, 'If you turn against those principles, we'll be your worst nightmare.'"[16]

It is at this very point that Robison's influence on Huckabee was greatest. Being guided by principle over all other considerations has shaped Huckabee in both his pastorate and his politics. He said, "If I were to make decisions based on self-preservation or political preservation, then I would become everything I want to change."[17]

***

Huckabee's response to that day in August 1980 was twofold. First, he was enamored with it all. Richard Land, also present at the event, said, "It was there that Mike caught a new vision for the potential of faith in politics and faith in public policy. There were a lot of younger evangelicals who had been raised to believe that politics was dirty business and the last thing a Christian would do is get involved in politics."[18] (Land would eventually become the president of the Ethics and Religious Liberty Commission of the Southern Baptist Convention.) The event with Reagan seemed to be a natural progression from the Explo '72 candle lighting, which, ironically, had also happened in Dallas. What impact for good can one man have on the world? Just take the first step and find out.

Second, Huckabee's response to all the momentous events—heady for anyone, let alone a young man in his twenties who was charting his course in life—was to accept the call to pastor a church in a town of ten thousand in the middle of Arkansas. In so many ways, that doesn't make any sense. One might guess that it was due to the influence of Adrian Rogers's win in the SBC that perhaps Huckabee dreamed of going back to Arkansas and bringing the conservative resurgence to his home state. But though he was a conservative, that wasn't his agenda.

In one year's time, Huckabee had watched as his mentor helped propel two men—Rogers and Reagan—into a presidentcy, each in his own realm. And throughout the 1980s, the effects of each man's presidency would ripple and bring about revolution. Huckabee wanted to help change the world, the "revolution" Bill Bright had spoken of eight years earlier at Explo '72. The question was, into which realm would Huckabee leap? The call to a pastorate seemed to answer that question.

―――――

As Huckabee celebrated his twenty-fifth birthday at the end of August, national news coverage of McAteer's Roundtable stated: "Religious Conservatives Launch Bid to Influence Presidential Politics."[19] *Newsweek* magazine followed suit, placing Jerry Falwell on the cover of its September 15 issue, to accompany the lead story: "A Tide of Born-Again Politics."[20] From the vantage point of thirty years later, such headlines seem unremarkable—religious conservatives and religious candidates do this routinely. But at that point in time, the "preachers and politics mingle" theme of the news story wasn't commonplace. Many considered it sacrilegious, but nobody considered it routine. Something new was in the air among religious conservatives.

On November 4, Reagan defeated Carter and won the right to govern the nation. The revolution had begun.

―――――

"Another One Bites the Dust" played continuously on the air in the fall of 1980, but John Lennon would soon knock it off the number one perch with his first single in five years. His "(Just Like) Starting Over" released at the end of October and ushered in renewed speculation of a Beatles reunion. Were the 1970s going to experience a renaissance?

―――――

Mark Chapman, another twenty-five-year-old from the South, had also walked down a "born-again Christian" path in the early 1970s. Like Huckabee, he had been exposed to multinational parachurch ministries making a big impact on the world. Chapman served with the evangelical humanitarian organization World Vision in their work with Vietnamese refugees. Chapman processed the refugees at Fort Chaffee in Arkansas, the same location where thousands of Hurricane Katrina refugees would arrive in 2005 for processing by the administration of Governor Mike Huckabee. Then Chapman entered Covenant College in Chattanooga, Tennessee, with a girlfriend he thought he'd marry. However, his life unraveled from there: he dropped out of college, struggled with suicidal thoughts, and became a drifter. Earlier, he had been a major fan of the Beatles, but now his unstable mind began to fixate on what he deemed the hypocrisy of John Lennon's telling everyone to "imagine" a world without materialism while living an opulent lifestyle. Chapman also began to dwell on and despise Lennon for his 1966 statement "Christianity will go. It will vanish and shrink. I needn't argue about that. I'm right and I'll be proved right. We're more popular than Jesus now. I don't know which will go first, rock 'n' roll or Christianity. Jesus was all right but his disciples were thick and ordinary. It's them twisting it that ruins it for me."[21]

On December 8, *Rolling Stone* photographer Annie Leibovitz snapped her famous photo shoot of Lennon and Yoko Ono in their apartment. Then Lennon and Ono went to go do some work in a music studio across town. As they left their apartment building, Chapman walked up to Lennon, pulled out a pen, and requested an autograph. Lennon obliged. Six hours later, when the couple returned home to the Dakota apartment building, Chapman once again approached Lennon, this time pulling out a .38 caliber handgun. Chapman shot five times, hitting Lennon four times in the back. The doorman of the Dakota shouted, "Do you know what you've just done?" and Chapman replied, "Yes, I just shot John Lennon."

Chapman sat down on the sidewalk, took out a copy of *The Catcher in the Rye,* and waited for the police to come and arrest him.[22]

Huckabee, the consummate Beatles fan, remembers Lennon's assassination quite well. "I was getting ready for the day," he said, "and I had the radio on to the local KOTN radio station in Pine Bluff. Buddy Deane, the 'Morning Mayor,' did the mornings and he was breaking the news that Lennon had been shot the night before. It was especially poignant because Buddy Deane knew the Beatles—he was the number one DJ in Baltimore and MC'd some

Beatles events in those days. Buddy in fact was the inspiration for the film 'Hairspray' and had a cameo role in the movie. Yes, I remember that day very well."[23]

The 1970s were definitely over.

CHAPTER 18

A PASTOR FOR ALL SEASONS

1980–1985

> The church . . . finally said, "Why don't you
> just stay and be our pastor?" And I did.[1]
>
> —MIKE HUCKABEE

BY THE TIME CHIEF JUSTICE WARREN BURGER SWORE
Ronald Reagan into office in January 1981, Immanuel Baptist Church in
Pine Bluff, Arkansas, had called Huckabee as its pastor. Although he had
been an organizer and attendee of key political events within the newly
formed Religious Right, he did not get pulled into political office or the
Moral Majority movement. Though opportunity presented itself, Huckabee
did not work in any formal capacity within these types of organizations
during the 1980s. And it would be another ten years before he announced a
campaign for public office.

So naturally, a question that comes to mind is, why did Huckabee go
back to Arkansas and spend a decade pastoring churches after the euphoria
of all these events and the election of Reagan? Was the pastorate the reason
he went home? What options did he have?

First, while working for Robison, he made such a strong impression on
influential people who saw him that doors of opportunity began to fly open.
If he had ever considered a career in law, a wealthy and very powerful Texas

lawyer offered to pay his way through school. Why didn't Huckabee take the offer? Was it a tough decision? "No, not at all. I didn't want to be a lawyer," said Huckabee.[2] Obviously, the bottom dollar of future salary played no part in Huckabee's decision-making process.

What about being a full-time pastor? Huckabee has said in numerous places that he wasn't completely interested in that career path. His true passion was Christian communications.[3]

So did he consider Christian broadcasting? Certainly, but you don't just go into broadcasting without an immense base of financial support. Preachers entered broadcasting only if they already had a revenue stream coming in the mail based on their crusades. As for being a full-time operations man, working for a Christian broadcasting station, Huckabee's better option for doing that would have been to remain in Dallas. Central Arkansas was not exactly the epicenter of the Christian broadcasting world.

What about combining pastoral ministry *with* Christian broadcasting? Well, that might work at a large church in a major urban area, but to plan on doing so in a small-town Baptist church, in Arkansas, in 1980—that didn't make much sense. At the very least, such a trail would have to be blazed by a pioneer. It would take the right church (some might say, a desperate church) and the right pastor, who both understood the operations side of the work *and* had the giftings for standing in front of the camera. Besides, Huckabee clearly said he was not thinking about full-time pastoral ministry.

What about serving in both Christian broadcasting and itinerant evangelism (crusades and revivals), as James Robison did? Yes, that option was very much on Huckabee's mind. As he recounted in a 1990 interview, "I had every intention of being in full-time evangelism-communications. The two complement each other greatly."[4] But to succeed to the point of being able to support a family, you would have to get a good base of support established fairly quickly. You would need to create an "evangelistic association" through which the income and expenses flowed. Your calendar would need to be filled up quickly with preaching engagements, and a good portion of those would need to be at sizable churches that could give a larger amount of "love offering." You would need to hire staff who could help with the logistics of the ministry. The question was whether your support could stay ahead of your expenses. Sure, Robison had wealthy benefactors in Texas who believed in his ministry and put money into the organization. But Huckabee had seen other evangelists attempt to go out on their own, only to have the operation fold due to a lack of funding. The communications side of his work could help pay the bills *if* the work remained regular, but how many "ifs" could a family man take before the burden of the unknown became too great? The son of Dorsey Huckabee knew how to work hard, but he also was averse to bills not paid on time. Without a sense of divine leadership, there would be no wisdom in positioning your family in such a risky path.

Finally, what about the vision of going into Christian broadcasting *and* itinerant evangelism, but knowing that you would keep an eye open for a move into politics? Would such a plan be evidence of double-mindedness? Could those two worlds overlap? Was it a pollution of the pulpit?

Consider the words of James Robison, from the May 1979 rally, coming just before Huckabee left his mentor and returned to Arkansas: "Someone said, 'Preachers ought not mess with politics.' Brother, when a preacher does his business, he messes with everything."[5]

Robison charged the preachers in his audience to both preach the Bible *and* speak on issues that could fall under the label of "politics"—issues that preachers had too often avoided, in Robison's opinion. Though there are some who conflate the kingdom of God with the kingdom of man—and make a mess of both—Robison seemed to understand the difference between the two. And yet, he urged pastors, the spiritual leaders of their community, not to allow an artificial dividing line to be constructed between the two spheres. They were to pull the muzzles off their mouths and start using their oratorical gifting to influence both kingdoms simultaneously. Huckabee heard Robison loud and clear. The mentoring of Haskell Jones and James Robison mingled together into a united vision for what Huckabee was to do with his life. As a result, Huckabee would move to Arkansas to serve Jesus and his fellow citizens—and he didn't plan on getting hung up on the particular vocational label he would be wearing in the process.

––––––––––

Huckabee did consider going straight into politics. Part of his motivation for moving from Texas to Arkansas was a possible attempt at the Fourth District

House of Representatives seat in the 1980 election.[6] Such a campaign, however, could not have had much chance of success. The Fourth District had never once elected a Republican since its creation in 1875, and was unlikely to do so for a rookie who would only become age-eligible a few months before the general election (the U.S. Constitution mandates a congressman be at least twenty-five). Would the GOP have even allowed an underage candidate into the primary?

That said, the current congressman, Beryl Anthony Jr., was finishing up his first term of office, so the power of the incumbency would not yet have been indomitable. Anthony hailed from El Dorado but also had a connection to Hope, Arkansas, because he'd married the sister of future hometown celebrity Vince Foster, deputy counsel to the Clinton White House.

And this is where the Huckabee history gets interesting. Before Anthony, the Fourth District was represented by Ray Thornton, a congressman so popular he easily could have won reelection. But being so popular, he decided he would run for U.S. Senate, attempting to fill the empty seat of former senator John McClellan, who died in office in 1977. Arkansas officials decided that until the special election to replace McClellan was held in November 1978, a "caretaker" would be appointed to immediately fill his seat, but that person would be ineligible to run for the office. So McClellan's seat would be open for the first time since 1944. Three major Democrats jumped into the race for their party's nomination and nearly split evenly their party's vote: David Pryor (34 percent) defeated Jim Guy Tucker (32 percent) and Thornton (31 perent). Tucker, having lost in the primary, was available when Jimmy Carter called and asked him to head up the ill-fated conference on the family. But had he become a U.S. senator that year, he would not have become the governor who, because of scandal, resigned his office to then lieutenant governor Huckabee.

As for Thornton, he had given up his congressional seat to run for Senate, so his loss in the Senate primary meant that he and his staff now needed to find new jobs. One such staff member was his young press secretary in Washington, DC, Jim Harris, who was married to Huckabee's older sister, Pat. The couple had met in 1975 when Jim worked for the *Hope Star* and Pat did her student teaching. Upon Thornton's loss, they left DC for Arkansas, settling in the border town of Texarkana, where Jim took a position as the editor of the local paper. Being on the border of both Texas and Arkansas, he had to cover the politics of two different states. As a result, both George W. Bush and Bill Clinton know Harris by name, literally. "If Mike were to become president one day, that would make three," Harris said. "Not bad for a small-town newspaper editor."[7] Eight years later, the Harris family welcomed the Huckabees to Texarkana, and they all attended the church where Huckabee pastored. Then, when Huckabee became governor, Jim worked on the communications and media team for nearly the entire length of the administration.

All that to say, Huckabee came back home from Texas in 1979 to run against freshman congressman Beryl Anthony—who had just defeated his brother-in-law's boss. But upon further consideration of the situation, he chose not to run. Some people run for office with little or no chance of winning, simply to secure name recognition for a future election cycle. But Huckabee said he's never done this; he always entered into a race believing he could win. So his sitting out in 1980 seems mostly a decision that the time was not right. It would be best to save his firewood for another cycle—perhaps 1982?

———

But there would be no 1982 Huckabee campaign. Midterm elections never go well for the party of the president, so 1982 did not calculate to be a good time to unseat a now two-term Democratic congressman, in a district that had never elected a Republican. Once again, the district looked unwinnable. And since the Huckabees had brought their second son, David, into the world in 1980, the increasing financial responsibilities of fatherhood demanded prudence. Then, in 1982 the Huckabees received some "sugar and spice" into their family with the birth of their daughter, Sarah. The Huckabees adored their children and sought to make wise choices in order to be able to provide for them. As one author later noted, "from 1973 to 1982, the United States suffered through three recessions, two energy crises, inflation and high unemployment—a disillusioning time to establish a career."[8] Yes, and a terrible time to launch a political campaign.

But on a positive note, by 1982 Huckabee was already experiencing the joys of successful pastoral ministry in Pine Bluff. His ministry was off to a great start, and the people were in support of his innovations. Huckabee believes in the idea of staying where God has put you and working in the areas where God is revealing signs of His blessing. In contrast to the appearance of a closed door for a congressional career, the door of Huckabee's pastoral ministry seemed wide-open.

If Huckabee was ever to leave his fledgling pastorate to enter politics, 1984 appeared to be the year. Reagan's "Morning in America" ads conveyed an optimistic message that the nation had turned a corner and was poised for a rekindling of traditional values.[9] Reagan returned to Reunion Arena in 1984 to speak at a prayer breakfast. He talked about the relationship between religion and politics: "The truth is, politics and morality are inseparable. And as morality's foundation is religion, religion and politics are necessarily related. We need religion as a guide. We need it because we are imperfect, and our government needs the church because only those humble enough to admit they're sinners can bring to democracy the tolerance it requires in order to survive."[10] In other words, Reagan delivered a speech with one of Huckabee's favorite messages, that we shouldn't force a separation between politics and religion. But Huckabee wasn't even present at that meeting with Reagan in 1984. Only five years after serving as a midwife at the birth of the Moral Majority and only four years after considering a run for Congress, Huckabee now found himself busy enough with all the successful duties of being a pastor and father.

———

Huckabee got himself into that pastorate in Pine Bluff through the back door.[11] Immanuel asked Huckabee to do "pulpit supply" for them and to preach at their upcoming revival. Pleased with his preaching, they asked him to serve as their interim pastor while they searched for their next minister. The remainder of the story is self-explanatory. After hearing him preach week after week, Immanuel offered him the full-time position. With a future in politics now looking doubtful, he took stock of the situation in Pine Bluff and committed himself to the church.[12]

Within a few months of his tenure at Immanuel, Huckabee began leading the church to become an affiliate station of ACTS, a satellite television network then owned by the Southern Baptist Convention. As an affiliate, they would broadcast both network programming and local programming. All of the shows were either religious, family-friendly, or focused on community events.

This was new ground for churches in Pine Bluff, and it did not come without resistance. As a 1990 denominational press profile of Huckabee explained:

> From that moment he felt that this was what he had been searching for all of his life. Southern Baptists had not had anything which tied the local church and community together in this unique way. When Huckabee first mentioned the possibility of a television ministry for Immanuel, many in the community laughed. But in February of 1981, the church began working toward developing this ministry. Huckabee said, "The Lord overcame all the problems and the ministry became a reality."[13]

Realizing that Sunday nights were a dead space of activity in people's lives, and a bit depressing, too, as the new workweek approached, Huckabee created and hosted a show called *Positive Alternatives*, which focused on uplifting stories and people from right there in Pine Bluff. Such broadcasts made him a pastor "for all of Pine Bluff," said Garey Scott, Immanuel's youth minister at the time.[14]

For Huckabee, television was only a means to the end goal of impacting the community outside the walls of the church. Broadcasting tied the church to the community and led to more people coming to church—his own, and the other churches too. Huckabee did not care to build a personal kingdom. The stronger all the churches in Pine Bluff became, the better the entire community would be. He believed mass communications could break down walls of separation that kept the churches from uniting together for greater effectiveness.

Two other side effects of the broadcasting ministry also emerged. First, Huckabee began to receive and accept an endless stream of speaking requests, both locally and throughout the state. Bruce Rodntick, a staff member at Immanuel, remembers Huckabee speaking more than twenty times a month.[15] For Huckabee, this was the start of what has now become nearly four decades of speaking several hundred times per year.

A second effect of the broadcasting was that Huckabee had to confront racism within the church. If you are going to broadcast community programs promoting gospel unity, then you can't turn right around and close the door of membership to African-Americans. However, Immanuel had never before had a black member, and when a young man expressed a desire to follow Jesus Christ and be baptized into the church, the issue became real. A number of members explained how that just wasn't done at their church, and that the man needed to go to church with his own people. Huckabee recalled what happened next: "I actually stood before them on a Sunday morning and said 'If the young black man who came isn't welcome, then neither am I. This is the Lord's house, not ours. He is welcome to come and if that's a problem, then you are welcome to go.' About seven old men got up and walked out. They later threatened the church and me. But we baptized him—that's for sure!"[16] This courage to stand against racism at the threat of physical harm and loss of livelihood came when Huckabee was hardly thirty, and had three young mouths to feed at home.

Huckabee also broke down racial divides among Pine Bluff ministers. Wherever need arose, he was simply color-blind. Dwight McKissic, an influential African-American Southern Baptist pastor now in Texas, also served in Pine Bluff during this time period. "I remember visiting with Mike about some pastoral issues in my career. Not only did he take the time; he also provided me some encouragement and counsel I needed, and some favors I needed."[17]

———

During his college days at OBU, Randy Sims's parents would ask him where he was going to church. Since he often went where Huckabee was preaching, he'd tell his parents he was attending a Missionary Baptist church. His father, at the time a music minister at Immanuel Baptist in Pine Bluff—the very church Huckabee would later pastor—would respond, "A Missionary Baptist church!?" Years later, after Sims's father had moved to a different city, he would tell Randy about all the good things he was hearing from Pine Bluff. He told Randy, "They've got this new young guy who is so good and the church is doing great." Randy said, "Yeah, Dad, I know. That's my friend

Mike Huckabee. The same guy you complained about when I went to hear him at his Missionary Baptist church."[18]

———

One key to his successful leadership was to create a culture of optimism using his favorite verse, Philippians 4:13: "I can do all things through Christ who strengthens me" (NKJV). Huckabee knew that sometimes God allows trials and defeats as a means to refine Christians. That said, he also believed God can take an almost-dead church and turn it around for another season of faithfulness and fruitfulness. When the people of Immanuel called Huckabee, they did not believe their church would be around in another five years. In fact, that may have been why they were willing to call such a young minister—what difference does it make if you're desperate?[19] The first thing he did was convince them that God was capable of doing anything, and there was no reason to assume their church had to die.

Even so, another leadership principle Huckabee brought to Pine Bluff was his idea of finding one's unique place and purpose. As he had done years before at Boys State, Huckabee looked to separate the church from the pack by doing things that weren't already being done by everyone else. The gospel is the same for everyone, but "if all a church is doing is duplicating what other churches are doing in programming, it is wasting its time and a lot of money. Every church needs to find its own unique ministry in the community."[20]

After experiencing twenty years of decline, Immanuel grew each of the five-plus years Huckabee pastored the church.

CHAPTER 19

TEXARKANA

September 1986–1991

> As the years passed, I became increasingly convinced
> that most people wanted me to captain the Love Boat,
> making sure everyone was having a good time.
>
> **—MIKE HUCKABEE**

SOUTHERN BAPTIST CHURCHES ARE AUTONOMOUS UNITS.
Though they associate together for common causes and missionary support,
there is no ecclesial hierarchy over the local congregation. Nobody outside
the congregation itself determines who the pastor will be. Therefore, when a
Baptist church finds itself in need of a pastor, the normal protocol is to form
a "pastor search committee," to begin collecting résumés, and then to receive a
recommendation from the committee that the members will vote on.

In the spring and summer of 1986, First Beech Street Church in Texarkana,
Arkansas, contacted Huckabee to gauge his desire for becoming their next
pastor. He was not interested. Things were going well at Pine Bluff, as the
church was growing and joyful. Besides, Pine Bluff had done the one thing
he really desired—the television broadcasting ministry. So he simply told
Beech Street that he could not consider the offer unless the church would
consider building a television ministry. The pulpit committee responded by
saying that Huckabee's Pine Bluff television ministry was the reason he had

appeared on their screen, literally, and that they wanted him to replicate this ministry at their own church.[1] So the Huckabees loaded up their belongings and their three children, and they moved 150 miles southwest to begin ministry in a new city.

To be sure, the two churches Huckabee pastored had their differences. Whereas Immanuel was on life support when he arrived, Beech Street already had health and vitality. Texarkana also had a bit more affluence and a white-collar professional core. Huckabee learned, however, that although greater education and salary can put lipstick on personal messes, underneath it all a pastor still deals with people in need—addictions, death, heartbreak, and pains that must be addressed. He shepherded through births, funerals, weddings, legal troubles, and gut-wrenching decisions about end-of-life care.[2]

Huckabee said pastoral ministry prepared him well for serving as governor because he had been a firsthand witness to the social and moral problems and pathologies present in every social stratum of life. He had seen the devastating effects of personal addiction and individual excess. Huckabee developed an eye for pragmatic solutions *and* a heart for the personal narratives of the pain. He dealt with people who, like the weary travelers from the Eagles hit "Hotel California," had succumbed to the allure of what they thought was paradise, only to wake up and find themselves in a prison of their own addiction. Abstract social issues developed names and faces as he became invested in people's lives.[3]

Huckabee's pragmatic-realist vision of life became solidified during his pastoral ministry, because he saw it does nobody any good to talk about society's problems in an overtly ideological manner that doesn't actually impact anyone's life. "During my teenage years and early adulthood, I longed for a faith that would catapult me above the pressures and problems of daily life," he wrote. "Somehow it never worked. I now realize the sun shines on the just and unjust alike, and it also rains on the good as well as the bad."[4] A person's life often capsizes—as when Janet got cancer as a newlywed—and real-life solutions are needed, not empty rhetoric. And people in pain need a human touch to help get them through.

All of this ties into the style and heartbeat of Huckabee's pastoral ministry. He believed the doctrine and ethics of Christianity could become more palatable to a watching world if a genuine attempt was made to be more winsome. The following quote sums up his philosophy of Christian leadership, whether in ministry, politics, or anywhere else:

We've not been very good at depicting the evangelical Christian faith. We've done a lousy job, sometimes focusing more on what we seem to be against than what we're for. And I think that's our fault. I think we've done a lousy job of communicating warmth and heart. We've come across many times as being harsh and intolerant. And for me, being a person of faith is an absolute admission of my own frailty and my complete understanding that the human condition is a very fragile one. And, if anything, it has made me far more sympathetic to people, whether they are addicted to drugs or addicted to alcohol or food for that matter. And I understand that we are all pilgrims struggling on this pathway.

Be careful about being overly harsh with someone who falls and stumbles, because, you know, I'm one step away from joining them down there on the turf. That doesn't mean that I am just cavalier about what I think might be the right and wrong of certain lifestyles. But certainly it doesn't mean that I should be overly judgmental and harsh and, frankly, mean-spirited. And I sometimes think we've all, in my realm, been guilty of that.[5]

Rick Caldwell also served as a pastor and thinks the key to his friend's successful ministry went beyond his excellent communication abilities. "He was so good at communicating with the people but also very compassionate about being involved in their lives. And as a pastor, he didn't settle for just pastoring his own flock. He was also concerned about connecting the church with the community. He would become a pastor to the community, and people of different faiths even embraced him—the non-evangelicals."[6]

As a result, the Beech Street church prospered under Huckabee's leadership, growing from an average attendance of five hundred in 1986 to more than eight hundred in 1990. The programs he used were similar to those employed at Pine Bluff. He emphasized strengthening the Sunday schools as a means of one-on-one interaction, Bible teaching, and outreach. The church finished the development of its family activities center and became intentional about using it for outreach. And as already noted, the church developed a television broadcasting ministry, again using the ACTS network, as Pine Bluff had done. In addition to the network programming, the church inserted more than thirty hours of local news, sports, Bible studies, worship, and talk shows. All this flowed from Huckabee's vision for impacting his community: "The traditional ways that we have gone about reaching people will no longer work. If we are going to reach 'the baby boom generation' we must institute new methods. It is essential that we do whatever it takes to reach people for Christ."[7]

By 1988, the ground began to shift nationally on religious television broadcasting, casting doubt on whether it would continue to be an arena for expressing a positive Christian witness. First, the Southern Baptist Convention decided to sell the ACTS network, divesting themselves of both the costs and the fruit of the ministry. Though Huckabee served as president of the Arkansas affiliates, he received no advance warning and only learned of the decision when a newspaper called to ask him for his response. "It was something of a shock to me to learn that the Trustees of the Southern Baptist Radio and Television Commission have voted to transfer the operation of the ACTS Television Network to a private for-profit corporation," Huckabee told reporters. "In the past we have had a good solid vehicle for communicating the gospel."[8]

Second, this was the season of sexual and financial scandal among televangelists. Jim and Tammy Faye Bakker and Jerry Falwell brought shame on and discredited the entire group of broadcast preachers. As one historian noted, "Televangelists fell on hard times. In the wake of the scandals, audience ratings dropped. So did revenues. As donations to the ministries declined, layoffs were imposed and broadcast airtime was cut back. Public opinion polls registered sharp shifts from favorable to unfavorable. The great electronic tent show of the eighties, if not struck, was collapsing."[9]

Even preachers like Huckabee, who never fell into sexual sin or committed financial fraud, still had to defend themselves against the caricature created by the scandalous behavior of others. As a result, whereas a young, talented preacher in 1978 might have entertained righteous ambitions about using television for evangelistic purposes, such an ambition would be the farthest thing from a young person's mind in 1988. The luster had been removed.

Connected to the televangelism scandals was the demise of the Moral Majority. Not that men like Jerry Falwell committed scandal themselves, but in the swirling vortex of shame, everyone suffered. Operations such as the Moral Majority required major funding, and the financial appeals often took place on the television broadcasts. In the fall of 1987, Falwell announced his resignation from the Moral Majority. "I will not be stumping for candidates again," he said. "I will never work for a candidate as I did for Ronald Reagan. I will not be lobbying for legislation personally."[10]

The Religious Right was still evaluating what had happened during Reagan's two terms in office. They had helped propel him into the White House but now were wondering what they had gotten out of it. In 1988, Pat Robertson decided the best way for an evangelical leader to influence the next president would be if an evangelical leader actually *became* the next president. Huckabee took notice of this shift, from Reagan's "I endorse you" in 1980 to Robertson's outreach to evangelicals as, in essence, "I come from you." In Huckabee's 2008 campaign, he would make similar statements. Robertson ran a spirited campaign but came in third behind the eventual nominee, George H. W. Bush, and second-place finisher Senator Bob Dole, who then became the nominee years later. The Religious Right never became enthused about either of these men, leading to GOP election losses to Bill Clinton in 1992 and 1996.

It is fascinating to see how Huckabee managed to avoid the waxing and waning of two different conservative movements during the 1980s. As a twenty-five-year-old in 1980, he could have moved right on up the national ranks of either televangelism or the Religious Right (or both at the same time). Instead, he went small and local and became a pastor for a decade. True, he became involved in local television broadcasting, but this did not connect him on a personal level to the scandalous behavior of others. As for the Moral Majority types of organizations, though Huckabee had never lost interest in politics and government, he also did not spend the 1980s helping to build up institutions that would mostly dissipate by the end of the decade.

Another of Huckabee's favorite scriptures is Proverbs 3:5–6: "Trust in the LORD with all your heart and lean not on your own understanding; in all your ways submit to him, and he will make your paths straight." His own life story during the 1980s illustrates the message of these verses. A decade worth of full-time local church ministry (ironically, the one career option Huckabee had no intention of pursuing) became the very means for him to avoid being caught up in the scandals of others or giving himself to building up short-lived religious-political institutions. Instead, he was able to spend those years in fruitful service to others, the effects of which continue to this day in those two cities. The churches he pastored are still serving their communities long after he left. And yes, they still offer television broadcasting.

On the other hand, there were some negative aspects to Huckabee's pastoral ministry. He described how hard it was to keep the church thinking outwardly and on mission. His "Explo '72" vision of Christians changing the world with the gospel would not allow him to slip into a pattern of quiet and comfortable pastoral ministry focused solely on internal matters at best, or petty bickering at worst. "In my early years of ministry, I was quite idealistic, thinking that most people in the congregation expected me to be the captain of a warship leading God's troops into battle to change the world," he wrote. "As the years passed, I became increasingly convinced that most people wanted me to captain the Love Boat, making sure everyone was having a good time."[11]

On October 3, 1991, then governor Bill Clinton stood alongside his wife, Hillary, to announce his campaign for the Democratic nomination for president. The next week, the Arkansas Baptist State Convention newspaper printed a letter from Huckabee, then the president of the convention. Huckabee, writing about a recent trip he had taken to Guatemala, wrestled with righteous discontent as he contemplated his own middle-class, status quo, American Christianity. He wrote:

> Most good hunting dogs in Arkansas have a much nicer place to stay than those people have for a worship service. A single piece of rusted tin on a hinge was the door. The walls were chicken wire with sticks and corn stalks filling in the gaps. . . .

For so many of us, abundant life would be a nice church facility, a well-educated pastor and staff, a diverse program offering all kinds of recreational and social activities for the members to enjoy. We would insist that our restrooms were sparkling clean, that parking was close to the building, that the pews were comfortable, and the length of the service timed so as not to infringe on the personal schedules. . . .

Yes, maybe we'll teach our Guatemalan friends a few things about mission strategy, church building, and evangelism, but they may well teach us a great deal more about the good shepherd who came to give us life and give it more abundantly.[12]

Huckabee looked at the poverty-stricken Guatemalans who struggled in this world. They worked hard to improve their condition, yet they also had their eyes on the world to come. Huckabee seemed to be thinking, *Now*, this *is real Christianity!*

Six weeks later, Huckabee gave his final presidential sermon at the state's annual convention. He exhorted the delegates to be on the lookout for warning signals indicating spiritual disease in the convention or the local congregation. He said, "We endanger the cause of Christ when we trivialize our faith into ministerial minutia. It's an unhealthy sign when church people are more interested in how we spend $25 of church money than in where an eleven-year-old spends eternity." Huckabee warned that pastors become bowed not under the pressure of spiritual battles but under battle over the color of choir robes, Wednesday night menus, and air conditioning.[13] Even as he spoke these words, he was in the midst of soul-searching over his own future.

It wasn't for want of numerical growth that Huckabee grew disillusioned with pastoral ministry. Nor was he embittered or burned out. Instead, he began to wonder if he was really prepared to give a lifetime of service within the local church. Now, to be fair to congregations, one of the tasks of shepherding sheep is to guide them onward, with patience and a long-term perspective. If Huckabee's sheep needed to be awakened from their middle-class slumber and pettiness, it was his job and calling as a minister to prod them.

After a decade of pastoring, Huckabee had not changed in his opinion of the power of Scripture or the importance of preaching. But he began to realize that if he wished to keep his job, he would have to devote so much of his time to keeping the sheep happy. Or he would have to work hard to change the culture and the mind-set of the sheep—and that would take the commitment of a long pastorate—maybe even a lifetime. Is that what Jesus was calling him to do? The fact that it would be hard work didn't scare him off the task. In fact, he wasn't scared off at all. Rather, something else— something outside of local church ministry altogether—had begun to grab his attention once again.

During the final two years of his ministry at Beech Street, Huckabee's presidential service to Baptists across the entire state of Arkansas created an itch for a broader constituency and a different sphere of ministry than the pastorate of one local church could provide.

CHAPTER 20

CAN'T WE ALL JUST GET ALONG?

1989–1991

> No, seriously, this *is* Bill Clinton.
>
> —BILL CLINTON

CHURCH HISTORIANS HAVE FILLED ENTIRE BOOKSHELVES with volumes written to describe the twentieth-century battle for control of the Southern Baptist Convention (SBC), so it would not do justice to the complex history of the nation's largest Protestant denomination to attempt a retelling of that story here. Suffice it to say, two sides fought for the future identity of the denomination.

Mainline, liberal, moderate, conservative, evangelical, fundamentalist—party labels meant different things depending on who used the term. Even the name for the battle differs depending on who is doing the talking. "Conservative resurgence" or "fundamentalist takeover"? Honest moderates, now mostly residing outside the SBC, today can admit that there really were sincere theological divisions and that their progressive agenda was the historical newcomer to the denomination. But for their part, the moderate group warned against "fighting fundamentalists" who saw every issue as a hill on which to die. Honest conservatives today will admit as much, that it wasn't always easy to keep fellowship with those coming to the battle from the far right. As one denominational leader said years later, "Once the battle was over, we could acknowledge, privately, that what the liberals said about us was true—half our troops *were* 'crazy uncles' who you didn't want to let get behind a microphone."[1]

The national battles that had taken place since Huckabee was a toddler began to spill over into the state Baptist conventions right about the time Huckabee took his first pastorate in Arkansas in the early 1980s. Then, with the forming of the Cooperative Baptist Fellowship in the 1990s, moderates found a new denominational home and moved away from the SBC battlefield. But each Baptist state convention is autonomous—partnered with the national convention, but not under its control. So even as the national battle wrapped up, the stateside battles were just beginning. Each state convention, local association, and individual church had to answer the question, "Whose side are we on?"

It was into this context of a denominational civil war that, in the fall of 1989, Mike Huckabee became the youngest-ever president of the Arkansas Baptist State Convention.

⸻

What does it mean to be the president of a Baptist state convention? First, this position does not pay a salary, so the person who holds it (normally a pastor) doesn't quit his regular job. In that sense, they are "honorary" positions—though that word can convey the wrong idea, that the position influences very little. That is not the case. The exact duties of the president vary from state to state, but the essential work is (1) to serve as a public face of the convention, (2) to appoint volunteers to the various committees that oversee the convention's entities, (3) to preside over the annual meeting of the convention, (4) to meet with Baptists across the state through continual traveling to meetings, and (5) to cast a vision to the Baptists of the state, inspiring them toward a set of united goals for mission.

Though in modern times, a "layperson" (non-pastor) rarely holds the office, such was not always the case. James Philip Eagle (1837–1904) served as president of Arkansas Baptists from 1880 to 1904, even as he also served as the governor of Arkansas from 1888 to 1892. And for good measure, the national Southern Baptist Convention elected him president three times (1902–1904).

Pastors of smaller churches— the kind of churches that make up half the convention—are seldom elected. Given the Southern Baptist's prohibition against a woman preaching, no state convention has ever elected a woman as president—though the state constitutions probably do not explicitly forbid such an election.

State conventions hold an annual meeting, typically in the fall, where delegates from member churches gather to worship and fellowship together, conduct convention business, and approve strategic plans for united mission efforts. It may seem odd to outsiders, but Baptists have a longstanding tradition of not looking favorably on those who campaign or orchestrate votes for the elected offices of a convention. Such elections are supposed to come as delegates are moved in their hearts at the moment of the convention. That is to say, Huckabee did not campaign for the position of state president.

Baptists hardly even remember they have a convention until ninety days before an annual meeting, and then a flurry of action and talk ensues. During the lead-up to the 1989 meeting, the secular press reported on meetings being held with talk of a takeover of the convention. A newsletter called "A Conservative Voice in Arkansas" began to be printed by a pastor in northeast Arkansas, in reaction to the perception by some that the newspaper sponsored by the state convention was biased against conservatives. Years later, Huckabee would tell the *New York Times* that the entire chain of events was "far more political than anything else I've ever been involved in."[2]

First Baptist Church in Little Rock hosted the meeting in November amid great discussion about the election of the next president. On the third day of the convention, "the sanctuary of Little Rock's First Church was full from the outset of the fourth session . . . on both the ground floor and in the balcony." The largest ever number of delegates—1,602—had registered by that point. The floor was opened up for nominations for president: "Dennis Swanberg of Hot Springs nominated Ronnie Floyd, pastor of Springdale First Church. Del Medlin of Cabot nominated Mike Huckabee, pastor of Beech Street First Church in Texarkana."[3] Floyd, a pastor in northwest Arkansas, was the conservatives' nominee. On the other hand, Huckabee was the nominee who would say things like, "If all the 'liberals' in Arkansas Baptist churches held a meeting, they could meet in the corner booth of a Waffle House and still have room for guests."[4]

Delegates cast their votes: "808 to 443. Huckabee received 64.6 percent of the 1,251 ballots counted."[5]

At the close of the meeting, president-elect Huckabee gave the benedictory prayer. "He told them that, despite the tension surrounding the presidential election, there was no personal tension between himself and Ronnie Floyd," the paper reported. "He said that the lordship of Christ is the 'common ground' on which all Arkansas Baptists should come together, and he declared, 'There is a place for everyone in the state convention.'"[6]

Both Huckabee and Floyd would later admit their theology did not differ from one another's, but Floyd said that the conservatives "were not sure Mike was committed enough."[7] Although Floyd never became the president of the Arkansas convention, he continued to lead his church to spectacular growth and effectiveness. And he wound up serving his denomination in key leadership roles, including his service as the president of the bigger ship, the national convention (2014–2016).

"The 1989 meeting of the Arkansas Baptist State Convention at First Baptist Church, Little Rock, may have been the best state convention held in many years," the editor of the Baptist state paper wrote in an editorial. "The election of Mike Huckabee, pastor of Beech Street First Church, Texarkana, as president of the state convention assures Arkansas Baptists of conservative leadership which will be fair to everyone in the convention."[8] In that last phrase, Sneed tipped his hand to reveal his view that Floyd would have made appointments to committees based on his own network of "conservative" pastors—and that Huckabee wouldn't. To borrow a phrase from the world of secular politics, Huckabee favored a bipartisan approach.

Huckabee's presidency began in earnest, as he began crisscrossing the state in an attempt to bring unity. He declared his top goal to be "to reestablish trust, friendship and a sense of common purpose among Arkansas Baptists."[9]

To people who wondered if their new president was sufficiently conservative in theology, Huckabee responded,

One legitimate concern expressed is that we remain faithful to God's Word. You elected a conservative president last year. My belief in the inerrancy and infallibility of God's Word didn't start when it became politically expedient. No one in this state has successfully shown my views to be any less "conservative" than anyone theologically. I remain convinced that, in our state and in our institutions, we need not lose sleep over the confidence Arkansas Baptists have to the veracity of scripture.[10]

The more contentious issue related to Huckabee's presidential appointments to committees. Following the playbook used on the national level, if Huckabee were a "true conservative," then he would use his position as president to only appoint Arkansas Baptists who had been given clearance by the conservatives. To effect a conservative takeover of the convention, one group or the other would need to shut out the other side from participation in the governances of the entities. Huckabee countered this view.

It continues to be my conviction that if we are willing to accept the financial contributions of a church and seat its messengers at our convention, then we have a moral obligation to ensure that its members are not excluded from consideration and participation in the rest of our processes—including representation on denominational entities. If we really believe that a church or its pastor is not "orthodox" enough for us, then let's have the integrity to challenge their seating as messengers and have the decency to return their gifts to the Cooperative Program. No one should be forced to pay if he isn't going to ever get to "play."[11]

Some people, even some from outside of Arkansas, never forgot Huckabee's refusal to fall in line with the "conservative resurgence" plan for appointments. Hal Bass, now a professor of political science at Ouachita Baptist University, said Huckabee was the moderate's candidate, "but I wouldn't say he was considered a moderate. . . . Certainly, he wasn't in the trenches fighting on behalf of the conservative resurgence. That wasn't who he was. That wasn't the fight he wanted to make."[12]

Huckabee advocated the use of technology so that more congregations could come together at the annual meeting, via satellite. In another example of his blue-collar populism, he recognized that "conventions are often more representative of pastors with convention budgets than many rank-and-file Baptists, unable to take three days off in the middle of a week to attend. Imagine the possibilities when churches could send its full number of messengers without bankrupting the budget by having to pay expenses of distant travel!" His advocacy of technology here was for leveling the influence between rich and poor churches. Huckabee also played to his fellow Arkansans' sensibilities in being cast as losers compared to other states. "We in Arkansas are often sneered at for being 'last' in per capita incomes, teacher salaries, and the like. If we can pull off this bold effort, the Christian world will certainly not say of Arkansas Baptists that we are last!"[13] In the end, things did not work out to make it a reality, but the plan was visionary for its time. Later when he became the governor of Arkansas, he would use the same approach—implementing new technological advances to create greater efficiency and less frustration for constituents.

Huckabee presided over the next year's annual meeting, this time held at Immanuel Baptist in Little Rock, pastored by Rex Horne, now the president of Ouachita Baptist University. Immanuel served as the home church for the governor of Arkansas, Bill Clinton. Huckabee had a humorous encounter with Clinton one day when the governor called him to speak about a concern. Clinton understood that, like himself, one-fourth of Arkansas was Southern Baptist. He wanted to maintain a good relationship with the Baptists and reached out to Huckabee for some counsel on a matter. Thinking it was a friend playing a prank on him by impersonating the governor, Huckabee cleared his throat and began doing his own spot-on impersonation of Clinton. The real governor said, "No, seriously, this *is* Bill Clinton." Eventually Huckabee realized it was, in fact, the governor on the phone, but not before establishing his credentials as a bona fide Clinton impersonator.[14]

Rex Horne, pastor of Immanuel Baptist in Little Rock, made national news in 1998 when denominational leaders in the SBC publicly questioned how the church could allow Clinton to be a "member in good standing" even after the sexual scandals of that year. But those events were still a lifetime away on the night in 1990 when Huckabee stood before Horne and the delegates to address the Convention with his sermon "The Ten Commendations."

Huckabee began his address by pointing out the failure to communicate. "We've said a lot about each other, but not enough to each other." He painted the denominational discord in terms of divorce: "Should our denomination go through a divorce, no one wins and everyone loses." The crowd turned jubilant with applause and agreement when he hailed the sacrifice of bivocational and small-church pastors: "The greatest work among us is probably performed by the bi-vocational pastor and the pastor who serves as his own staff." In one sweeping statement, he affirmed both orthodoxy and orthopraxy: "It doesn't embarrass me one bit to let you know I believe that Adam and Eve were real people. What does embarrass me is when we draw lines of fellowship over the application and interpretation of the Bible rather than over the authority and inerrancy of the Bible." Finally, he urged the delegates to turn away from fault-finding: "Trying to decide who's wrong or even who's most wrong won't solve our crisis. . . . We can break rank with the prevailing opinion of a budget item and yet still break bread with each other when the vote is over."[15]

Huckabee's message caused "the messengers, who had filled every available seat and stair and were sitting in the aisles" to rise "for a prolonged and heartfelt standing ovation." Sneed wrote, "Arkansas Baptists owe a debt of gratitude to President Mike Huckabee. Much of the harmony that our state convention enjoyed was a direct result of the excellent spirit and good-natured humor displayed by President Huckabee. Huckabee's presidential message placed the controversy confronting the Southern Baptist Convention in proper perspective. This is an address that every Arkansas Baptist needs to read."[16] Following present-day custom among Baptists, the 1990 delegates voted by acclamation to give Huckabee a second year of office.

Huckabee found an opportunity to speak to national events in February 1991, due to the onset of what became known as the First Gulf War:

Our world is at war again, and with it comes the stinging reminder that people are by nature sinners. If the humanists were right in espousing the "universal goodness of man," there would be no war or cause for war. . . . None of us want a war, but neither do we want the consequences of doing nothing while a demonic despot overruns neighbor nations and vows to annihilate others. . . . The reluctance of the world to rise up against the death machine of Hitler's Nazi Germany resulted in millions of innocent men, women, and children being gassed.[17]

During his second year, Huckabee continued his work of unifying Baptists. That task was made increasingly difficult, however, whenever relationships within the national SBC disintegrated. At the June 1990 annual meeting of the SBC, the conservative candidate for president won again—a succession that had begun in 1979. The moderate voting bloc had worked hard and had hoped that they could win with their candidate, Daniel Vestal. But Pastor Morris Chapman defeated Vestal by a wide margin. That meeting would mark the beginning of the end of two groups under the same tent; in August 1990 the moderates held an inaugural meeting that led to the formation of the Cooperative Baptist Fellowship (CBF).

Huckabee responded to the national events in his newspaper column:

What impact will recent events in the Southern Baptist Convention have upon us here in Arkansas? Good question. The answer, however, is not mine to give. . . . The "L" word that may characterize our greatest threat is not "liberalism," but "legalism." . . . Legalism is not limited to the theological camp of the conservatives, moderates, or anyone in between or beyond. . . . A legalist questions everyone else's motives and mission but never sees a need to question his own.[18]

What made Huckabee, admittedly a theological conservative without any reservation, nevertheless respond to the denominational controversy in such manner? How was he able to maintain deep friendships with people on both sides of the denomination aisle? The answer is that Huckabee's background in the perpetually divisive Baptist Missionary Association created within him a strong desire to unite on big ideas and issues. "The background that I have come from has had a major impact on the way I respond to the current controversy in the SBC," he wrote. "I don't want to give up my energy to things as small as those that we debated over in the BMA." The newspaper explained some of those BMA log-jams: which version of the Bible was correct to use, the length of one's hair, and whether or not church buildings should have kitchens on their premises. "I think that legalism is as big a curse as liberalism. Both are devastating to the gospel of Christ," Huckabee said [19]

In his 1991 swan song sermon as president, Huckabee spoke on "Seven Warning Signals for Arkansas Baptists" and hinted at where his own future might lie. He warned against isolationism: "There is a dangerous tendency of evangelicals in general and Baptists in particular to complain about the spiraling decline of the values of our nation and the integrity of those who lead it, but who at the same time feel that Christians 'shouldn't get involved' . . . We cannot change the world if we refuse to participate in the institutions of society that dictate its direction." We get a foretaste of Huckabee's future political stump speeches as he speaks about "a battle to salvage our culture and our very civilization from a worldview that thinks man is good and God is dead."[20]

Delegates to the meeting gave Huckabee a resounding standing ovation and thanked him for his peace-driven presidency. Huckabee's tenure as ABSC president can be summed up in his analysis and approval of the SBC's 1991 annual meeting—which he found to be a small step in the direction of peace and harmony. "Whenever Baptists gather, there's certain to be some disagreement over various issues. It's not wrong to disagree—it's just wrong to be disagreeable."[21]

Only thirty-six, Huckabee believed the ABSC presidency had been a great honor but felt it certainly could not be the apex of his professional career. In one of his final President's Corner columns, one can see hints of where his mind was leading him. "It's time for the torch to be passed. Two years ago, messengers attending the Arkansas Baptist State Convention placed upon me the mantle of this office and in so doing gave me one of the greatest privileges and challenges one can have. Arkansas Baptists represent one in every five Arkansans, and when as a body we speak (or fight) it's worthy of attention. Fortunately, we've done more speaking than fighting during these past two years!"[22]

With one in five Arkansans holding membership in ABSC churches, Huckabee considered what his own next career step might be. With so much acclaim for his leadership coming from such a large number of his fellow citizens, he considered whether he had a base of support for a run for a statewide public office. With Clinton's announcement and potential departure from Arkansas, political machines across the state began to stir into action. By the time of the ABSC meeting, Huckabee had already sought the counsel of old friends from college—guys who had told him, "Give me a call when you jump into politics and run for office."

CHAPTER 21

EXPERIENCING GOD

> The defining moment for me was as I thought about who was
> making public policy. I came to the conclusion that a lot of
> people that were making it had no clue how real people lived.[1]
>
> —MIKE HUCKABEE

IN ONE OF HIS LAST NEWSPAPER COLUMNS WRITTEN AS THE
president of Arkansas Baptists, Mike Huckabee told of an insightful question
posed to him by a Christian layman: "Do you preachers think you're the
only ones God can move around? Why is it when a preacher goes to another
church, it's 'God's will,' but when a layman moves to another church, he's a
'church hopper'?" Huckabee said the man's question helped him a lot. "As
people come or go at our church, I've learned not to take it so personally. If
they can say that they have come because the Spirit of God led them, or that
they have left for the same reason, then we are all there by the same hand
of the same God. The most important issue is not whether we are employed
full-time by the church, but whether we are confident that we are where we
are by divine destiny."[2]

In this one paragraph, Huckabee intersected two theological themes central to his own biography: God's will and the nature of Christian ministry.
Huckabee used this man's particular question—"Is it ever okay to leave and

go to another church?"—to hint that he was thinking about leaving full-time pastoral church ministry. More important, he believed individual Christians could make this kind of decision—personal and private, yet having public consequences—with the confidence that they were following the will of God.

What does Huckabee mean when he talks about "the will of God"? This question relates specifically to the decisions a Christian makes in areas of life not explicitly defined by Scripture. How does a Christian know what to do?

In 1990, a Southern Baptist pastor and denominational leader published a book titled *Experiencing God: Knowing and Doing the Will of God*. Christian books on this subject are common, but Henry Blackaby's became a publishing phenomenon, selling more than seven million copies. The book, better described as a Bible study workbook with questions and blank lines for writing down answers, taught Blackaby's vision that knowing God's will was related to knowing God intimately and getting on board with what He was doing. The Huckabees studied through the book together. They read things like "We don't choose what we will do for God; He invites us to join Him where He wants to involve us." Or "The truth is that God can do anything He pleases through an ordinary person who is fully dedicated to Him."[3]

After Huckabee entered politics, his interaction with Blackaby became personal when Huckabee invited him to dine at the governor's mansion. Blackaby recalled what the governor told him that night: "He said that while he was the pastor of a church, the Lord had begun to impress on him that He wanted to use Mike in new ways. Huckabee had trained to be a church minister, and that is what he had been doing. But as he and his wife began to study *Experiencing God*, it became clear that God was leading him to resign from the great church he was leading and to run for governor of his state."[4]

Knowing that Blackaby's teaching influenced the Huckabees helps us better interpret his statements where he tips his hand and reveals how he makes life decisions.

For example, God's will does not preclude sacrifice, suffering, or risk. For Huckabee, the guitar-selling poverty of his early days of marriage came to his mind when trying to decide whether to enter politics. "I was pastor of a large and growing church, president of Arkansas Baptist Convention, constantly being looked at by megachurches to come and be their pastor. I was running a television station as well as a church—and life was good," he said.[5]

And the satisfaction with his life went beyond vocational fulfillment. His family had stability and happiness there in Texarkana. "You've got to understand something. We had a beautiful house and our kids were in great schools—and doing great in them too. Janet and I felt like God had already given us so much—beyond our dreams and beyond the comfort level we had known growing up in Hope."[6]

So his running for Senate would risk upsetting these comforts, but Huckabee believed God's will for his life might involve walking down a path where personal happiness and financial security diminished, not increased.

Huckabee made this explicit when he talked about the actual night he and Janet made the decision to enter politics:

One night, after struggling for weeks about what to do, we took a long walk around our neighborhood, talking and trying to sort things out. If the goal of being a Christian was to be comfortable, we had arrived. But was that where we were supposed to stay? Could I simply say, "I'm a believer" and then kick back and take the world as it came? Jesus told us to be salt and light so our lives might have some kind of impact that will improve the world.

We made our decision that night. The following Sunday, I announced my plans to resign from the ministry, effective the first Sunday in February.[7]

A second principle Christians use for interpreting God's will is to ask, "What do other people think of this? Do they concur?" This would never be an ultimate factor in making a decision, but it does play a part. Once, an interviewer asked why a church—even a small church—would have made him their pastor. Huckabee responded: "I didn't know I couldn't do it. . . . I felt like, Well, if they asked me, I must be able to do it, or they wouldn't be asking me."[8] We can agree this principle doesn't apply universally in all situations. But for Huckabee, how else does an eighteen-year-old preacher decide whether he should be preaching the sermons at a particular church, except to get up and do the duty on a given Sunday? Huckabee had been in Baptist churches long enough to know that if a congregation didn't want to hear any more of your sermons, they wouldn't.

Related to the last, a third principle is that your own perception of your aptitude shouldn't be the starting point for discerning God's will. Moses evaluated his speaking abilities and told God to find another messenger to stand before Pharaoh. Huckabee said, "It's not about just, Do I have the ability or the experience, but if others have the confidence, then maybe God has a reason."[9]

When asked in 2015 why he thought he had what it took to be the president of the United States, Huckabee gave a multi-angled response. "I think some people who run for the office of president can't handle it, to be honest"—the "it" referring to the actual serving as president. "I always say the most dangerous man in the room is the man who doesn't know what he doesn't know. There's a certain level of wisdom and experience necessary— and I don't think there's any fast track to some of that."[10]

So, outside of pure narcissism, how does anyone look in the mirror and see a future president? Huckabee's Christian faith informs his answer: "I look at it in light of Philippians 4:13, 'I can do all things through Christ who strengthens me' [NKJV]. It's been the verse that I've depended on since I was fifteen. I really do look at it like that—anything that I am empowered to do and have been thrust into, I'll be able to handle. I believe that I have a source that is beyond me that will be able to make it work."[11]

Too often, people misunderstand what Huckabee means when he speaks about being led by God to run for office. He isn't making a prediction that God is going to give him *victory*, only that God has led him to run the race. Huckabee knows that God is free to act however He desires, and it may be His desire for a person to both campaign for office *and* be defeated in the campaign. His ways are not our ways.

Finally, where does personal ambition fit into all of this? Is political ambition anathema to the Christian faith? It can be, but it does not need to be. Consider what Huckabee wrote about then president Bill Clinton in 1997:

> Although President Bill Clinton and I obviously differ greatly on political issues, in many ways the president represents what Republicans promote in their public policy: self-determination, setting goals, and overcoming adversity on your own. Young Bill Clinton was poor and disadvantaged, but from the time he was young, he was focused like a laser on becoming president of the US. It's what he wanted; it's what he worked for and

sacrificed for, and through the years he managed to remove all the barriers to his goal. While there are 260 million Americans who can say whatever they want about him, he'll sleep in the White House tonight and the rest of us won't. In that way, Bill Clinton's rise to success epitomizes the American dream.[12]

Coming from similar economic backgrounds, both Huckabee and Clinton put personal ambition to work in getting themselves to high positions. Would either of them have made those achievements without ambition? Absolutely not. So for Huckabee, ambition itself is not wrong. But what is the result of the ambition? The apostle Paul wrote, "It has always been my ambition to preach the gospel where Christ was not known" (Romans 15:20).

When asked how he would advise a young person who is equally interested (and has aptitude) in both politics and the ministry, Huckabee said he would recommend politics, because "the ministry ought to be something you ought to be so compelled to do, where you wouldn't be comfortable doing anything else." Beyond that, however, Huckabee would also say, "Don't deny the fact that there is a ministry in politics." He doesn't think there should be such a wall of division between clergy and laity, nor a false dichotomy between "secular" and "sacred" service to God. Huckabee asked, "Does he feel like one is serving God and one is not? If pastoring is serving God then what is politics? Is that not serving God? Are you abandoning God? If that is what is thought, then you don't understand what serving God means because it's not true that serving God in the church is the only way to serve God."[13]

When influential conservative political blogger Erick Erickson entered a program of study at a seminary, he told the *Atlantic* "he felt 'called' to learn more about the faith that forms the backbone of his world view. 'Some of my most-read posts involve faith. At some point, I just accepted that I have a ministry, even if I never get in a pulpit.'"[14]

Not everyone agrees with Huckabee's take on mixing ministry and politics. Hugh Hewitt, a conservative radio host and author, argues that Christian pastors should keep far away from politics. He wrote, "If you are a seminarian who wants to plan a ministry career that will intertwine with politics, as Jerry Falwell or Pat Robertson has done, please put it [Hewitt's book] down." Hewitt reasoned, "Influence in the world is difficult to obtain and requires skills and disciplines that are not at all like those I have observed in the great leaders of the church." In other words, pastors shouldn't enter politics because they won't be good at it, which, by his earlier sentence, implies that Falwell and Robertson were not entirely good at it. Hewitt continued, "It is true that a very few pastors have on a very few occasions served the church and the world at the same time. Augustine, Thomas More, and Thomas Becket, as well as the pastors of revolutionary America, are examples of such unique individuals." So Hewitt acknowledges that there are exceptions to the rule, but that for the most part pastors should stay in their area of specialized expertise and skills. The people who can wade into both waters are a rare find and have "extraordinarily talented intellects," according to Hewitt. He knows such people and counts them as his good friends. But outside that circle, Hewitt thinks pastors mostly act as rubes when they enter into the public arena. "If you are ordained, leave the world to others, and tend to your flock," Hewitt wrote. "Both will be better served as a result."[15]

Beyond the simple elitism implied in Hewitt's argument, he also assumes a sharp divide between secular and sacred ministry. Contrast that with the viewpoint of Charmaine Yoest, an executive campaign staff member for Huckabee's 2008 campaign and now the president of Americans United for Life. Yoest said, "I'm a believer in politics. I think that it can be a noble calling if you bring principle to it. Politics is the essence of how people come together, live, work, worship and negotiate the rules of our living and our life together. Politics can be a really high calling to be a part of that and as Christians, I think we have to take that very seriously. I know Mike does and I respect him for that."[16]

Huckabee also does not make such a sharp division between secular and sacred callings. He believes that all Christians are called to serve Jesus, and some people will choose to do that in full-time vocational ministry within a local church. But Huckabee does not believe that pastoral ministry is a greater divine calling to serve than any other vocational choice. He says, "Even though everyone talks about how I left the pastorate for politics, I tell them, 'The pastorate was my detour, not my destination.'"[17]

The pastorate may have been a detour, but it also provided the source of inspiration for Huckabee's vocational pivot into politics. His statewide travels and interaction during his two years spent as the president of the Arkansas Baptist State Convention brought continual streams of encouragement from people who saw his potential role in government. He recalled how "people started saying . . . 'have you ever thought about running for office? Have you ever thought about getting involved in politics?' Well, the truth is, I had thought about it. I loved politics."[18]

That was the positive encouragement he needed. But it was also during Huckabee's tenure as president that Governor Bill Clinton called him to ask him for assistance, and in the process helped reawaken Huckabee to the idea of his entering politics. At the time, Joycelyn Elders served as Bill Clinton's director of the Department of Health. A few years later, as Clinton's surgeon general of the United States, Elders would make national news for her intemperate comments advocating masturbation education for public school children. And she traveled the country to dedicate new Planned Parenthood abortion clinics, being a strong and vocal advocate of abortion.

Elders got her start in controversial speechmaking while back in Arkansas. Huckabee recalled, "While I was president of the ABSC, we were pushing for a pro-life bill. That is when, in a committee meeting, Elders said, 'Preachers need to get over their love affair with the fetus.' Needless to say, it went nuclear. Clinton called me and asked me would I be willing to sit down with Elders to discuss why that statement was so very offensive. I agreed to do it and he set up the meeting. After my visit with her, I went home and told Janet 'We need to get out of the stands and on the field if people like her are setting policy that will affect our kids.' In many ways, it was the tipping point for me."[19]

Which is to say, the brash mouth on an appointee of Bill Clinton helped ignite the fire of Mike Huckabee's political ambitions.

Finally, there is one response to Huckabee's announcement that carried special weight. One week after he announced to his parents that he was moving away from pastoral ministry to run for the United States Senate, his mother, Mae, was rushed to the hospital. A ruptured aneurysm in her brain would nearly kill her that day. Though she lived on until 1999, she never regained her full health. But in that one week she still had left before the aneurysm took part of her mental capacity away, she wrote a letter. It is dated December 30, 1991—the day before her son made the announcement to his church, a "no going back" moment for the Huckabees. Mae wrote of her love and support for her son and her desire for him to always "seek and do God's will." Here is an excerpt of this final coherent word from his mother:

> Dear Mike,
>
> We realize that we do not have a gift with words or the gift of saying the right thing at the right time, but we do want to say a few words at this time. Of course, you realize that this is your earthly mother and father speaking and not your Heavenly Father speaking. . . .
>
> We are so very thankful to God for what you both have turned out to be, and we always thank God in our prayers for this.
>
> Now that you both are grown up, married and are parents yourselves, we have tried hard not to tell you what to do with yourselves, etc. . . . (even though it is hard sometimes), and it is because of this that we have not interfered with any of your decisions. Instead, we will swallow real hard and pray very much that God will help you both in everything you do.
>
> To make a long story a little shorter, we love you both so very much, ask for your forgiveness wherein we have failed you, and *shall continue to pray that you both will always seek and do God's will.*
>
> With much love,
> Mom[20]

Mike Huckabee has been around long enough to know that praying for God's will to be done doesn't mean your life will be free from pain and sorrow. Mothers have strokes and become incapacitated. A new wife has cancer.

Husbands sell sentimental items in order to buy peanut butter and to pay bills, Huckabee believes that following God's will does not mean that you always get what you want. As even Jesus prayed the night before his death, "Father, if you are willing, take this cup from me; yet not my will, but yours be done" (Luke 22:42).

PART 4

THE CITY OF MAN

CHAPTER 22

YOU CAN'T ALWAYS GET WHAT YOU WANT

1991–1992

> I really thought I wanted to get into politics, but now I just
> don't know if I like politics at all. I just don't know.
>
> **—MIKE HUCKABEE**

MONTHS BEFORE TELLING HIS PARENTS AND CHURCH FAMILY
about his idea to enter politics, Mike Huckabee talked the decision over
with friends and potential supporters. Rick Caldwell remembers the phone
call: "Hey, I want to come by and see you. I want to tell you something,"
Huckabee said. "I know this comes as a shock, but I'm thinking of running
for the Senate."

Caldwell asked, "The state senate?"

Huckabee responded, "No, the United States Senate."[1]

Randy Sims got a call too. "Hey, it's Mike. I'm thinking about running
against Dale Bumpers," Huckabee told him. "And you need to help me." Sims
became one of Huckabee's county chairmen for that election, a position he
has held for all the rest of his campaigns too. "He is my most expensive friend
I've ever had," Sims joked.[2]

When Huckabee told his plans to his brother-in-law, Jim Harris, he tried to persuade him otherwise. "Don't do that—you can't win," Harris said. "Not only is Dale Bumpers still very popular in the state, but with Bill Clinton running for president, there's going to be a very large Democratic turnout in the general election."[3]

Harris's prophecy raises an important question—Did Huckabee sincerely think he could defeat Bumpers? Bumpers first won election to the Senate in 1974 by knocking off the beloved Fulbright in the Democratic primary—the very same week the Huckabees were wed. Before that, Bumpers had been the governor of Arkansas (he was the governor who sent Huckabee a personal letter of congratulations after Boys State). Then, in the general election of 1974, he defeated the Republican challenger by winning 85 percent of the vote. Commenting on his victory, *Time* magazine wrote, "Many to their sorrow have had trouble taking Bumpers seriously . . . Dandy Dale, the man with one speech, a shoeshine, and a smile."[4]

In the general election of 1980, Bumpers defeated Republican challenger Bill Clark by a margin of 57 to 43. This would be the closest a Republican ever came to Bumpers. In 1986, Bumpers faced off against Asa Hutchinson, then the state chairman of the Arkansas Republican Party. Bumpers again earned reelection, this time winning with 62 percent of the votes, 170,000 more than Hutchinson.

Despite this history, Huckabee must have thought he would be able to find at least 85,000 more votes than Hutchinson had been able to muster. Remember, Arkansas had not sent a Republican senator to Washington, DC, since Reconstruction ended in 1877. Did Huckabee really think he would be the first? Or was his 1992 campaign a sacrificial lamb designed to build name recognition for himself, making him a more viable candidate for a future election—perhaps a U.S. Congressional seat? This is a common political strategy for political newcomers and, most would argue, nothing to be ashamed of doing.

In hindsight, you could even make the case that Huckabee was a brilliant chess strategist, seeing two or three moves ahead of the present. This scenario posits that Huckabee believed Clinton would win the White House in 1992, pulling current lieutenant governor Jim Tucker into the governor's seat in Little Rock. That would immediately create a vacancy in the lieutenant governor's office; Arkansas would follow protocol and hold a special election to fill the vacancy. And a Republican with statewide name recognition might get lucky and win the election, moving into the lieutenant governor's office. In fact, that is exactly what *did* happen, so one cannot be faulted for taking that as a working hypothesis of what Huckabee planned to achieve in his campaign against Bumpers.

But when asked if the above scenario correctly described what had taken place, Huckabee responded emphatically that he had never run a race that he didn't expect to win and desire to win. "I wish I was that smart, to have thought two or three moves ahead," he said. "But I'm not. And I really did think I would beat Bumpers in '92."[5]

"Yes, Mike ran to win," Lester Sitzes affirmed. He served as Huckabee's chairman for Hempstead County and saw firsthand Huckabee's determination to defeat Bumpers. "He wasn't thinking about anything beyond getting elected and doing good as the senator from Arkansas. That was his sole aim."[6]

Randy Sims said, "I looked at him and I said, 'Do you really, really think you're going to win this?' And he did. He was convinced he was going to win it. I knew we'd have to work hard to get it done."[7]

Huckabee's boxes of archived records from the 1992 campaign reveal his genuine intent and plan to win the election. He had mapped out a county-by-county grassroots organizational system to make his case to the people. Huckabee knew up front that he would be outspent five to one or even ten to one, but he intended to make up for the lack of funding through sweat equity and retail politics. For a first-time candidate, the campaign showed a high level of organization and personal investment into the process. No friend was left uncalled. No volunteer sat on the sidelines waiting for something to do. The paper trail alone offers enough evidence that Huckabee was "in it to win it."[8]

Pundits, conservative or liberal, didn't give Huckabee any chance against Bumpers. Sitzes remembers inviting John Brummett, a liberal-leaning newspaper editor from Little Rock, as a speaker for the Rotary club in Hope. It was Brummett who in 1991 had made a prediction about Huckabee's potential in politics based on Huckabee's leadership within the Arkansas Baptist Convention. Brummett wrote, "He's the kind of young man who might succeed in secular politics."[9] Now, however, Brummett told Sitzes, "Your buddy Mike is a good guy, but he doesn't have a future in politics." Sitzes replied,

"I'm going to tell you one thing John, just remember this—Mike Huckabee grows on you. Get to know him and he'll grow on you."[10]

Sitzes also brought John Starr, a conservative columnist in Arkansas, as a guest speaker. Starr said nearly the same thing to Sitzes: "Huckabee's a good guy, but he doesn't have a future in politics." Sitzes responded the same way he had to Brummett: "Mr. Starr, I want you to remember one thing. Mike Huckabee grows on you." Sitzes said that in one of Starr's final columns before his death in 2000, he admitted that he thought Huckabee was a good governor. Sitzes' word had proven to be true.[11]

On a personal level, the campaign helped the Huckabees discover who their true friends were. "What we were least prepared for was the abandonment of the people we thought were friends," he said. "We expected broadside opposition from the Democratic-party people, political opponents. . . . But there were others, people we had been through the fires with, and they turned on us immediately. For some of them, they were Democrats first and Christians second. How dare I not only run for office, but the real insult was that I would run as a Republican!"[12]

Huckabee remembers being pained by one family in particular. He had performed weddings and funerals for them; he had supported them when they had trouble with the law and in medical crises. Yet their yard displayed signs for his opponent. While he could understand being philosophically opposed to voting Republican, he was stung that they would so openly work to defeat him when he had stood by their side through so much.[13]

Huckabee had always known about the Arkansas Democratic machine, but now he saw it in operation up close and personal. Jim Harris recalled one campaign stop in a town in southeast Arkansas. Huckabee went there to hold a news conference and answer questions from the media, but the local paper didn't show up. Not wanting to have wasted the time and gas spent for the trip, Huckabee drove over to the offices of the newspaper, accompanied by two reporters from other newspapers who traveled with him that day. They all walked in together and sat down, waiting to see the editor. But she wouldn't meet with them—she didn't even acknowledge they were in the building.

"Huckabee said he was just going to wait until she came out," Harris recalled.

Finally she emerged and candidate Huckabee said, "I thought you might like an interview." But Harris said the editor curtly replied, "We don't do interviews," and then abruptly turned around and walked back to her office. The other two reporters looked at each other and asked, "What newspaper doesn't do interviews of candidates?" "This editor was so beholden to the Democratic ticket that she did not want to let her readers even be exposed to the message from the other side," Harris explained.[14]

Not everyone responded negatively though. Huckabee wrote about how an anonymous sender mailed him postcards featuring encouraging Scripture verses. Only after the campaign would he learn that the postcards came from a young wife and mother who had been a parishioner at Beech Street First Baptist Church in Texarkana.[15]

The volunteer corps who made up Huckabee's campaign gave it their best effort. Sims remembers putting up campaign signs all day long and even into the night. "Yes, at midnight, way out in the middle of wherever in Conway, Arkansas," Sims said. "And Mike used to come by here and change clothes before going on to a next event. Whenever he came through Conway, he would run to our house and get freshened up."[16] Huckabee's campaign lacked a touring coach bus or enough dollars to make constant hotel lodgings affordable. But, from his days as a Baptist pastor, he *did* have good friends in every town and city. If Huckabee were to become the next U.S. senator from Arkansas, the victory would be the result of countless sacrifices made by common, everyday people throughout the state.

Huckabee said that his 1992 campaign strategy and messaging was "cookie-cutter Republican" in its approach: "You're going to have a biographical spot. 'Hello, I'm Mike Huckabee . . .' And then you'll immediately start talking about 'Let's cut taxes' and 'Let's get the government under control'—all these issues that, quite frankly, all the Republicans already all believe. So you don't move anybody."[17]

Huckabee also took his cues from the playbook of the national cultural wars being fought that year. As such, he utilized more right-wing rhetoric than was helpful for building a victorious voting bloc. That's not to say he spoke words untrue to his real convictions at the time. But there seemed to be a lack of sophistication in his answers; even mere silence would have been more useful for explaining his positions on some subjects. For example, when responding to a written Associated Press questionnaire about the AIDS epidemic, he stated that government should "isolate the carriers of this plague. It is the first time in the history of civilization in which the carriers of a genuine plague have not been isolated from the general population, and in which this deadly disease for which there is no cure is being treated as a civil rights issue instead of the true health crises it represents."[18]

That statement took on a life of its own and continues to be used by opponents to this day. Given that AIDS was perceived as a medical crisis almost entirely limited to the homosexual community, people caricatured his statement as latently homophobic. Huckabee's comment seemed, to many, to be a recommendation that the government lock the gay community in concentration camps. He meant less than what critics say he said, but he has been walking back from that comment for over two decades now.

In another example, Huckabee jumped into the national conversation over whether taxpayers should fund the National Endowment for the Arts. The NEA had recently sponsored some artwork that nearly everyone—whether they liked the artwork or not—considered blasphemous to the Christian faith. In 1990, while Huckabee served as president of the Arkansas Baptists, the convention unanimously passed a resolution "in opposition to the policy of the National Endowment of the Arts in funding pornographic and anti-religious artistic presentations."[19]

The problem, however, was that Senator Bumpers was only nominally linked to the NEA funding battleground. Bumpers said the art was in poor taste but voted to continue the NEA's funding. But the issue didn't have a lot of traction with potential swing voters in Arkansas. Ironically, Huckabee is a big supporter of art education within the schools, and that positive message might have won him some support among middle-class voters concerned about the lack of a well-rounded education in the public schools. But instead of running on that positive message, his campaign painted Bumpers as a supporter of pornography.

Max Brantley, an ardent critic of Huckabee through the years, said, "In that race, I thought he managed to pigeonhole himself as strictly a religious conservative—abortion, pornography, and the NEA funding." As Brantley explained it, however, though Arkansans are overwhelmingly religious in practice, "it doesn't necessarily follow that they're kind of down the line on all the issues that the hard core religious right kind of take as a matter of sort of marching orders."[20]

Though it is doubtful that any path to victory existed for Huckabee, even one that moderated his rhetoric on social issues, it is a fair assessment to say that Huckabee never again ran for Arkansas office using the full script of the national culture wars. "In terms of public comments that are clearly derogatory toward gays and lesbians or persons with HIV/AIDS, most of those comments come early in his career," author Jay Barth told the *Boston Globe* in 2007. "That is not to say he became a progressive on the issue, but he talked about them less."[21]

———

Huckabee won the spring Republican primary easily with more than 40,000 votes and 79 percent support over the challenger, David Busby. Clearly, he had a base of statewide support, stemming from his Arkansas roots and his Baptist convention presidency.

Once he became the official nominee of the GOP, Huckabee traveled to California for an event at the Reagan Library, hosted by President and Mrs. Reagan. This was the first time Huckabee had been alongside Reagan since the August 1980 rally in Dallas. Could Huckabee "win one for the Gipper" in Arkansas?

He didn't. As the election results came in that night, the good news was that Huckabee had earned an extra 85,000 votes more than Hutchinson had done in losing to Bumpers six years earlier. The bad news, however, was that this was a historic day for Arkansas—the chance to vote an Arkansan into the White House. And based on the huge turnout at the polls, it appeared that nobody was missing their opportunity. Even though Huckabee received 100,000 more votes than Hutchinson had, he still lost by nearly the same 60 to 40 margin. Bumpers received 553,000 votes to Huckabee's 366,000.

———

The night of the loss, Huckabee thanked his supporters and spoke to their hearts, telling them that the fight had not been in vain. Then, after he left the cameras and crowds behind, he crashed—physically and emotionally. "That's the lowest point I've ever seen Mike," Sitzes recalled. "He had pneumonia, though hardly anyone knew. He was trying to be strong for everybody. But as soon as the election was over in Little Rock—across town from where Bill Clinton was celebrating—Mike traveled back to Texarkana and entered the hospital. I sat by his side. He told me, 'I really thought I wanted to get into politics, but now I just don't know if I like politics at all. I just don't know.'"[22]

Huckabee's finances, not pneumonia, proved to be the greatest post-campaign concern for the Huckabees. They had burned through their life savings, which admittedly was not much, but now they had nothing. Without a job in hand and with a mortgage still to pay, financial stress ensued. "They almost lost their house," said Sitzes. "They were broke; there's no other way to put it. And to hear Hillary Clinton talk about being broke—what a joke. Mike and Janet were broke for real—everything was leveraged. It was not a good situation."[23]

As the Huckabees began to rebuild and figure out the next step of their journey, they still had to buy groceries. Huckabee took whatever work he could find. That's when Huckabee bumped into the wife from the family of former parishioners who had put Bumpers signs in their yard. She approached her former pastor in the aisle and asked if he would be a reference for her in her job search. Huckabee remembers being too stunned to answer coherently, muttering something like, "I will do everything I can to help you," while thinking, *like you did everything to help my opponent*. He said, "She had worked so hard to keep me from getting a job, and then had the audacity to turn around and ask me for help getting her one. Those were some of the tough moments."[24]

The Rolling Stones' hit "You Can't Always Get What You Want" sums up Huckabee's feelings in the aftermath of the election loss. But, to paraphrase the Beatles instead, Huckabee knew he'd "get by with a little help from his friends."

Sitzes sat by his friend as the antibiotics did their work against the pneumonia. "We talked about all the pain of the election. But then I told him—and this is best friend to best friend—I said, 'Mike, there's a reason for all this. You'll see.'"[25]

CHAPTER 23

EVEN THE LOSERS GET LUCKY SOMETIMES

1993–1996

> We all know there's a political machine. It runs over
> ordinary people. You've been the victim of it time and time
> again, but now it's time to unplug the local machine.
>
> **—MIKE HUCKABEE**

THE DESPONDENCY THE HUCKABEES FELT AFTER THE 1992 campaign loss did not last long. The same night that brought such joy to the Clinton family, sending Bill to the White House as the next president, also sowed the seeds for Huckabee's future in politics. With Clinton moving out of the governor's mansion in Little Rock, Arkansas, lieutenant governor Jim Tucker moved in and assumed the duties of the office. He had actually been doing many of those duties before that time anyway, as Clinton had been out of the state, campaigning for president, for at least an entire year, if not longer.

Looking back on that period, Huckabee reflected, "I didn't lose my fire, my zeal, I lost an election. But I've always said politics is a process, not a single event. . . . You have to look at this as something for the long haul. . . . Your goal is not simply to win an office, it's to effect the change in policy that you want to see happen. And you can't do that with one single election."[1]

In other words, if you can't effect change with "one single election," then an election loss is not a final loss. Put it behind you and look up to see the next opportunity coming. That sounds like a cheesy motivational poster, but Huckabee knows the truth of it from his 1992–1993 experiences.

No sooner had the Huckabees put leftover Senate campaign posters into storage than Asa Hutchinson came to Huckabee with a proposition. Since Jim Tucker had moved up to the governor's office, the lieutenant governor's position sat vacant. Hutchinson appealed to Huckabee to declare himself a candidate for the special election to be held at the end of July 1993. Of course, whoever won this election would have to stand for reelection the next year, so even with a victory, this might only be a one-year gig. Plus, the likelihood of a Republican winning the special election was not very great. Arkansas had elected only one Republican to the position since the office was first filled in the 1920s. The Arkansas lieutenant governor and governor are elected separately in Arkansas, so it was possible for two different parties to fill the spots. The lieutenant governor is mostly a ceremonial office, presiding over the Arkansas legislature, giving commencement speeches, attending funerals, and so forth. The work and the pay were considered part-time. Lieutenant governors were not inclined to move their families to Little Rock, but would opt instead to set up an apartment in the city and simply commute back and forth. In other words, the job would involve days away from his family, for little pay and only a remote chance for the job to develop into a long-term vocational path.

So Huckabee jumped right in and geared up for his second campaign in nine months. But what would be different this time? His competition was a Democrat named Nick Coulter, and the election seemed his to win or lose. "Oh, was it ever," Huckabee said. "He was Clinton's chief legal aid in the governor's office. Harvard educated. Brilliant attorney. He was the Barack Obama, the heir apparent to Bill Clinton. The coming new generation, with all the money that the Clintons could raise—and they raised all his money for him right out of the basement of the White House. Clinton's fund-raiser, Mark Middleton, was making calls every night to get Coulter's money. He had millions—and this for a lieutenant governor's race!"[2]

Huckabee knew he would be unable to compete with the Coulter–Clinton fund-raising, so he got right to work mobilizing a grassroots campaign. But this time around, he had a secret ally in the fight, someone with a vast reservoir of Arkansas-based political knowledge and the desire to earn money.

Huckabee tells the story of receiving a call from Dick Morris, a campaign strategist and advisor to the Clintons. "I picked up the phone and Morris said, 'Look, I think you're a fascinating individual and you have real potential. I want you to be in that lieutenant governor's race, and I think I can help you win. I don't agree with some of your positions, but that's okay. I'll make enough money off you, so I can live with it.' Huckabee appreciated his candor, being just straight up about it all—that was refreshing. "So we talked and really hit it off. Here was a New York Jew and an Arkansas Baptist boy, the most unlikely odd couple you can imagine. It was a Felix and Oscar relationship to be sure. And we had great rapport. Dick didn't try to change me. He didn't tell me to stop being pro-life or to quit being so Christian. But he helped me take what I believe and what made me tick and turned it into election issues which would help me win."[3]

Morris ended up working for Huckabee in the 1993 campaign, and then in his reelection campaign of 1994 and reelection-for-governor campaign of 1998. Morris also led in Bill Clinton's successful reelection campaign of 1996, after having the ear of the president more than anyone else did in 1995— according to George Stephanopoulos, who served in the White House at the time.[4]

Huckabee won the July 1993 special election and became lieutenant governor. He did so by the slimmest of margins, beating Coulter 50.85 percent to 49.15 percent (151,502 to 146,436)—a margin of only 5,000 votes.

Huckabee has never forgotten the lessons learned in that election. In analyzing the 1993 election, Morris said, "The mistake Republicans always make is that they are too much of a country club set. What we wanted to do was run a progressive campaign that would appeal to all Arkansans."[5]

In contrast to the cookie-cutter Republican ads and messaging Huckabee had used less than one year earlier, Morris worked hard to develop campaign advertisements that would depict Huckabee in a more moderate light, more in line with the values of Arkansas voters.[6] Morris also taught Huckabee the principle of looking for the wedge issues. "Dick had the attitude that when you take a poll and find an issue with 90 percent support, that may not be an issue that you want to run on, because the fact that 90 percent of the people supported it doesn't mean that it actually means anything to them. They're already either going to vote for you or against you," Huckabee explained. "For example, the message 'I'm going to cut taxes,' spoken by every Republican in a campaign. Most of them don't actually do it, but they all say it. In contrast, it's better to look for the wedge issue."

Huckabee said a good example of this was Bill Clinton's promotion of school uniforms as an issue in 1996. Why would a president of the United States care about school uniforms? The answer is that there were millions of mothers out there who had concluded that a school uniform would lessen the likelihood that her child would be bullied, picked on, or criticized for his or her clothing. This issue moved voters who were not necessarily going to vote for him prior to the wedge issue. "That kind of strategy was Dick's genius," Huckabee said.[7]

Morris also changed the visuals. He depicted Arkansas as a state run by the Democratic Party. In one of the advertisements Morris created, an electrical cord can be seen being pulled out of the wall. "The message was simple," Huckabee said. "We all know there's a political machine. It runs over ordinary people. You've been the victim of it time and time again, but now it's time to unplug the local machine.

"The Democrats went nuts when that ad came out. Nuts," Huckabee said. "They did not want to believe there was a political machine, but everybody knew it. I didn't say it was Bill Clinton. You didn't have to. Everybody knew."[8]

Going into election day, Morris had a good idea that Huckabee would win. He tells the story of how Dick spent the day in a room at the Camelot Hotel in downtown Little Rock. With pencils, notebooks, and a calculator in hand, Morris would receive bits of data sent in from polls throughout the state as they closed. Huckabee remembers that at 8:30 p.m., when only 15 percent of the precincts had reported, Morris congratulated him on the coming win. He even predicted that Huckabee would end the night with 51 percent of the vote. An hour and a half later, Huckabee told his supporters he was declaring victory. And yes, the prediction about the 51 percent was exactly right.[9]

When asked whether he thinks he would have won the election without Morris's help, Huckabee said, "Probably not. . . . I mean, he wasn't the only factor. It was a grassroots effort by many people. But we were able to stop the Democratic machine somehow. But probably not without Dick."[10]

Now that he was elected, it was time to show up for work. Huckabee put on his suit and headed to the office of the lieutenant governor—his new office. But when he reached the door and pulled on the handle, nothing happened. The door "seemed to be jammed or blocked," Huckabee said.[11]

"Oh, we've designated that room for a committee meeting," Huckabee was told. But a few minutes later the story was something different. What was going on? Huckabee discovered that the door had been nailed shut from the inside, and not just with one or two nails, but all around the entire door frame. This wasn't a random act of vandalism or a prank gone too far. The secretary of state for Arkansas controlled the use of that building, and he had allowed (or requested) the door to be nailed shut.

Apparently, the idea of a Republican crashing in on the government was more than some people could handle. After all, Huckabee was only the fourth Republican since Reconstruction to be elected to a statewide consti-tutional office. His very presence in the capitol represented something the Democrats were not yet prepared to accept. For the next fifty-nine days, Huckabee pulled a table and chair into the hallway outside his door and used the makeshift office to conduct his business. The nails eventually came out and the door was opened. But once inside, Huckabee discovered that all the office furniture was gone. And before Huckabee had taken over the position, the staff had spent the entire remaining budget for the year. What was worse, the ornery behavior was systemic throughout Little Rock. It took him four months to get letterhead made because the requisitions office kept rejecting his request. Finally, he just took out his wallet and paid for some to be made at his own expense, bypassing the blockage.

As for Gov. Jim Tucker, Huckabee said that they got along well with each other. "In fact, I had a much better working relationship with Tucker than he had experienced with Governor Clinton. The two of them had been rivals for years."[12]

When it came time for reelection one year later, Huckabee had a much easier time securing a victory. He earned 58 percent of the vote over his Democratic challenger, Charlie Cole Chaffin. Though the Clintons had once again assisted Huckabee's opponent, the help failed to secure a victory for the second election in a row. Dick Morris again gave campaign strategy to Huckabee, even as he was also coaching Clinton on his messaging in support of the midterm elections. This was 1994, the first midterm election since Clinton was elected. Newt Gingrich had offered his "Contract with America" as a campaign promise from the Republicans, and the national results of the election would reveal a backlash against the Clintons. Plus, there had already been scandals in the White House, and some Arkansans felt that the Clintons were embarrassing them. None of the three Hope, Arkansas, friends who came to Washington with Clinton to serve in the White House (McLarty, Watkins, and Foster) had made it to the midterm elections. The point being, 1994 was a good year for Republicans due to Clinton's miscues and policies.

As for the effects of the rough treatment Huckabee received from Democrats, he believes the incidents helped him in his 1994 bid for reelection. "The Democrats unintentionally transformed me from a vile Republican to a friend of the common folk. People in Arkansas . . . may be yellow dog Democrats, but deep down there were a lot of people who seemed to say, 'I didn't vote for him, and I don't like Republicans, but he won the election—so let's treat him right.' They were embarrassed for their own party at the kind of treatment I was receiving, and the sympathy worked in our favor."[13]

Huckabee settled into the duties of being lieutenant governor, although those tasks did not provide a full sense of achievement for someone who longed to make a real difference in the world. So, when Senator Mark Pryor announced, in the early months of 1996, that he would be vacating his seat in the U.S. Senate, Huckabee decided to enter the race. He was leading in the polls in the spring and appeared to have a good chance of winning in the fall. Having been in the statewide spotlight for four years, certainly his chances would be better this time around than they were in 1992.

But becoming a United States senator would *not* be in Huckabee's future. In May 1996, Jim Guy Tucker was convicted of fraud in a Whitewater-related case. The Arkansas Constitution forbids a convicted felon from holding office, so Tucker stated he would be resigning his office on July 15. Both the conviction and Tucker's decision to resign surprised many people, including Huckabee. It was at this time that Huckabee turned away from the idea of running for the Senate. He told *World* magazine, "Putting that aside has been very difficult. When you've worked so hard for something, you funnel every ounce of your energy toward it, and your fingers are all but touching the prize, then abruptly something changes the whole structure of the world for you: Do you keep reaching or do you withdraw your hand?"[14]

Tim Hutchinson stepped into Huckabee's spot on the Republican ticket and won the election, becoming Arkansas's first Republican senator in more than one hundred years. Hutchinson had less name recognition than Huckabee, yet still won—giving every evidence that Huckabee himself would have won.

Instead, with forty-five days to prepare for becoming the forty-fourth governor of Arkansas, Huckabee began to assemble his staff and prepare his vision of governance. The press said he would be an "accidental governor," and people predicted his tenure would be short. It was still assumed that Arkansans didn't want Republicans in Little Rock. In the Arkansas House, eighty-eight out of the one hundred representatives came from the Democratic Party. In the Arkansas Senate, twenty-eight out of thirty-five were Democrats. Little Rock was the domain of the Democrats.

It is fascinating to consider how close Huckabee came to never making it into statewide elected office. Nick Coulter should have won that 1993 campaign, and probably would have had anyone taken Huckabee seriously. Dick Morris should have been working for Democrats alone, except that was not his economic style. He had Arkansas-specific skills for hire, and Huckabee was a willing buyer. Morris's working both sides of the aisle led to Huckabee's 1993 win. Had Huckabee lost, that would have been his second defeat in nine months. Who can say what would have happened to his political career after a second loss? For certain, he would not have been in a position to take over for Tucker and become the governor. So, in a very real sense, all events in Huckabee's life after the 1993 election victory came about because of that 51–49 vote. Had 2,500 voters marked their ballots differently and voted for Coulter, Huckabee's ascent to the governor's office and candidacy for the president of the United States would have never happened.

After the campaign loss in 1992, Sitzes told Huckabee "something good will come of all this." And something good *did* happen. Had Huckabee not run for the Senate, he would not have earned statewide name recognition or built up a grassroots organization of support. In other words, Huckabee's victory over Coulter in 1993 sat on the foundation of the failed 1992 campaign against Bumpers. The loss bought the win. As the title of Tom Petty's song declares, "Even the losers get lucky sometimes."

Furthermore, it must be noted that Jim Tucker's conviction may never have happened had it not been for the national political scene. Because of the desire to discover and convict the Clintons of crime in the Whitewater investigation, a significant amount of time and resources were spent on the investigation. And part of that effort led to peripheral convictions—like that of Jim Tucker. If not for the Clinton-related scandals, Tucker would have served out the remainder of his term of office, and then Lieutenant Governor Huckabee would have run and likely won a seat in the U.S. Senate. Huckabee would have missed his opportunity to be used where his executive skills were best put to use—in the pressure-filled work of the executive branch of Arkansas government.

Under pressure, indeed, from the very first day.

Mae and Dorsey Huckabee.

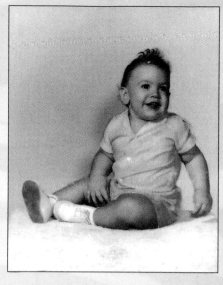

"Hucka-baby."

Pat and Mike
Huckabee
(c. 1961–1962).

All suited up for
a family portrait:
Dorsey, Mike, Mae,
Pat (c. 1963).

The Huckabees pose with their baby cousin (1964).

Pat and Mike Huckabee stand at attention in their home on 2nd Street, with fresh uniforms signaling the start of another year of Girl Scouts and Cub Scouts.

Mike is standing just to the left of the coach on the right, Bobby Joe Lee, whose son Robin played on the team (c. 1962).

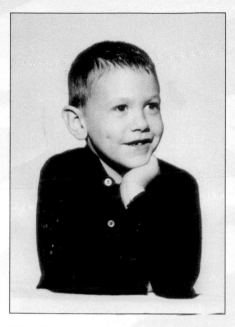

Mike Huckabee, early elementary school picture.

Mike Huckabee, late elementary school picture (c. 1967).

Huckabee the wishful Beatle, age twelve, continuing to learn guitar, after receiving his first one (leaning against the couch) as a Christmas present two years earlier. The photo was taken in the Huckabees' home on 2nd Street.

With television star Hugh O'Brian, when Huckabee was chosen, along with a small number of other high school sophomores, to attend O'Brian's leadership camp in Florida at the Space Center.

Huckabee and his Bois d'Arc Boogie Band (Huckabee is second from the left in the back row).

During Boys State in the summer of 1972, Huckabee practices the art of political handshaking with a young man who became a lifelong friend, Jonathan Barnett.

Huckabee sits in the seat of power after winning the governor's spot at Boys State in the summer of 1972. Standing directly behind him is Rick Caldwell, Huckabee's good friend.

Huckabee in the fall of 1973, his senior year. Lester Sitzes says, "It took Mike an hour to get his hair perfect like that."

Huckabee as a smooth senior at Hope High School.

Mike and Janet (McCain) Huckabee on their wedding day—May 25, 1974.

The wedding of Mike and Janet Huckabee. Left to right: Johnny and Pat McCain House, Janet (McCain) Huckabee, Mike Huckabee, Mae Huckabee, Dorsey Huckabee.

Mike and Janet
Huckabee, with
lifelong friend
Alan Foster.

The young evangelist in the
mid-1970s.

Graduation day for Mike
Huckabee, Ouachita Baptist
University, spring 1976.
Though Huckabee finished
his coursework in December
1975, Ouachita did not have
a winter graduation. The man
shaking his hand is OBU
president Daniel R. Grant.

Backyard picture on Mother's Day (c. 1979). Left to right: John Mark Huckabee, Mike Huckabee, Janet Huckabee, Pat Harris, Jim Harris, Mae Huckabee, Dorsey Huckabee.

Christmas (c. 1984). Front row, left to right: a Harris cousin, John Mark Huckabee, David Huckabee. Back row, left to right: Jim Harris, a Harris cousin, Pat Harris, Janet Huckabee, Sarah Huckabee, Mike Huckabee.

Interview with Dave Woodman (KARK-TV, Little Rock) during the 1992 Senate race.

Huckabee at the Reagan Library in Simi Valley, California, with former president Ronald Reagan and first lady Nancy Reagan, during Huckabee's 1992 Senate campaign.

Huckabee speaking at a 1992 campaign rally in Little Rock.

During Huckabee's term as lieutenant governor, his sister, Pat Harris, was recognized as the teacher of the year in Arkansas. Left to right: Jim Harris, Pat (Huckabee) Harris, Gov. Jim Tucker, Janet Huckabee, Lt. Gov. Mike Huckabee.

Huckabee family dressed to the nines for Mike Huckabee's momentous day of inauguration as governor of Arkansas—July 15, 1996.

Huckabee and first lady Janet, in the late 1990s.

First lady of Arkansas Janet Huckabee addressing citizens while her husband hams it up with a thumb of approval to the photographer.

Mike Huckabee Papers, Ouachita Baptist University Archives

Huckabee being sworn
into his second term
of office as governor
in 2003, by Arkansas
Supreme Court chief
justice Dub Arnold.

Official portrait of
Governor Mike Huckabee.

Huckabee
with a winning
team of Little
Leaguers in
2004.

Front row, left to right: Sarah, Mike, and Janet Huckabee. Back row, left to right: David and John Mark Huckabee.

Janet and Mike.

Left to right: Governor Mike Huckabee, First Lady Laura Bush, President George W. Bush, and First Lady Janet Huckabee, for a formal dinner together (c. 2005–2006).

Huckabee at book signing for *Quit Digging Your Grave with a Knife and Fork* (2005).

Governor Mike Huckbee demonstrates to students how much extra weight he used to carry around, by carrying a student who weighed the same amount as he had lost (c. 2005).

Huckabee with an Asian delegation (c. 2006).

At Magic Springs Theme Park in Hot Springs, Arkansas (c. 1996–2000). Mike Huckabee is in the front row, hands definitely gripping the safety bar. Janet Huckabee is in the seat behind him, definitely not gripping the safety bar.

Mike Huckabee Papers, Ouachita Baptist University Archives

Huckabee, with one of his trophy fish caught in the rivers of Arkansas.

Mike Huckabee Papers, Ouachita Baptist University Archives

Governor Huckabee fishing on the Arkansas River in Little Rock, Arkansas, with the dome of the Arkansas capitol in the background (c. 2005–2006).

Mike Huckabee Papers, Ouachita Baptist University Archives

Left to right: Jet, the wonder Labrador, and Mike Huckabee, duck hunting at Hampton's Reservoir near Stuttgart, Arkansas.

Bob Robbins, the number one radio DJ in Arkansas for the past thirty years or more, giving Huckabee a gift of a pair of boots. Note the painting of former Arkansas Governor Bill Clinton behind them.

Mike Huckabee Papers, Ouachita Baptist University Archives

Huckabee gives a commemorative knife to the president, who comically looks at it with a note of concern. Left to right: President George W. Bush, Governor Mike Huckabee.

At a music festival (c. 2004). Left to right: Janet Huckabee, Willie Nelson, Mike Huckabee.

Huckabee playing with members
of his band, Capitol Offense.
Next to Huckabee is Rick
Calhoun and then Gordon Caffey.

Huckabee playing the
bass guitar at a blues
festival (c. 2005).

Mike Huckabee
enjoying a visit
with Bon Jovi's
Richie Sambora
and Henry
Juszkiewicz, CEO
of Gibson Guitar
Corporation.

CHAPTER 24

UNDER PRESSURE

July 15, 1996–November 1998

> It was a bombshell. Everyone was stunned. There was a moment when no one really knew who the governor was.

—RICK CALDWELL, MIKE HUCKABEE'S FRIEND FROM BOYS STATE AND OBU

WHEN MIKE HUCKABEE BECAME ONLY THE THIRD REPUBLICAN since Reconstruction to take the oath of office as governor, he faced a hostile legislature composed of 80 to 90 percent Democrats. Further, the media in Little Rock were neither unbiased nor Republican. It is no surprise, therefore, that he had plenty of critics from the left that no amount of winsomeness and personal charm could overcome. But he also regularly found himself in battle with colleagues from the right who disagreed with Huckabee's pragmatic approach to governance.

The next three chapters cover Huckabee's three terms of office from 1996 through 2007. No attempt is made to cover every policy, program, and event in the state of Arkansas over the course of that decade. Instead, we will focus on some broad themes, initiatives, and events that aid in our understanding of the principles that led Huckabee in his duties as the chief executive officer of the state. In doing so, one may discern how Huckabee would also lead the United States of America. The particulars change from year to year, but the principles remain the same in a person led by conviction rather than politics or party.

Queen's song "Under Pressure" ends with a passionate appeal for people to slow down from the pressure of modern life long enough to notice and care for those who are going under. Tornado survivors, school shooting victims and their families, impoverished kids, murderers and relatives of the murdered: being a state governor brought Huckabee into contact with a never-ending stream of people affected by tragedy and trial. The pressure on them created pressure on him to govern well. How would he hold up?

One thing is for sure: the stress of governance hardly ever stripped Huckabee of his sense of humor. His philosophy, both in life generally and politics specifically, is "Take God seriously, but don't take yourself too seriously." Huckabee attributes this way of looking at life as an inheritance from his father.[1] It served Dorsey well as a fireman in stressful situations, and it would serve his son well while governing the state.

Since Huckabee was polling 20 percentage points higher than the Democratic candidate was in his 1996 campaign for U.S. Senate, he seemed headed to Washington. Of course, as things turned out, Huckabee changed course and wound up as the governor. Either way, his father did not live to see the outcome of all the political motion surrounding his son that spring. "As he was dying," recalls Pat Harris, "Dad said, 'I know I'm not gonna make it, but I sure wish I could.'"[2] Dorsey died on March 31; Huckabee was sworn into office on July 15.

———————

Rick Caldwell describes the events in Little Rock on July 15 as both the "darkest *and* brightest hour" for the state of Arkansas.[3] Outgoing governor Jim Tucker, forced by the Arkansas Constitution to resign due to his Whitewater-related conviction, had set his resignation to be effective at noon that day.[4]

That morning, Huckabee's friends and family all arrived in Little Rock for the inauguration. Many people had already taken jobs with his administration and were in the process of moving to the city. But unbeknownst to anyone, Tucker came to the decision that it was in his best interest to hold on to his office, at least until he appealed the original conviction. After all, Arkansans voted him into office. He figured they would stand by him through this setback. Meanwhile, Huckabee was under the assumption that he would become the acting governor as of noon.

At 11:55, just five minutes before Huckabee planned to walk to the legislative chambers and be sworn in, Tucker called and told Huckabee of his decision to forgo the resignation. "It was a bombshell," Caldwell recalled. "Everyone was stunned. There was a moment when no one really knew who the governor was."[5]

That's when Huckabee took a strong stand of leadership and communicated to Tucker that this was unacceptable. "I would strongly disagree with the actions that you are taking today," Huckabee said to Tucker. "You are now going back on what you told the people, and it seems to me that your actions are being done in your interests, not in the interests of the people of Arkansas."[6]

Tucker's idea was to hold back the resignation but relinquish his duties to Huckabee for a temporary period until he had a chance to appeal his conviction. The state would be in leadership limbo until then, but Tucker would not lose his governorship.

Huckabee rallied the state legislature. Though a predominantly Democratic assembly, they sided with Huckabee against Tucker. The *New York Times* was on hand and wrote that the "Arkansas Capitol was enveloped by barely contained confusion and undisguised bipartisan outrage."[7] The legislature agreed that either Tucker must resubmit his resignation immediately or they would begin the process of impeaching him. An aide later described Huckabee as having "an incredible ability to focus" amid all the confusion, and another aide said "he had a very firm grasp of the Constitution" on that day.[8] Both of these characteristics served Huckabee well during the tense hours.

Huckabee had been scheduled to go on television at 5:15 p.m. and give a speech as the new governor, but his prepared, polished speech sat unused on his desk. Instead, after all the adrenaline rush, politicking, confusion, bewilderment, and stress put on everyone who had gathered that day, Huckabee stood in front of the camera and calmly spoke to the citizens of the state he was to govern for the next decade.

Without notes or preparation, Huckabee said, "Good evening, ladies and gentlemen. Tonight I fully expected to address you as the governor of the state of Arkansas." He then explained what had transpired and how he and the legislators would begin impeachment procedures against Tucker in the morning. Huckabee concluded, "Let me simply express to you we want America to see the best we are and come to understand Arkansas is truly a small but wonderful state with wonderful, wonderful people. God bless, and good night."[9]

Eyewitnesses to the speech were amazed at Huckabee's repose and off-the-cuff polish displayed in the speech. "I was astounded at his ability in such a crisis situation to display calm and to calm the whole state through that," said someone who was next to Huckabee. Another said, "All day long he had a right to be the most frazzled, but he was the calmest person in the building."[10]

In response to the united resolve to impeach him, Tucker relented and resigned. Huckabee was sworn in at 6:45 p.m.

> I, Mike Huckabee, do solemnly swear, will support the Constitution of the United States, and the Constitution of the state of Arkansas, and that I will well and faithfully discharge the duties of the office of Governor of the state of Arkansas upon which I am about now to enter, so help me God.[11]

The "so help me God" may be boilerplate language for some politicians, but when Huckabee spoke those words, he had his favorite Bible verse in mind, Philippians 4:13: "I can do all things through Christ who strengthens me" (NKJV). Huckabee said he has depended on that verse since he was fifteen. "I really do look at it that anything that I have been thrust into, I'll be able to handle because I believe that I have a source that is beyond me that will be able to make it work. The day of my swearing-in as governor when I gave that speech, it was 'Cameras on . . . Go'—and I did it. People ask how and I tell them it was as if I was lifted out of my body and God said, 'You're kind of over your head, kid, but don't worry. I'm God. I got this.'"[12]

Huckabee has seen Tucker a few times since that day and says they have a cordial relationship. "I don't have any harsh things to say about him or what he went through because I don't walk in his skin," Huckabee said. "I think there was plenty of deep pain and trouble for him and his family. . . . not something that any of us could celebrate."[13]

The chaos surrounding his inauguration had made the *New York Times*, and his administration continued to draw the paper's attention over the first few months of his being in office.

First, Huckabee refused to authorize a Medicaid payment for an abortion, stating that his first obligation was to obey the constitution of Arkansas, not the federal law. "The State Constitution includes an amendment banning the use of public money for abortion except when a mother's life is endangered," explained the *New York Times*. "The Federal statute requires that Medicaid pay for abortions that are performed on poor women in cases of rape or incest or threat to the mother's life." This situation involved a case of incest between a stepfather and his fifteen-year-old daughter who an official said was "likely developmentally disabled."[14] Huckabee said that neither the amount of the money involved ($430) nor the fact that he was pro-life determined his response. Rather, the state was currently involved in a lawsuit filed by an abortion opponent, and Huckabee's administration believed paying the Medicaid payment for this abortion would jeopardize their case.

In a *New York Times* story a few days later, he said, "This isn't the 1957 school crisis . . . This is the 1973 55-mile-per-hour speed limit. We were perfectly free not to lower our speed limit as Congress directed. But we were also free to lose every last dollar of Federal highway aid as a result." That article closed with this: "Ms. Brownstein [the attorney for the teen's abortion provider] said the supremacy clause does require Arkansas to yield to the Federal law."[15] This "state versus federal" dialogue should sound familiar, because Huckabee continues to have the same dialogue two decades later—though the precise items have changed.

Second, Huckabee ignored the pleas of the Dalai Lama, Mother Teresa, and actor Richard Gere to save a multiple killer from execution by lethal injection. The man, William Frank Parker, had converted to Buddhism while in prison (hence the appeal by the Dalai Lama and Gere). Twelve years earlier, however, he had shot to death his ex-wife's parents and attempted to kill his sister-in-law. Then, he took his former wife hostage and drove her to a police station in an Arkansas town, before shooting her and an officer (they would survive). Huckabee refused to commute the man's sentence to life imprisonment. The Supreme Court of the United States did not take the case, so Parker was executed.

From 1964 to 1990, no capital punishment took place in Arkansas. And there have been no instances of it since 2005. In the fifteen years between, 27 people were executed: 19 white, 8 black, and 1 Latino. Clinton oversaw 4, Tucker 7, and Huckabee 16 (11 white and 5 black). Of those executed under Huckabee, 6 were in his first term, 7 in his second term, and 3 in his third. Not much can be gleaned from these facts alone, due to the back-and-forth nature of capital punishment's constitutionality or public approval. Neither citizens nor politicians seem to have a firm resolve on the judicial aspects involved, and a governor plays only a small part in the process. People tend to agree with capital punishment more in theory than they do in its actual application, given the racially tinged discrepancies in how executions are handed down by the courts.

Evangelical leaders often are not as pro–capital punishment in private as they are in public. Roman Catholic leaders, less constricted by the opinions of their donors, find more freedom to support the official anti–capital punishment teaching of their church. An evangelical politician, however, knows he gains very little in critiquing the practice. A progressive view goes against the prevailing sentiment of the evangelical and conservative base.

Huckabee has often stated his opinion that there is racial bias within the judicial system as a whole, and in matters of capital punishment in particular. But when he served as governor, he didn't have the luxury of ivory-tower ethical debate. Real criminals sat on death row—and many of them had lock-shut cases of proven guilt for heinous crimes. In such cases, Huckabee fulfilled his obligation as the chief enforcer of state law and authorized the executions. In the case of Parker, the murderer-turned-Buddhist, Huckabee was called to act just three weeks after his inauguration.

Huckabee said that many of the workers in the governor's mansion were inmates of the Arkansas penal system. "Nearly every inmate was there for murder," Huckabee said. "Interestingly, one of the things you learn is that they are the best inmates of all. The people who are there for murder, chances are they did it as an act of passion when they were seventeen, and now they are in their forties or fifties—they've long since mellowed out." Huckabee jokes that he was more afraid of his own staff hurting him than he was of the inmates. "It's a weird dynamic. One of those things that you don't expect the public to fully understand, but you do learn, is that people can make horrible mistakes—but it doesn't mean that they are permanently horrible people. In essence, my kids grew up around people who had committed murder."[16]

Another point here is that becoming the "first family" and living in the governor's mansion took some getting used to—and it wasn't always pleasant. Once *other* folks are putting away your laundry, Huckabee said, that's the end of privacy. Even the refrigerator is not your own. He and his family quickly learned that once they stepped beyond their bedroom doors, they were in a public area—and they were never, ever alone, what with tour groups and staffers traipsing through during the day and troopers patrolling at night and in the early morning hours. As Huckabee said, "There's no such thing as stepping out of your bedroom in your underwear and going down to the kitchen."[17]

A more explicit form of privacy invasion directed against the governor involved people taking great pains to know his family's private business. They'd grab a receipt to see how big a tip he had left for the waitress. They'd go through the trash on the curb, looking for an incriminating receipt or an old tax return. Or they'd pretend to be from the education department in order to look at his kids' academic records.

His children lived in a fishbowl enough as it was, without people taking opportunity to invade their privacy. By this time, their oldest son, John Mark, was in college, while David and Sarah were in high school and junior high, respectively. Huckabee guarded his time with his children, blocking out time for meals alone with each of them and taking them on special trips. To this day, they all have a very close relationship, and though they are spread out geographically, the Huckabees see their children (and now grandchildren) on a very regular basis. Though it is hard to be a pastor's kid, let alone the child of the governor—and the young Huckabees experienced both—they have no bitterness about the life they lived growing up. It provided them with many opportunities they otherwise would not have had, and because their parents gave them lots of their time, they don't feel like they were cheated of parents because of the vocational choices made by their dad.

Earning his living in politics, Huckabee was glad to know who his friends were, and it was good to have a church family to call home. Rick Caldwell helped on both counts one night while standing in the kitchen of the governor's mansion. "We'd gone out to dinner, and now we were eating ice cream out of the box with a spoon," Caldwell said. Huckabee admitted he didn't know where they were going to attend church. They'd been in Little Rock a few weeks, and didn't know where to land. Caldwell mentioned to him about a young friend who was starting up a new church. "It wasn't real big or anything," Caldwell said, "maybe a hundred people meeting in a warehouse." Caldwell said his pastor friend got a call at six o'clock the next morning saying, "We want to let you know that Governor Huckabee is planning to bring his family to attend your church." The pastor, Mark Evans, figured it was Caldwell playing a gag on him until Huckabee showed up with his family. They fell in love with the church and raised their family there; Huckabee played bass in the band. "Now the church runs a couple thousand people—one of the leading churches in Little Rock," Caldwell said. "Which, of course, I attribute to Mike's great bass playing in the worship team."[18]

People say that one of Huckabee's greatest strengths as governor was that he would work to build relationships with people—on both sides of the political aisle. Huckabee obliged anyone who wanted to "come and let us reason together" and never let the party label stand in the way. "He used those connection-making skills he had developed as a pastor to work with people throughout the Arkansas government," Jim Harris said. "As a result, he got legislation passed. He was willing to negotiate—especially since he worked with such a lopsided legislature. Democrats ran the place!"[19]

Harris recalled how some hard-line Republicans told Huckabee they would rather not pass any legislation at all than to compromise with the Democrats. And Democrats would often say the same thing, in reverse. But Huckabee coached them on a better way, the way of actual governing with what you were given to work with.

One problem Huckabee faced, however, was a lack of Republicans qualified to run state agencies. Some Republicans wanted him to "clean house" and move out all Democrats from appointed positions of employment. But Huckabee knew that, since Democrats had not given Republicans many opportunities to gain experience in running the state over the past generation, there weren't enough Republicans to fill all the spots. So he left Democrats in positions all over the government, much to the chagrin of some in his own party. Besides that, just because a person was a Democrat didn't mean that individual had turned in his or her citizenship. As he'd done in his days as president of the Baptist convention, Huckabee chose to work with a wide spectrum of people, not just his own brand.

Huckabee's friend Randy Sims remembers how Huckabee began to appeal to Sims's colleagues at his work in banking and finance. Though Democrat by DNA, once they met Huckabee in person, they became fans. "I mean, he had such magnetism, such a way of relating to people," Sims said. "The ability to remember names or to remember the name of a mutual acquaintance. Or to just be a regular guy with them. It was just an incredible gift that he had."[20]

In governance, Huckabee started with something small yet extremely practical—improving the process for car registration. Before his reforms, you would have to go down to your county courthouse to prove your vehicle had been assessed. Then you brought your car to a service station where someone would check the basics—your taillights, blinkers, and so on—for a small fee and give your vehicle a "pass" or "fail" mark. Then you would take all this paperwork down to the revenue office, wait in line forever, and finally you were done (unless you had missed something small in the process). And none of this could be accomplished or explained online, because the state didn't have a website for that yet. Since this entire process could take up to a full day, people had to take off work just to get their car registrations renewed. So Huckabee eliminated the unpopular inspection and streamlined the process, receiving instant affection from his fellow citizens. And within a few years as governor, he had so invested in technology and online tools that many of the forms people once stood in line for could be completed online. By 2000, people across the nation were bragging about Arkansas's achievements for being a leader in "e-government."

Huckabee next turned his attention to the plight of uninsured children. Who was going to look out for kids born into lower-middle-class homes—too poor for private insurance but too wealthy for Medicaid? Huckabee's administration created the ARKids First program to provide insurance for kids who fell into this economic demographic. *Time* magazine noted that his program "helped reduce the percentage of uninsured Arkansans under 18 to 9% in 2003–04, compared with the 12% for the nation and 21% for neighboring Texas."[21]

Then, at the end of 1996, Huckabee campaigned in support of a one-eighth-cent sales tax to support the programs affecting the environment and conservation: the Arkansas Game and Fish Commission, the Department of Arkansas Heritage, the Department of Parks and Tourism, and the Keep Arkansas Beautiful Commission.

To create awareness for the benefit of the tax, the Huckabees loaded up in a boat with some staff and traveled from one end of the state to the other, stopping at each point they could to drum up support. (Technically, the governor rode in the bass boat while the first lady skimmed down the river on a jet ski.)

"I campaigned for Amendment 75 and we won," Huckabee said. "We used that money to completely rebuild our state parks system, fight pollution, purchase thousands of acres that are now set aside to remain natural, and create friendly and affordable places for families to enjoy the outdoors."[22]

Huckabee admits that it seemed paradoxical, at least in Arkansas at the time, for a Republican to care about the environment and conservation. And yet his favorite environmental hero, Teddy Roosevelt, was a Republican—though a lot has changed since 1900.[23] Huckabee used populist, blue-collar reasoning to support his vision of well-maintained public lands and lakes. He said that in a state where "you have a lot of people who can't afford memberships in expensive hunting and fishing clubs . . . you never want there to be this sense that you had to be a person of affluence in order to experience just the scenic beauty of a state."[24]

One of the first appointments Huckabee made after becoming governor was to appoint Lester Sitzes, his best friend since childhood, to the state's Game and Fish Commission. Doing so fulfilled a promise he had made to Sitzes, an avid sportsman, as they came home from Boys State in 1972.

Sitzes predicted that Huckabee would one day become the real governor of Arkansas. "And when you do," Sitzes remembers saying, "just remember to put me on the Game and Fish Commission." Huckabee agreed, and a promise made is a promise kept. Now, the Bois d'Arc lake is part of the "Dr. Lester Sitzes III Bois d'Arc Wildlife Management Area," named in honor of Sitzes and a lifetime dedication to leaving the outdoors in better condition than he found it (aka the Scout's pledge).

The "Dr." in front of Sitzes' name is for his dentistry. When you go into his office in Hope, just blocks from Hope High School, you'll find wall after wall covered in either Huckabee memorabilia or pictures of Sitzes with dead deer, ducks, or flopping fish. And if you ask him for his thoughts on his best friend, Mike Huckabee, you won't be disappointed with the stories he can share.

———

As Huckabee began his first term, it quickly became apparent that he would need all the help he could pull together in handling the media in Little Rock. The state of Arkansas was full of small towns with newspapers that would be happy to get news and photographs from the governor of the state. A lot of them, however, had come to depend on the news outlets in Little Rock providing them with coverage of what was going on. That worked fine when the sitting governor was a Democrat, but the process began to break down once Huckabee came into office. "They seemed only interested in the news if it was something negative about Mike," said Jim Harris. "If you did something good, that wasn't news."[25]

Huckabee hired Harris and Rex Nelson, formerly an editor with one of the conservative newspapers, and together they worked with a communications staff dedicated to getting the news out directly to newspaper editors throughout the state. "E-mail had come along at about that time, and so we'd use that to send them news and pictures," Harris said.[26] This doesn't sound too revolutionary now, but it was at the time, and it enabled Huckabee to keep the knowledge of his administration's progress from becoming Little Rock's best-kept secret.

Huckabee's relationship with the media became polarized—some were fair and others were not. Max Brantley, longtime editor of the *Arkansas Times*, worked his way into the latter category. "We were so clearly identified by him as being his enemy, his foe, that anytime anybody had anything they wanted to gripe about, they came to us with it," Brantley said. "So we broke a lot of stories about Huckabee that he didn't like."[27] Once Brantley was known as the editor who printed news unfavorable to the governor, more of that kind of material gravitated in his direction.

About five years into his being governor, Huckabee wrote, "I have become increasingly amused by editorial writers and self-appointed political reformers who think they know how to solve all the problems faced by the government." He vented his frustration that those who could never understand the complexity of governing continued to bring "attacks," "baseless allegations," and "frivolous lawsuits" that distracted him from his work.[28]

An ongoing narrative about Huckabee is that he has thin skin, or even worse, he's just a jerk, especially in his relationship with unfriendly media. Brantley said, "You could ask people who are a lot more admiring of him than I am, and they would tell you Huckabee has a thin skin. That's not a good thing to have in politics because people can give you a lot of grief sometimes."[29]

There seems to be a grain of truth to the idea that early on in Huckabee's career as governor, he had such negative interaction with a few members of the media that it set him on edge against them. When asked whether he had thinner skin at the beginning than he did at the end of his term, Huckabee said, "Yeah, that's probably true. In the first few years of politics you know it's going to be rough, and you know there's going to be the criticism. But if it's legitimate criticism, then you say, 'I deserve that.' But when it's ridiculously unfair—so untrue, so manufactured—then it's hard for it not to be frustrating and hard not to react to it. You want to challenge the reporter and ask, 'Why did you say that? That's not true and you know it wasn't true.' And, of course, they view that as having thin skin. I view it as being bold and trying to make them accountable for their actions."[30]

For Huckabee, the issue was not that the journalists were coming from the left or were Democrats, but that he perceived them to be unprofessional and had flawed ethics. Huckabee's lifelong habit of making friends out of enemies suddenly had no effect on these people, and it frustrated him. Huckabee eventually cut off Brantley from having any access to the governor's office.

"It doesn't have the same emotional effect on me it once would have had," Huckabee later said. "I became more frustrated about the lack of professionalism than I was worried that it's going to change people's perception. Nobody's getting news from one source anymore anyway. So what if somebody is saying I've kicked little puppies and beat up little girls at school? Only a limited number of people are actually going to see that, and of those who do, a very limited number will actually believe it. You just have to remind yourself of that when you read things about yourself on the Internet."[31]

———

In March 1997 a system of tornadoes struck throughout the southeastern United States. Altogether, seven F4 tornadoes touched down, three of them in the state of Arkansas alone. As they ripped through Arkansas, they killed twenty-five people, making it the deadliest tornado outbreak in the state since 1968.[32] Much of downtown Arkadelphia, the Huckabees' college town, was destroyed. President Clinton and Huckabee toured the devastated areas of Arkadelphia together, dishing out hugs and the promise of emergency disaster relief.

One year later, in March 1998, another tragedy occurred, although this time it was not a natural disaster. Two middle school students in the town of Jonesboro brought semiautomatic rifles and handguns to their school, stolen from the grandfather of one of the boys. They set up their weapons on a hillside overlooking the school, and one of the boys ran into the building to pull the fire alarm. As the teachers and students exited the building, the boys took aim and fired on them, killing five and wounding ten. *New York Times* columnist Frank Rich asked the question, "Why do they do it?" He then quoted Huckabee, who had spoken of a "culture where these children are exposed to tens of thousands of murders on television and movies."[33] Huckabee answered that question in more depth in a book published that year titled *Kids Who Kill*.[34] Brenda Turner, chief of staff for Huckabee, recalled the pastoral sensitivity Huckabee brought to the scene in Jonesboro. With no cameras or reporters around, Huckabee went from person to person, holding them up literally with his arm and spiritually with his prayers. It was a town in pain, and Huckabee brought a full measure of empathy for the situation.[35]

Many actions of a governor are entirely ceremonial in nature. But some-times the ceremonial acts have such an energy to them that they affect the real-world conversation and actions of others. In his 1997 State of the State address, Huckabee proclaimed a year of racial reconciliation for Arkansas. He said, "Let every one of us make it our priority to bring reconciliation, not so much that we can force it or legislate it, because we cannot, but that we begin in each of our own lives to purpose in our hearts that we will not harbor anger, hostility, prejudice, bigotry, and racism toward any person."[36]

Two years earlier, the Southern Baptist convention had offered up a resolution of reconciliation—contrition and apology—for the denomination's acceptance and promotion of slavery during its founding in the 1840s. Also included in the contrition was an admission that Southern Baptists had been slow to support the civil rights movement of the 1960s. At the time of this resolution, both Clinton and Huckabee were members of Southern Baptist churches.

Dwight McKissic remembers how, during Huckabee's early years as governor, his old friend and pastoral colleague "awarded the University of Arkansas at Pine Bluff (HBCU) two million dollars from his discretionary fund to assist in building them a new football stadium."[37] This school, a his-torically black university, had used facilities of much poorer quality than some of the other state universities. "UAPB had always been a stepchild in the University of Arkansas system," Huckabee said. "It had always gotten shortchanged, but we remedied that. Now they have ten to fifteen thou-sand people come to these facilities for their annual homecoming, and the event is a great source of pride for the school."[38] McKissic wrote, "The over-all funding that UAPB received from the Arkansas State government during Gov. Huckabee's term in office far exceeded the funding received during Bill Clinton's governorship in Arkansas. Gov. Huckabee appointed over 300 African Americans to boards, commissions and state employment positions during his tenure as Arkansas governor."[39]

Huckabee also steered money, a "disproportionate amount of health care dollars," to the Delta regions of Arkansas, where a higher number of minori-ties live and where low wages keep the area poor and less developed in terms of infrastructure and health care. The annual budget became one way in which Huckabee showed he meant what he said when he talked about racial reconciliation.[40]

Huckabee recalled an encounter he had several years after leaving office, while passing through Arkansas and eating dinner with some friends. He looked up from his table and saw Hank Wilkins Jr., an African-American member of the Arkansas legislature during Huckabee's administration. "He came over, gave me a big hug; we talked awhile. He said, 'I was talking with some guys just a few weeks ago, and we got to talking about all the governors we had worked with over the years. We all agreed that you were the best one we ever worked with. It's true; you always kept your word. When you told us you were going to do something, we never had to worry. You'd actually do it. Every time. Every word. And you listened to us—you cared and you made things happen.'"[41]

On September 26, 1997, Huckabee shared an outdoor stage in downtown Little Rock with a number of distinguished guests to commemorate the fortieth anniversary of the "Little Rock nine" event. In the battle for the integration of the Little Rock schools, Central High in Little Rock was the epicenter of segregationist hostility. Nine African-American students attempted to attend but were turned away at the door by the Arkansas National Guard. Now, forty years later, the same nine people, now middle-aged, came together with the citizens of Arkansas to commemorate the pain of the past and to call for an ever-increasing reconciliation of the races. The son of Thurgood Marshall was in the audience. On the platform sat President Bill Clinton, First Lady Hillary Clinton, and Governor Mike Huckabee and the First Lady of Arkansas, Janet Huckabee.

"At this schoolhouse door today, let us rejoice in the long way we have come these 40 years," President Clinton said. "Like so many Americans, I can never fully repay my debt to these nine people. For with their innocence, they purchased more freedom for me, too, and for all white people."[42]

Hillary Clinton rose to speak. "Unlike the other speakers that you will hear from, and unlike the Little Rock nine, I did not grow up in Arkansas. I saw what happened in Little Rock in 1957 from my suburb outside of Chicago where I went to a school that was all white. Where I lived only with white people. And as I sat in my living room and looked at the television set, I didn't know what to think. It not only was an issue for those who lived in Little Rock and in Arkansas; it was an issue for the United States. And it took me some years to realize that what happened here, and the courage and perseverance of the Little Rock nine was directly related to my own life."[43]

In contrast to the Clintons, Governor Huckabee was relatively unknown outside of Arkansas at the time of the 1997 commemoration. The Clintons had first entered the governor's mansion eighteen years earlier, but Huckabee had arrived only fourteen months prior. But with national and international media covering the event, Huckabee walked to the podium and delivered a powerful address.

Essentially, it's not just a skin problem, it's a sin problem. Because we in Arkansas have wandered around in ambiguity, all kinds of explanations and justifications. And I think today we come to say once and for all that what happened here 40 years ago was simply wrong. It was evil, and we renounce it. . . .

What is really tragic that we today come to renounce is the fact that in many parts of the South it was the white churches that helped not only ignore the problems of racism, but in many cases actually fostered those feelings and sentiments. And today, we call upon every church, every pulpit, every synagogue, every mosque in every part of Arkansas and the rest of the world to say never, never, never, never again will we be silent when people's rights are at stake. . . .

Let me remind us: Government can do some things, but only God can change people's hearts. Government can put us in the same classrooms, but government can't make classmates go home and be friends when school is out. Government can make sure that the doors of every public building are open to everyone. Government can ensure that we share schools and streets and lunch counters and buses and elevators and theaters. But let us never forget that only God can give us the power to love each other and respect each other and share life, liberty and the pursuit of happiness with every American, regardless of who he or she is.[44]

Ebony magazine called Huckabee's speech "perhaps the strongest statement of the day."[45] And the *New York Times* said, "Of Thursday's speakers, it fell to Huckabee, Arkansas' Republican governor, to issue the strongest denunciation of his state's past sins."[46]

———

On that day back in July 1995 when Jim Tucker had reneged on the promised resignation, he told Huckabee, "The people of Arkansas voted for me. *Over four hundred thousand of them elected me governor.* They didn't elect you."[47]

So in 1998, when it was time for Huckabee to face reelection, it would actually be his first campaign for governor. Since his losing Senate campaign in 1992 (60 percent to 40 percent), he had won the statewide lieutenant governor's race twice, in 1993 (51 percent to 49 percent) and 1994 (58 percent to 41 percent). But would Arkansas now elect him outright as governor? Dick Morris, again Huckabee's counsel, said the polls looked good for Huckabee.

When the votes were all counted, Huckabee had won by a margin of 60 percent to 39 percent (the exact opposite of his 1992 loss). He had earned 421,989 votes from his fellow Arkansas citizens. Over four hundred thousand of them had elected Huckabee as governor.

CHAPTER 25

LIFE IS A HIGHWAY

1998–2002

> Our people deserve good roads.
>
> —MIKE HUCKABEE

FRESH FROM HIS VICTORIOUS 1998 REELECTION, MIKE Huckabee gathered with his advisors and took stock of his first partial term of office. They agreed his poll numbers were strong, indicating that the citizens of Arkansas generally liked the way the administration conducted itself in those trying first few years. They discussed what political roads needed to be traveled during the second term of office.

The issue of "legacy" came up—what did Huckabee want his legacy as governor to be? What did he want the people of Arkansas to remember him for?

In governing, a leader can choose to be passive, acting mostly in reaction to current events, natural disasters, and problems presented by constituents with the loudest voices. Or a governor can be proactive in leadership, putting forth a positive vision of where he or she intends to take the state. Huckabee determined to lead proactively.

Recent statistical information from the Arkansas State Highway and Transportation Department led Huckabee to ask tough questions about the conditions of Arkansas's infrastructure. He heard reports of roads and bridges crumbling. New roads needed to be built and old roads needed expanding and repaving. Everywhere one looked, the transportation infrastructure of Arkansas was keeping people from getting safely where they needed to go. This cost citizens extra dollars out of their pockets for car maintenance and fuel, in addition to the safety issues involved with poor roads.

So Huckabee began to envision at least one priority he would make in this first full term of office. He would fix the roads. Doing something practical like this wouldn't be the path to international fame, but it would be just the thing needed in order to get Arkansans safely where they needed to go. And that was reason enough for Huckabee to tackle this challenge.

The best calculations estimated it would take five years and $950 million dollars to fix the worst 60 percent of Arkansas roads, roughly 400 miles.[1] Together with the Arkansas State Highway and Transportation System, Huckabee rolled out the "Pave the Way" campaign for creating public support for a ballot initiative to fund the work. If Arkansas voters wanted a safer road system, then they would vote for its funding.

As in most states, Arkansas had used the pay-as-you-go method for regular road maintenance and rehabilitation, and the state repaired only what they could afford in each annual budget. But with the magnitude of the improvements now needed, a new method was necessary. Huckabee and the highway department reasoned that borrowing some money to fix more roads sooner would be cheaper than fixing them through the pay-as-you-go system. It made logical sense.

Throughout the spring of 1999, Huckabee worked hard in urging the Arkansas legislature to support the funding of the roadwork. The legislature voted by an overwhelming margin of 85 to 14 to increase the state gas and diesel taxes by three cents per gallon, with the tax money going straight into roadwork. Analysts calculated this would raise $44 million per year.[2] Legislators also gave authorization, by means of a 95 to 1 vote, for the highway commission to sell bonds, but only if the public first approved of them through a ballot initiative. In both of these votes, Huckabee earned overwhelming bipartisan support from the duly elected representatives of the citizens.

Next, Huckabee took to campaigning for the initiative, hitting the road and going out to the people to make his pitch. He treated the task as the political campaign that it was and raised money for public relations to get the word out about the need for supporting the initiative. "I do not wish to leave Arkansans bouncing along on poorly maintained highways," Huckabee wrote. "Our people deserve good roads and so do those who are visiting our beautiful state." He also explained to the voters how the ballot initiative did not raise the taxes of a single Arkansas citizen: "Voting yes will not increase taxes. Voting no will not decrease taxes."[3]

When the measure was put to a vote in June 1999, Arkansas citizens approved the plan by a vote of 80 to 20 percent, marking the first time in fifty years they had authorized taking on debt for highways. Roadwork began by the end of 2000, and the bonds were paid off within a decade. By the time of its completion, this would become the largest highway project in the history of the state. As a result, by the end of the term, the citizens of Arkansas nicknamed Huckabee "the highway governor."

Huckabee's relationship with the media improved remarkably since his first days in office, as journalists realized just how knowledgeable the governor was about how they did their work. He understood broadcasting, journalism, tight deadlines, and the need for timely quotes. What's more, he surrounded himself with staff who had extensive backgrounds in journalism and used them to reach out to the media. "Help the media do their jobs," was the idea.

Alice Stewart, the director of media and communications for Huckabee's 2008 and 2016 campaigns, came to Little Rock in 2000 to work as the weekend anchor and news reporter for KARK (NBC). "[Governor Huckabee] was really good to all of us who were tasked with covering politics and Arkansas government," Stewart recalls. "If I had a question, he was usually available for an on-camera interview. There were times I remember where he would call me back personally, or have his staff connect with me—getting me the information I needed. He always took the time to answer my questions and was very open and transparent."[4]

That's not to say that everyone in media wanted to play nice with the Republican governor. Huckabee recalls how during the 1998 campaign, it seemed that he was getting an immense amount of front-page coverage, but all of it was negative. Was that simply his perception? Curious, he tasked Rex Nelson, his chief of staff and the former editor of the statewide newspaper *Arkansas Democrat-Gazette* with analyzing the coverage. Nelson began keeping detailed records. "Rex found that in the seventeen days leading up to the election, there were eighteen front-page news stories about me," Huckabee recalled. "And every single one of them was a negative story. It was unbelievable. Worse, some of them were just conjecture."[5]

For example, the Huckabees finally decided to sell their home in Texarkana. They still wanted a place for their family to go outside the governor's mansion, and so they found a little cabin up on Lake Greeson that was owned by an elderly couple. The husband was showing signs of Alzheimer's disease, and the wife had been diagnosed with cancer. They hated to sell the cabin, having saved up over the years for the land and then having built the cabin with their own hands. But their children helped them relocate closer to family in order to take care of them in their declining health. The Huckabees closed on the sale of their Texarkana home, realizing a profit, and immediately reinvested the money into the cabin to avoid paying capital gains taxes. One of the newspapers got wind of these real estate transactions and published a speculation story, just ahead of the election, asking how it was that the governor could have purchased the cabin. Did a wealthy donor secretly put some money in the Huckabees' pockets for the purchase? When the newspaper contacted the elderly couple and questioned them about their activities, Huckabee was appalled. Such an intrusion was unthinkable.[6]

In Arkansas there exists a mechanism for citizens to file an ethics complaint against an elected official. The filing of a complaint doesn't necessarily mean the official is guilty of the charge, but it does provide an opportunity to move potential corruption out of the shadows and into the light. The Ethics Commission would pursue the lead and investigate, or the complaint might even merit the attention of journalists, who would report on the story of potential violations.

Throughout his ten years in office, fourteen ethics complaints were filed against Huckabee. In response, Huckabee twice sued the commission itself, claiming that it "has been misused as a weapon against Republicans" and that he had been "unfairly attacked regarding his ethics history while governor of Arkansas."[7] Most of the complaints were dismissed, although five of them came with admonitions from the commission. He was charged a thousand dollars' fine in one of the cases.

Without either getting into the details of each ethics complaint or brushing them all under the rug, what do these allegations tell us about Huckabee?

First, in what seems to be the most significant infraction, in which the Huckabees had to pay the fine, the commission charged Huckabee with failing to declare a payment he made to himself from his campaign. The payment itself was not in question at all, just the record keeping of the payment.[8] The Huckabees paid the thousand-dollar fine and learned the lesson: stay on top of your records.

In another example, the commission found Huckabee did not disclose $23,500 worth of royalties from speaking engagements undertaken before he became governor. But the commission ruled this an "unintentional failure to disclose."[9] Again, it was deemed sloppy record keeping.

Then there is the issue of gifts. People claim the Huckabees enjoyed too much the getting of gifts, however legal they may have been. Max Brantley said the Huckabees seemed to expect that copious amounts of gifts would be coming their way, and Brantley thought this was problematic, or at least unprofessional. Now, Huckabee's political enemies readily admit that he simply cannot be bought, that if the gift-givers had a quid pro quo expectation, they were going to be disappointed. Nevertheless, when the Huckabees filed their gift disclosure reports, the list of gifts and givers ran too long, according to the critics. Cowboy boots, a chainsaw, dental care (a Lester Sitzes donation), suits, dress shoes for the kids, flowers for the governor's mansion, free rental of bass boat—Huckabee had many friends who gave him many things.[10]

Another alleged ethical lapse still being discussed on social media fifteen years later is how a fund set up to pay for maintenance at the governor's mansion wound up being used to pay for some panty hose for Janet, a doghouse (for Jet, his Labrador retriever) and Taco Bell for the kids.[11] After these receipts were brought to light, the Huckabees promptly reimbursed the account.

Then there was a time that a friend donated seventy thousand dollars' worth of furniture for the governor's mansion. At first, Huckabee said the furniture would be his to take with him when he left. Complaints ensued, and Huckabee reversed his position and said he would leave the furniture behind.[12]

Another complaint surfaced when Janet's friends told her they wanted to help the Huckabees get set up in a house after they left the governor's mansion. What would she need? Did she have a mixer? What about bath towels? Silverware? After living in government housing for a decade, it was true that the Huckabees would be, in some sense, "starting over" when they left. So Janet went to a department store to set up a registry to help her friends know what she needed. She entered her information into the computerized gift registry and when it asked her to state the occasion for the registry ("baby" or "bridal" being her only two options), she chose "bridal." People took umbrage with what they said was Mrs. Huckabee claiming to need the same perks as a new bride. "My wife has friends; she has lifelong friends. They wanted to do something for her," the governor responded.[13] There was no claim that something wrong had been done—only that it seemed distasteful.

Do allegations of wrongdoing equal wrongdoing? Or, when the Huckabees were shown to have failed to turn in a receipt for a purchase made—a purchase that in and of itself had no ethical taint—does this display a pattern of unethical behavior? Or is it instead a very occasional lack of good record keeping? Out of the ten thousand purchases made or income received by the couple and their three children, spanning a decade, there are only a handful of times when the Huckabees were shown to have made an error in either judgment or bookkeeping.

As for the receiving of gifts from friends, remember that as the governor of Arkansas, the Huckabees were under obligation to document every gift they received. And they did so. But gifts, such as a weekly delivery of fresh flowers, given to the governor's mansion by a millionaire friend, also fell under the critics' scorn. Though they were unsuccessful in their search for quid pro quo, there were plenty of receipts for donated floral arrangements.

In 2000, everyone knew that the governor's mansion was in serious need of renovation and expansion. The rooms were too small for the state functions required of a governor, and the living quarters offered little creature comforts to the family of the chief executive. Janet Huckabee took charge of administrating the renovations and went to work planning the vision and budget for the project.

An immediate question, however, was what would happen to the first family while the yearlong renovations took place? The mansion would be uninhabitable. Advisors looked around Little Rock for appropriate housing—big enough for the Huckabee family while also having adequate security. The rental price for such a residence would not come cheap. But the Huckabees had a different idea, a whimsical plan that would not only save the taxpayers money but would also bind the hearts of everyday Arkansas citizens to their first family. The Huckabees would move into a "triple-wide"—a manufactured house to be put on the grounds of the governor's mansion. After all, one out of eight Arkansas families lived in a manufactured home, so this was an established part of Arkansas family culture, even if some in Arkansas didn't want to take pride in that fact. Furthermore, the Huckabees knew it would be easy to find an Arkansas company who would donate the triple-wide in return for the marketing exposure the industry would receive.

So a triple-wide was shipped to Little Rock for the Huckabees, with a banner that read "My other home is a mansion" on the back. From the start, they knew they were going to be smeared by the elites, but it didn't matter—it was the right thing to do. Besides, given the houses they had lived in growing up, how could they be housing snobs anyway?

In her trademark humor, Mrs. Huckabee explained the situation to the *New York Times*. "'This is *not* a trailer . . . Trailers are pulled behind a pickup truck . . . We are not having a trailer on the mansion grounds.' Nor is it, she explained, a mobile home, since the Huckabees are not going anywhere.

"'Is it a double-wide?' she continued. 'The answer is no. It's a triple-wide. So get it right, O.K.?'"[14]

After Jay Leno made several weeks of jokes about the situation, the Huckabees videotaped a segment with the host of *The Tonight Show*, to dish it back out to him.

Leno said, "I hope you're not too upset with some of the jokes."

Huckabee responded, "I tell you what, Jay, we feel so good about it, I'm going to send you a full set of Firestone tires for your car." He described the size of the home as "large enough so that we could get you and your chin inside."

Huckabee didn't want Arkansas citizens to feel like second-class American citizens, even if they came from modest backgrounds or lived in manufactured housing. He said, "One of the things we want to do is to show that people in Arkansas aren't all that sensitive about people making light of us. We know who we are."[15]

Heading into 2002, the Huckabees geared up for another round of campaigning. If reelected, this would be the governor's final term of office, being term-limited by the Arkansas Constitution. Would this be his final campaign for elected office, or would there be a future for him after Arkansas? He wasn't sure yet, so he planned to enjoy every minute of the 2002 campaign.

Not every politician thinks that the campaign trail is fun, but Huckabee does. Both friend and foe admit that he is one of the greatest practitioners of "retail politics." That means Huckabee is good at the daily grind of meeting crowds of new faces a day and giving a stump speech with fresh enthusiasm, even after he has given it one thousand times before. In this regard, both of the Huckabees are very similar to Bill Clinton: they are extroverted and they take genuine delight in meeting people.

"I freely admit, I love the excitement of campaigning," Huckabee wrote. "It's the thrill of the unknown. The frantic pace. Some of us are crazy enough to enjoy it; others see it as a necessary evil. George [H. W.] Bush had great disdain for campaigning. Bill Clinton, on the other hand, is in my same camp in this regard. We both like people, and in campaigning the ultimate goal is to be with people—to share your views, listen, sympathize, and persuade. There's also the sense that you always have to be at a peak performance level. You never know when you'll slip."[16]

The line "You never know when you'll slip" helps raise a justified point of criticism, and one that Huckabee admits to. Sometimes, he can talk too much and needlessly get himself into trouble. And when he does, it usually happens because of his use of metaphors and colorful exaggerations that are either scatological or slightly naughty. Which is to say, Huckabee is capable of creating Southern metaphors on the spot, but that ability can become a political liability.

"I'm more spontaneous when it comes to expressing myself. I know what I believe. I have deep convictions. I don't have to sit around and say, 'ok, let me think how I answer this because I need to be so afraid that it's what they want to hear.' I know what I believe and I am comfortable in that conviction, so I'm going to express it spontaneously. Frankly, sometimes that gets me in trouble. Probably my greatest vulnerability is that I tend to speak freely."[17]

Sometimes, the comments are risqué in a 1950s sort of way—no vulgarity, but with a hint of the forbidden. Like the time he was explaining to reporters about who it is who shows up to hear his band, Capitol Offense. Huckabee said, "I keep hearing about these bands that have girls throwing their underwear onstage. . . . But given our demographics, we're more likely to have old men throwing their Depends at us."[18] Or consider this line at a Values Voter conference: "Nancy Pelosi said, 'We're gonna know what's in this bill when we pass it.' I said, 'Really? That's like saying I'll know what I just ate when I passed it.'"[19]

Or there was the time Huckabee was being interviewed for a profile in the *New Yorker*. The author wrote about the exchange she shared with him: "I joked with him once that I would write about his (fictitious) affair with Nancy Pelosi. He e-mailed back, 'The only thing worse than a torrid affair with sweet, sweet Nancy would be a torrid affair with Helen Thomas. If those were my only options, I'd probably be FOR same-sex marriage!'"[20]

The point is that Huckabee's strength, when used to excess or carelessly, can also become his weakness. Huckabee seems most willing to toss out these zingers when in a room chock-full of like-minded folks—as though there aren't reporters sitting in the room or social media making his lines go viral.

The night of the 2002 election was unusual in that it brought both joy and disappointment to the Huckabee home. The joy was because Mike won reelection, defeating Democrat challenger Jimmie Lou Fisher. The race was closer than the 1998 election, but still comfortable, as he won 53 to 47 percent.

The night also brought disappointment, however, because Janet Huckabee lost in her bid to become the secretary of state for Arkansas. "She ran in large part because she had personally tried in vain to recruit people to be a candidate for these empty positions," Huckabee said. "She's very politically active and believes in public service—stemming from her own mother's service as the county clerk of Hempstead. Janet has this real sense about how people ought to run for office."[21]

The Huckabees took a lot of criticism at the very idea of them both being in statewide elected office, but her 62 to 38 percent defeat ended all that anyway. "She would have made a wonderful secretary of state," Huckabee said.[22]

Janet Huckabee remembers how hard it was during the election season because she was also finishing her baccalaureate degree and the renovations on the governor's mansion. "That was a busy time, a difficult few months," she recalled. "We each had our own campaign office and our own bus. One time we passed on the interstate. I called and asked where he was. He said, 'Oh I'm going down I-30.' I was too, so we waved at each other as we passed—traveling down the highway."[23]

CHAPTER 26

ANOTHER BRICK IN THE WALL

2002–2006

> I took an oath to uphold the Constitution of the state of
> Arkansas, and our highest court clearly has told us it's the duty
> of the state to ensure equal educational opportunities for all
> students. . . . It's not a matter of what we like or might want.
>
> **—MIKE HUCKABEE**

THROUGHOUT HIS YEARS AS GOVERNOR, HUCKABEE RESISTED
falling into a GOP goose step or becoming another brick in the wall of the
nostalgic-for-Reagan complex. The official Republican Party line on an issue
did not receive an automatic endorsement from Huckabee's administration,
nor did conservative talk-radio criticism count as much to him as the actual
real-world implementation of helpful policy. As a result, Huckabee often
received the label "prodigal son" or "wayward Republican" from friend and
foe alike. "I was never one to just pick up the company line and recite it,"
Huckabee told a reporter. "I hate that—I think it's repulsive. And politics
has become more and more where you're handed this script and told, 'Don't
improv.'"[1]

The Huckabean tendency to jettison conservative groupthink became
even more pronounced during his final four years as governor. Arkansas
term limits its governors, so after winning his 2002 campaign for reelection,

Huckabee knew he had just four years to accomplish unfinished business. One established priority for his final term would be to improve the level of education within the state. The Huckabees had a vested interest in public education, as their own children attended public schools from kindergarten through twelfth grade. What was good enough for the children of Arkansas was good enough for the governor's children. But what would educational reform look like? How much political capital would have to be spent to accomplish anything? Should his reforms be modest or bold?

Many of those questions were answered for Huckabee when, just sixteen days after his 2002 election victory, the Supreme Court of Arkansas thrust the issue of education onto the top of his priority list. In *Lake View School District No. 25 v. Huckabee*, the Court declared unconstitutional the state's procedures for school funding and ordered the governor and legislature to produce a more equitable system. The basic problem was that each school operated with funding from three sources—local, state, and federal. Affluent school districts, of course, had more financial resources and hence, had better schools. But the idea had been for state and federal monies to help level the playing field—to bring up the quantity of funding and quality of education in the poorest of districts. In 1992, the Lake View School District filed suit to force the state to take action to make things more equitable. Now, a decade later, the court had made its decision and it was time for the executive and legislative branch to respond. The court imposed a deadline of January 2004.

Space doesn't permit an entire chronicling of what happened over the next two years, and the educational reforms took the hard work of all three branches of government. That said, Huckabee's administration led in the efforts, even as some conservative legislators and citizens disagreed with a court they believed to be overstepping its bounds. Huckabee ignored the voice of the strict "party line" or "true conservative" pleadings and opted instead for solutions that worked to fix the problems.

Huckabee agreed with the direction of the court's analysis of the current system, being especially troubled by how the inequality too often fell along racial lines—minorities receiving the inferior educational opportunities. He set out to create and implement a solution. Many felt that too many districts existed in the first place, so consolidation became one mechanism for obeying the court's ruling. After examining all the school districts with fewer than fifteen hundred students, the Huckabee administration proposed to consolidate the state's 310 districts into just over 100 and to streamline the administration of the entire system.

Huckabee explained that because of the Arkansas Supreme Court ruling, "it's unrealistic to claim we can continue to exist under the current structure. . . . I took an oath to uphold the Constitution of the state of Arkansas, and our highest court clearly has told us it's the duty of the state to ensure equal educational opportunities for all students . . . It's not a matter of what we like or might want. It's a matter of complying with federal law and current budget constraints. Here in Arkansas, it's also a matter of complying with the orders of our Supreme Court."[2]

Huckabee admitted that his plan would probably not be politically feasible had it not been for the hand of the Supreme Court in pushing them all to act. "For example," he said, "the demands for additional rigor at the high school level will force us to make extensive structural changes that probably wouldn't have occurred otherwise. Boundaries we've lived with for years will cease to exist. Powers that traditionally were given to local superintendents will now be handled at the regional and state levels. And, yes, high schools will be forced to merge."[3]

In 2004, the legislature came back with their own plan, opting to consolidate only the very smallest of school districts (fewer than 350 students). The Court examined the work of the governor and the legislature and determined that they had walked down the path of compliance with the Court, so they closed the case. Huckabee said he had paid a price for advocating some of these positions, likening the experience to a tooth extraction without anesthesia.[4] Such was the freedom Huckabee had as a term-limited governor: he could make some unpopular decisions that he felt were in the long-term best interests of the state.

―――――

A second area of education reform Huckabee pushed during his years in office was to raise the performance of both the teacher and the student within Arkansas schools. In his first term, Huckabee created two programs—Smart Start (kindergarten to fourth grades) and Smart Step (fifth to eighth grades), which focused on improving students' math and reading skills. To quantify the progress, however, would mean more rigorous testing for the students, which in turn would lead to a higher expectation put on teachers to teach more effectively (or some would argue, to teach for the test).

These ideas were at the center of state and national debates at the time, as governors and taxpayers asked, "What are we getting for all our money?" and some teachers and administrators responded, in effect, "Stay out of our classrooms." Politicians continue to wage war for the public school classrooms, but the specific battles seem to change every few years. Some conservatives forget the origin of the "standards" movement, not remembering the battles their predecessors fought against teachers' unions who resisted the very idea of holding teachers accountable for the performance of their students.

In 2005, Huckabee responded to critics of President George W. Bush's No Child Left Behind program by saying, "It's the best thing that ever happened in education because it says we're not going to let children spend years and years and let taxpayers spend thousands and thousands of dollars only to find out when the kid graduates high school that he's basically a functional illiterate, that we're not going to leave him lingering back in those classrooms and that he or she will get a decent education and we will hold accountable those who are responsible for getting that child a good education."[5]

In 2005, Bill Gates, the chairman of Microsoft, addressed the nation's governors at the National Education Summit on High Schools. Gates warned them of the need to improve the quality of U.S. high schools because, at the current levels of academic preparation, U.S. students would not be able to compete with international students. The National Governors Association cosponsored the summit, and Huckabee served as the vice chairman of the NGA that year. He cited a study showing the importance of a challenging curriculum in high school as the key predictor for whether the student would finish college—trumping socioeconomic or racial factors. "This is about the starting line, not the finish line," Huckabee said.[6]

The point here isn't to analyze the complex question of whether these federal or Arkansas programs succeeded or failed. Rather, it is simply to place Huckabee's attempts within the historical context of the national conversation conservatives were having at the time. The current debate over Common Core is both heated and important, but it is not identical to the conversations about education that took place from 1996 to 2006.

––––––––––

A third area of concern for Huckabee centered on the educational opportunities afforded to the children of illegal immigrants. In 2005, he advocated on behalf of legislation that would ensure illegal immigrants could be awarded college scholarships or receive in-state tuition, no matter their citizenship status. This was not a popular position within his own political party. When Jim Holt, a Baptist minister and Arkansas state senator, sponsored legislation to deny benefits to immigrants, Huckabee called the bill "un-Christian," "race-baiting," and "demagoguery." In case he had not been clear enough, Huckabee said, "I drink a different kind of Jesus juice."[7] Holt responded by saying that state benefits and Christian charity could not "turn a blind eye to lawbreaking."[8]

Chad Gallagher, an aide to Huckabee at the time, remembers the immigration debates of 2005, describing them as "the moment I was proudest of the governor's leadership. He acted politically courageous by taking an unpopular stand—in a battle that he ultimately didn't win."[9]

Gallagher continued, "He reminded us that immigration is a federal problem and must be fixed on the federal level with a securing of the borders. But he said that as the governor of the state, he couldn't educate a child K–12, tell them about the American dream, and then not give them in-state tuition or a scholarship—even when they were the valedictorian of their class."

Despite Huckabee's hard work in favor of the bill, it was defeated. "He never blinked," Gallagher recalled. "We sat in strategy meetings where the governor heard reports from his best supporters, telling him to stay away from the bill. It may have been the right thing to do, but it was political suicide. The governor said, 'I understand your concerns and agree with you that immigration has to be overhauled, but that's not what this is about. This is about justice and injustice for those children. And I won't budge.'"

Gallagher said the way Huckabee stood on principle, forgoing the political calculations, was a defining moment. "I went home and told my wife, 'I already knew that I love and respect and support Mike Huckabee, but today I was most proud to work for him.' He didn't pander. He wasn't a politician. He took a lot of criticism, even from friends, but he was unwavering because he was doing it from a place of deep care and compassion and conviction. He didn't mind the heat because he believed he was doing the right thing."

During this final term of office, national praise began to be heard for the job Huckabee had done during his governorship. *Time* magazine put Huckabee on their list of the "Top 5 Governors" of 2005. They wrote that because of the financial turmoil and budget shortfalls plaguing states at the midpoint of the decade, "Today what makes Governors great is not the loft of their dreams but the depths of their pragmatism. . . . When it comes to raw political talent, there's not a Bill Clinton in this group. But these are the rainy days. And charisma doesn't keep you dry. A roof does. Meet the hardest-working carpenters of 2005."[10]

With those introductory caveats, the magazine said Huckabee "has approached his state's troubles with energy and innovation, and he has enjoyed some successes." They also noted how he had mellowed into a leader who knew how to unite people across traditional lines of division. "Huckabee is now a mature, consensus-building conservative who earns praise from fellow Evangelicals and, occasionally, liberal Democrats."[11]

Then, AARP followed suit and awarded Huckabee its "Impact Award," given to those who have done something extraordinary "to make the world a better place."[12]

Also in 2005, *Governing* magazine honored Huckabee by naming him its "Public Official of the Year," calling him "a true exemplar of the concept of compassionate conservatism." They wrote, "He has overseen breakthroughs in health coverage for children, education management, and school finances. He also sponsored the largest tax cuts Arkansas has ever seen, as well as the state's biggest road construction package. And the state this year racked up the largest budget surplus in its history."[13]

But even as Huckabee began to attract national attention and accolades, he also began to come under increasing attack by conservative groups. The Club for Growth expressed concern about the increases in state spending under Huckabee, calling him a liberal in disguise. In 2006, the libertarian Cato Institute graded him an F for his fiscal policies in Arkansas and an over-all grade of D for his entire time as governor.[14]

To this day, Huckabee has continued to wage war back and forth with these groups, and they have responded by pouring millions of dollars into campaigns against him. Some of the leaders come from Arkansas, giving them what they feel was a front-row seat to Huckabee's economic prodigality. Huckabee notes that many of these people come from incredible wealth, and he argues that they do not understand the way most Americans operate or what their needs are. They counter by stating that Huckabee's fiscal policies were of little difference from Clinton's (or Democrats' in general) and that his social conservatism in no way overrides his heterodoxy on economic and tax issues.

Huckabee responded by calling them the "Club for Greed" and chal-lenged the idea that *any* tax increase is a bad thing. On one hand, he believed that his record had been distorted by these groups. But on the other hand, he believed that even when the honest facts proved he had raised taxes or increased spending, his responsibility as governor called for him to provide safe roads and efficient schools—and that these responsibilities demanded someone pay for them. Indeed, the Arkansas Constitution required the state to operate under a balanced budget. Further, with the court mandating the educational reforms, the governor said he was obligated to take action—even when that expanded the size of the government.

Huckabee also explained his fiscal governance in terms of compassion trumping conservative ideology. Countering the claim that it's not the govern-ment's job to make sure lower-income kids go to school and have health care, he told the *New Yorker*'s Ariel Levy, "If the kid's sitting outside the door of the hospital choking with asthma, do I sit there and say, 'Oh, I'm sorry, I don't think, philosophically, government should get involved'? I'd much rather the kid gets help than I sit around and say I'm so pure in my ideology."[15] Huckabee preferred practical problem solving to worrying about political ramifications or philosophical conundrums.

Only time will tell whether the now-decades-old coalition between social and economic conservatives will hold together. The cracks in the wall of that relationship have already begun to form as each side explains exactly which values they consider essential for the Republican party and which ones can be jettisoned.

———

Behind the scenes, what kind of boss was Huckabee? What was it like to work for him? He claims to be a "very driven person" and that he expected "other people would really work hard" in their service to the citizens. But he denies being unfair or volatile. "No one will ever tell you that I yelled at them or screamed at them or berated them in front of others," he said. "You'll never hear that. I think quite the opposite. I always told my people that if they mess up, just make sure I heard it from them first—not the next morning in the newspaper."[16]

Huckabee said he expected his staff to make some mistakes, but to learn from them and move on. You don't simply move good people out the door after they have one bad week. True leadership, according to Huckabee, sometimes meant taking the fall for your staff when they made an honest error. He recalled a time when a member of his administration made a multimillion-dollar mistake. "It wasn't stolen money, just money that went into the wrong account. It made the state budget look bad—a very embarrassing event. The man was in my office in tears, knowing he was about to get fired. But I said, 'I'm not going to fire you. You were straightforward, and you told me what happened. We'll live with it. Let's just accept that I'm going to get blamed for it, but I'll live to fight another day.'"[17]

On the other hand, Huckabee said his staff knew that if they had finished ninety-nine out of one hundred assignments the governor had given them, then he would invariably ask them about the one yet uncompleted task. "They'd ask, 'How did you know?' and 'Why didn't you ask me about the others?'" Huckabee said. "I don't know how all that worked out, except that it's the mark of a good executive to have a feel for what's going on around you. You can't micromanage, like Jimmy Carter, but you do have to ask questions and do spot surveys to get a sense of how things are going—like the rock band who specified in their contract that no brown M&Ms were to be in their dressing room. They needed to see in an instant if the local crew had read the contract or not."[18]

In 2005, Huckabee gained national attention for three very different things. First, he led in a public ceremony of "covenant marriage," putting a spotlight on Arkansas's high divorce rate and offering an avenue for strengthening marriages.[19] Second, he ran a marathon and published a weight loss book as the capstone of a two-year turnaround in his health and obesity. As the *New York Times* wrote, "it was as if he simply unzipped a fat suit and stepped out."[20] Third, in the aftermath of Hurricane Katrina's devastation wreaked upon Arkansas's neighbors to the south, Huckabee earned high applause for the efficient compassion shown to the seventy-five thousand hurricane refugees who flooded into Arkansas in a matter of days.

On Valentine's Day, 2005, three to four thousand couples gathered with the governor at Alltel Arena in Little Rock, to celebrate their marriage vows and to consider the idea of Arkansas's "covenant marriage." Back in 2001, Huckabee signed legislation giving couples the ability to get married under a modified marriage license, the "covenant marriage" approach. This voluntary act signified that the couple had committed to each other and to the state of Arkansas that, if their marriage seemed headed for divorce, they would first receive counseling and that they would have to wait longer than a normal divorce settlement. Also, entering into a covenant marriage meant divorce would only be granted for abuse, abandonment, or adultery.

Critics said covenant marriage might keep people in abusive situations longer. Also, same-sex marriage activists picketed outside (and heckled inside) the arena, proclaiming the injustice of their not having the right to marry at all. Supporters of covenant marriage, however, agreed with the governor as he said, "There is a crisis of divorce here in Arkansas. . . . When it is easier to get out of a marriage than get out of a contract to buy a used car, clearly something is wrong."[21] Huckabee told the crowd that his marriage, though then over thirty years in duration, was not invulnerable to trouble. He said that covenant marriage simply offered a "speed bump" for couples who were rushing into divorce during times of marital stress and crisis.

Couples who were already married had the opportunity to convert their regular license into a covenant marriage license. The Huckabees, along with hundreds of the couples present that night, converted theirs, then renewed their vows and exchanged kisses.

Though many Arkansans thought the entire ceremony was corny, nobody could deny that Huckabee's moral leadership set a much higher bar for what to expect out of future governors. As Lester Sitzes told a reporter, "He's been true to his wife and never had any kind of—there will be no Monica Lewinsky or Gennifer Flowers—because Mike and Janet are what they are."[22]

—————

Second, Huckabee lost an incredible amount of weight, ran a marathon, and wrote a book to tell the world about it—and to encourage everyone to do the same. The impetus for Huckabee's weight loss and health crusade began in 2003 when his doctor warned him that he probably had only ten more years to live due to obesity and a lack of exercise. Huckabee and his sister, Pat Harris, remember the final ten to fifteen years of their own parents' lives, years Dorsey and Mae spent in sickness and poor health. Huckabee also reflected on the sudden heart attack and death of friend and former Arkansas governor Frank White—invariably brought on by his lack of a healthy lifestyle. Huckabee wondered if a similar fate awaited him.

Huckabee rejected the idea that he could not change a lifetime of bad habits, but he knew it would first take a change in his mind-set. He had to turn away from thinking obesity was acceptable. Indeed, in the religiously charged atmosphere of the South, gluttony has traditionally been an "acceptable sin" within the culture. After good Protestants let "wine and women" pass them by, they are less reluctant to forgo chicken fried steak smothered in gravy. Rex Nelson remarked that Huckabee would never be caught "hiking the Appalachian Trail," alluding to the 2009 sexual scandal of Huckabee's fellow

Republican governor, Mark Sanford of South Carolina. "Should he fall off the wagon, it'd be the buffet trail."[23]

Huckabee also explained the link between the South's lower income levels and their higher rates of obesity, noting that techniques like breading, frying, and drenching meat in gravy stretch the food further.[24]

Before he began waging war on his waistline, Huckabee's weight would peak at close to three hundred pounds in 2003. Things got so bad that Huckabee crushed an antique chair when he sat down at the table for a Cabinet meeting.[25] Something had to be done.

Huckabee cut out fried foods and sugar. He began taking short walks, only to find himself doubled over with heavy breathing. But then, the short walks became long ones, and colleagues began to notice. He declared his goal to be health and fitness, rather than weight loss.[26]

As he began to turn his own health around, Huckabee led Arkansas to pass legislation requiring all public school children to receive annual body mass index (BMI) checkups. The reports were sent home with advice to parents for combating obesity and a lack of exercise. Some conservatives chided him for creating a "nanny state" mind-set, noting that small government principles should just let people live with the consequences of their poor decisions. But Huckabee felt that when a child was clinically obese by the age of ten, it was the child's parents and the prevailing culture that were mostly to blame. Besides, he argued, the state budget had a vested interest in its citizens being healthy, given the large payments made for health care. The proverbial "ounce of prevention" among children would cost less than fixing the major medical problems of grown adults.

He continued the emphasis in 2004, with the launch of "Healthy Arkansas," a program for promoting changes in the culture and mind-set of his fellow citizens. And as he did so, Huckabee became the poster boy for the changes he was advocating. Pictures of the slimmed-down governor splashed across the newspapers, and people were shocked. When people saw him in person for the first time since losing the weight, they hardly even recognized him. Then, to add to the amazement, he ran a marathon in 2005—a great feat of physical accomplishment that took a team of new friends to give him the skills and encouragement he needed.

Alice Stewart, now Huckabee's director of communications, was a news anchor in Little Rock at the time, and an avid runner who trained people for marathons. Stewart approached Huckabee after the Little Rock "Firecracker 5K" event in July 2005, Huckabee's first 5K. "I was just real excited for him," Stewart recalled. "I had gotten a trophy and I gave mine to him because I was so proud of him for losing weight. I had struggled with weight myself, so he was being a great role model for people that struggle with diabetes and weight issues. I mentioned that he should run a marathon, and he looked at me like I was crazy."[27]

Huckabee came back to Stewart a few weeks later and asked for more information. "Look, if you want to commit to doing it, I will personally train you for it," Stewart told Huckabee. The governor signed on and went onto Stewart's disciplined schedule of running, pushing Huckabee into longer lengths with each passing week. Stewart recalled Huckabee's solid commitment: Once, the rain forced them to train indoors, but when they arrived at the governor's mansion to use the treadmill, they discovered it was broken. Stewart suggested putting off the training. "But he wouldn't hear of that. He sat down and fixed the treadmill, then got up and did his running. He didn't let anything get in the way. Honestly, if he hadn't been able to fix the tread-mill, he probably would have jogged in place for twenty miles. That's how committed he was to turning his life around and being a better role model for Arkansas citizens, especially the kids."[28]

As Huckabee celebrated his fiftieth birthday in late August (with sugar-free cake and no-fat ice cream, of course), Hurricane Katrina hit the Gulf Coast of Florida, on its way to crashing into Louisiana and Mississippi. By the time it dissipated, Katrina had become one of the deadliest hurricanes and the costliest natural disaster in United States history. Within days of the event, evacuees fled the affected regions. By automobile, plane, and even foot, tens of thousands of people headed north, often without anything but the clothes on their backs. People on medication were suddenly without their supplies, or money and proper identification to get a refill. Children who had been preparing to start school in New Orleans or Baton

Rouge were instead waking up on cots in places like North Little Rock or Birmingham.

All told, an estimated seventy thousand people came on their own or were shipped to Arkansas for shelter and relief, increasing the state's population by 3 percent in only five days.[29] Huckabee immediately went to work, signing executive orders that temporarily waived policies or restrictions that were of benefit to normal life, but were hindrances during this time of crisis. Huckabee told the state government workers to prioritize "people, not paperwork," taking care of the immediate need rather than worrying about whether or not a form had been filled out correctly.

Huckabee recalled the tension felt between his office and the White House administration over how to handle the evacuee situation. "The way the Bush administration handled Katrina, they got a lot of grief," Huckabee said. "They should have gotten a lot more. It was absolute incompetence. It was just disgusting. I had screaming matches with people at the White House over their unwillingness to let go. They wanted all the decisions to go to Washington first to be approved. On a conference call with Michael Chertoff, secretary of homeland security, I said, 'Mr. Secretary, you don't have enough people in Washington to approve what we're dealing with here. You have no idea. So you're going to have to trust us to get our jobs done and trust that we know what the heck we're doing. We're going to take care of our business, and if you don't want to reimburse us, then don't. But I'm not going to sit here and make people wait for eight hours in line to get some paperwork done so you can be happy about it.' Gosh, it was so frustrating."[30]

One of the practical decisions Huckabee quickly made was to spread out the refugees throughout the state. He said that the federal approach was to send them all to Fort Chaffee in Arkansas for processing, but there wouldn't be enough people in one location to handle the load. Huckabee decided that spreading out the children across the state meant no one school system would feel an undue burden, and no one hospital system would suddenly be overwhelmed with a surge in population. "We didn't warehouse people in big facilities," Huckabee explained. "If you put a bunch of people together like they did to five thousand people in the Astrodome, then if an infectious disease breaks out, you have five thousand exposures. If a fight breaks out, you have the potential for an absolute riot. You can't control that kind of mass.

You would have masses of strangers sleeping next to each other; how do you know who's a sexual predator? There's no privacy; there's no way to put a family together. So we did things differently. We created little communities of care and concern—small units where people could form a community and have their needs met, and then get on with the next step in their life."[31]

When asked to explain how he had the wherewithal to handle this crisis, Huckabee deflected the idea that it took a genius or an Ivy League education. "I always look at a problem and ask, 'How do you fix this?' and I think God gives you a vision and wisdom," he said. "Anytime you're in a situation that's so overwhelming, the first thing to do is to break it down into manageable little problems. When I had to deal with seventy-five thousand people, the first question was, where are there seventy-five thousand beds?"[32] Huckabee said the practical solutions flow from asking the right questions. For example, once the seventy-five thousand beds came into focus, he remembered the great number of church-run campgrounds throughout the state. The next step was to make the calls, offer liability protection for the camps, and then get the evacuees rolling into them. It all seems like common sense, which is to say, it sounds like the kind of good decision making anybody could have, or would have, made. Except that not all leaders responded with measures of efficiency and compassion equal to that in Arkansas.

"There's a difference between educated people and smart people," Huckabee said. "A lot of people are educated and not very smart. An educated person will try to figure out what studies show, what the empirical evidence is to answer a problem. But the smart person will just ask, 'What will work?'"[33]

Huckabee admits this commonsense "What will work?" approach came to him as part of his socioeconomic background. "When you grow up like I did, somewhat poor and in a redneck kind of world, then you learn to make due. You can't just go out and buy what you need. So what *will* work? If I can't have the ten-thousand-dollar solution, is there a ten-dollar solution? Honestly, I think a lot of it was watching my dad make things work that shouldn't have worked. So I consider it a compliment to be called pragmatic because that means you're going to get the job done. It may not be the conventional way, or the ideologically driven way, but you're going to get it done, and it's going to work."[34]

By the end of 2006, as Huckabee wrapped up his final term as governor, people continued to speculate about his viability for winning the 2008 GOP nomination for U.S. president. He had made many accomplishments in Arkansas to highlight his proven ability to lead, and political allies lined up to encourage him to pursue the White House. But he also had made enemies on both sides of the political spectrum, so Huckabee knew he would need every bit of help his friends could muster in order to win a campaign for president. And Huckabee never ran a race he didn't think he could win.

CHAPTER 27

WITH A LITTLE HELP FROM MY FRIENDS

January 28, 2007–January 2, 2008

> Reporters drove over to our barber and asked Speedy, "How much do you charge Mike Huckabee for a haircut?" Speedy, now in his seventies, said, "Well, it depends. Normally fifteen dollars—unless I have to give him some political advice."
>
> **—RICK CALDWELL, FRIEND OF MIKE HUCKABEE**

ON SUNDAY, JANUARY 28, 2007, MIKE HUCKABEE SAT across the table from moderator Tim Russert for an interview on NBC's *Meet the Press*.

"The 2008 race for the White House has begun," Russert said. "Sixteen candidates have already formed presidential committees. And this morning, it's decision time for our guest, the former Republican governor of Arkansas, Mike Huckabee. Governor, welcome."

"Thank you very much, Tim," said Huckabee.

"Are you running for president of the United States?" asked Russert.

"Tim, tomorrow I'll be filing papers to launch an exploratory committee, and yes, I'll be out there."

"Why?" asked Russert.

Huckabee kicked off his campaign with these words: "I think America needs positive, optimistic leadership to kind of turn this country around, to see a revival of our national soul, and to reclaim a sense of, of the greatness of this country that we love, and also to help bring people together to find a practical solution to a lot of the issues that people really worry about when they sit around the dinner table and talk at night."[1]

After serving ten and a half years as the forty-fourth governor of Arkansas, Huckabee would spend the next fifteen months campaigning to become the forty-fourth president of the United States of America. But first, he would need to win the nomination of his own Republican Party, and the list of potential candidates was getting longer by the day. The first step to the nomination is winning the affections of people in a few key states: Iowa, New Hampshire, South Carolina—it changes from election to election, but those are usually the important early ones. So Huckabee set off to campaign in these places, mostly concentrating himself in the cornfields and cities of Iowa.

When his campaign ended one year later, Huckabee picked up his laptop and penned a quick book, *Do the Right Thing*, released just days after Barack Obama defeated John McCain.[2] The book offers up a hearty serving of behind-the-scenes campaign anecdotes, fantastic material that makes for very enjoyable reading. There's no reason to retell an entire year's worth of anecdotes about eating pork-on-a-stick at Iowa fairs, drinking coffee in New Hampshire, or flying chartered airplanes through thunderstorms. So, leaving aside the chronicling of the "retail politics"—the shaking of hands, kissing of babies, and working of rooms, which Huckabee excels at—instead the focus here is on a few big themes that emerged during 2007. Particularly, the focus will be to explain reasons for Huckabee's campaign loss.

Six weeks after his announcement, an interviewer asked Huckabee for an assessment of the campaign. "It's going very well and I think we're gaining momentum . . . This is such a long, protracted presidential campaign." Huckabee countered the notion of there already being front-runners—Mitt Romney and Hillary Clinton—as declared by the pundits. "Right now the race is really sort of being framed by celebrity and money, but if those are the only two criteria to be president, then Paris Hilton would qualify as our next president."[3]

The ongoing war in Iraq hung large over the entire election season, only eclipsed at the end by the economic meltdown in the fall of 2008. In that same interview, Huckabee responded to a question about the current military strategies being employed by the Bush administration. Would Huckabee attack the policies of a sitting president from his own party? If not, did that mean he would cheerlead for the administration and lose credibility as an independent thinker? Huckabee diplomatically dodged both ditches. "I support the President's right as Commander-in-Chief to make the decisions that he feels like will work and General Petraeus is the person in whom he has placed his trust and the Senate has given unanimous confirmation to him. I don't know if it's going to work, but let's hope it does. I have to respect that he's looking at information that I don't have, and he has based this decision on those intelligence reports and the reports that he's getting from his generals in the field."[4]

Huckabee then added the human element from his own experience as governor. "I have concerns that we are overextending our National Guard and Reserve forces. We're asking so much of them that I fear we're going to stress them to the point of really breaking the system. These are supposed to be citizen-soldiers, but in many cases, they're now going for long, extended, and repeated deployments. That is a concern to me."[5]

The topic of Iraq would surface a hundred more times over the next year, and Huckabee's answers remained precisely the same throughout: avoid direct criticism of the president or of the initial decision to deploy to Iraq, and emphasize the need to take care of our troops. In this regard, Huckabee played to his strengths (empathy and practical help for people in need) and minimized his perceived weaknesses (military and foreign relations experience).

The debate season began on May 3 at the Ronald Reagan Presidential Library in Simi Valley, California. This first of nearly two dozen GOP debates featured ten candidates. Pundits took note of the visual spectacle of the crowded stage and began using the label "clown car" to describe the GOP nominating process.

Being a debate champion since high school, Huckabee showed up at nearly every one of these televised debates. He especially enjoyed the setting of this first event, standing on a platform alongside Reagan's Air Force One and in a building full of memories of the former president, who had died just three years earlier. Reagan's shadow of influence continued to be cast over Republicans as they sought for his heir apparent. What exactly it meant to be "like Reagan" seemed open to endless interpretation, as different parts of his long political career would be either emphasized or diminished. Nevertheless, if there was one Reaganism nearly everyone still agreed on, it was his doctrine that conservatives win elections when they build a "three-legged stool" coalition: defense conservatives, economic conservatives, and social conservatives.

Jerry Falwell, the patriarch of religious and social conservatism, died that same month. Huckabee could not break from the campaign trail to attend the funeral, but expressed his admiration for the man. He thought Falwell, and others like him, had been unfairly depicted in one-dimensional caricatures. "Critics and the media sometimes portray Dr. Falwell as a self-righteous and stuffy, closed-minded backwoods preacher. Nothing could have been further from the truth. In reality, he was one of the kindest, most genuinely humble, and compassionate human beings I've ever encountered. He had a trademark sense of humor, was a master practical joker, and treated the lowliest person in his presence with the greatest respect and concern."[6] During the 2008 campaign, Falwell's son, "Jerry Jr.," gave a strong endorsement to Huckabee.

Columnists took note of Falwell's passing as an opportunity to also sing a requiem for evangelical political engagement, the kind of activism the Moral Majority had kick-started thirty years earlier. Mark DeMoss, a public relations consultant for evangelicals and a former spokesperson for Falwell's Liberty University, countered the idea that the movement was finished simply because it now lacked key frontline leaders. He admitted, however, "there will never be such a single, dominant leader of the movement again."[7] DeMoss would go on to endorse and advise Mitt Romney in the 2008 and 2012 elections, and as of March 2014, he had already signed on board with Jeb Bush.[8]

If people thought Huckabee would get an automatic endorsement from every evangelical leader, they were gravely mistaken. For his part, Huckabee didn't think he had a birthright claim on anyone's support simply because of shared religious convictions. Even so, as he examined the other candidates' often-liberal stances, past or present, on key social issues, he believed he had a strong chance to earn evangelical endorsements. He was wrong.

Rather than finding any groundswell of evangelical support rushing in behind him, he kept hearing "soft endorsements" (public words of affirmation, short of a full endorsement) going out to Fred Thompson, Mitt Romney, and John McCain. Even Rudy Giuliani found evangelicals ready to back him. Only Huckabee seemed to be left without early evangelical support.

But the problem with some of these candidates was their problematic past stances on key social issues—they had flip-flopped around on the core concerns. And Giuliani hadn't even flip-flopped, still preferring a pro-choice and pro-gay position. By contrast, Huckabee had never wavered on any of these issues in ten years as governor, and you could go back farther in his private life to document his complete consistency over the decades. But in spite of all this, even someone like Paul Weyrich—who had known Huckabee since the WFAA rally in 1979 and who was a personal hero to Huckabee—endorsed Mitt Romney in November 2007. Huckabee responded, "It hurts that he has accepted some misinformation as fact . . . I'll bet in the late 70's and 80's Mitt Romney wasn't listening to cassette tapes of Paul Weyrich speeches like I was." The "misinformation" that Huckabee referred to was the idea that Huckabee left the Arkansas Republican Party in shambles.[9]

So what was the problem? Huckabee wasn't considered a "serious candidate"—he was labeled "unelectable." Why support such a candidate and waste your time and resources? Worse, some evangelical leaders figured that if they came out in favor of Huckabee and he lost, then the eventual nominee might hold it against them and keep them from coming to his own table.

Huckabee later wrote, "The days in which spiritual leaders like Falwell, Kennedy, and Bright had held fast to certain principles, drawn a line, and said, 'Here I stand' had passed. The 'movement' was no longer led by clear-minded and deeply rooted prophets with distinct moral lines; it had been replaced by political operatives who played the same game as any other partisan or functionary whose goal was to be included and invited."[10]

Huckabee thought of his mentor, James Robison, and the courage he had displayed in those 1978–1980 years. Robison had instilled in Huckabee a vision of boldness with words like these: "The prophets of old were rarely invited back for a return engagement. In fact, most of them were never invited the first time. They came to speak truth to power regardless of consequences."[11] Huckabee thought about Robison's words during the 2008 election, as he "witnessed those who blurred the lines of prophet and politician," he wrote. "One can be either or, but it's really hard to be both."[12]

———

When Huckabee spoke to two thousand Christians at the Value Voters Summit in October 2007, he told them, "The other candidates come to you. I come from you." The crowd gave him a standing ovation, one of a dozen he received during the twenty-minute speech.[13] The evangelical rank-and-file who had the opportunity to hear Huckabee loved him, even as the evangelical leaders waffled around, looking for a better candidate.

When asked to explain further why evangelical leaders tossed away their principles in favor of political expediency, Huckabee gave several reasons. First, "a prophet is not without honor except in his own country," he said, quoting Mark 6:4, the Bible verse used to describe how Jesus' hometown of Nazareth rejected him outright (NKJV). They had seen him grow up, so in their minds Jesus could not be the Messiah. In like manner, evangelicals had watched Huckabee for three decades—what made him think he was anything special?

Second, Huckabee believed some evangelicals couldn't envision their future importance as advisors to an administration who already understood their constituency. "It would prove that the president didn't really need us to be an advisor to him on what our constituency was thinking."[14]

Third, Huckabee said evangelicals can "fund-raise and justify their organization's existence so much better if Hillary is the president or Barack Obama is the president. Frankly, even if Romney had won, because then they would say, 'We need to represent evangelicals to Mitt Romney—he's not part of us.' But if a guy like me won, then they wouldn't need to represent the evangelicals to me, obviously—because I am an evangelical."[15]

Fourth, Huckabee factored in old-fashioned jealousy. He said, "There are people that don't want anyone to rise higher than their ranks. This is an especially big deal among Baptists in the convention. They're the highest-ranking figure in the Baptist world. So if a Southern Baptist becomes president, then he suddenly would become the highest-ranking activist—and the other guy is not."[16]

Fifth, some Southern Baptists who had fought in the trenches during the "conservative resurgence" of the denomination did not support Huckabee because of his record in Arkansas. Not his record as governor, mind you, but his record as the president of the Arkansas Baptist State Convention. "I don't know of conservative appointments he made, and I don't know of any contribution to the conservatives," one of the leaders told the press.[17]

In 2011, longtime Huckabee friend and fellow pastor Dwight McKissic decried this attitude:

> I was shocked that SBC pastors, by and large, did not rally behind Mike Huckabee. The reason Huckabee did not get SBC support is that he was reportedly sympathetic and cooperative to the "moderates" while president of the Arkansas Baptist Convention. I publicly endorsed Mike Huckabee. Had Southern Baptists wholeheartedly and enthusiastically embraced Huckabee, he perhaps would be President today. Consequently, same-sex marriages, the Mexico policy, the Health Care policy that funds abortions and bailouts would not be moving into the mainstream and becoming public policy. But because of the SBC's propensity to "strain out a gnat and

swallow a camel," we are now faced with these policy initiatives that most SBC pastors and pew-sitters disagree with.[18]

A final factor is that some evangelicals fear an evangelical White House would cause the media to get the false idea that everything the president did or said should be considered the "evangelical position" on the issue. Huckabee agrees that there isn't an evangelical consensus on dozens of issues, and that having an evangelical as president wouldn't change that fact. He said, "What should the marginal tax rate be? I don't even see that there is an evangelical position on that or on many other matters on which Christians can disagree. Some people will approach it as if there is. And if you don't have the same view that they do, you're not just politically incorrect; you're like an apostate."[19]

———

After McCain lost to Obama in the fall election, numerous evangelicals came back around to Huckabee in private and told him they regretted not having supported his candidacy. Paul Weyrich, a founder of the religious right, made his mea culpa before Huckabee had even ended his campaign. Weyrich, who would die by the end of the year, was seated in a wheelchair when he addressed a group of his conservative peers who had assembled in March 2008 to discuss the mess that had become of the GOP nomination. As a group, they were not excited about McCain. Weyrich said, "Friends, before all you and before almighty God, I want to say I was wrong." Journalist Warren Cole Smith reported what happened next as follows: "In a quiet, brief, but passionate speech, Weyrich essentially confessed that he and the other leaders should have backed Huckabee, a candidate who shared their values more fully than any other candidate in a generation. He agreed with [Michael] Farris that many conservative leaders had blown it. By chasing other candidates with greater visibility, they failed to see what many of their supporters in the trenches saw clearly: Huckabee was their guy."[20]

Huckabee had only gotten a little help from his friends, and the result was a losing campaign.

———

Throughout the campaign Huckabee emphasized his blue-collar background and made populist sound bites like "People are looking for a presidential candidate who reminds them more of the guy they work *with* rather than the guy that laid them off."[21]

On May 15, the candidates headed to Columbia, South Carolina, for a debate in the state that would play host to a key early primary. In a round of discussion about budgets and runaway congressional spending, Huckabee made the audience burst into twenty seconds of laughter with this off-the-cuff zinger: "We've had a Congress that's spent money like John Edwards at a beauty shop."[22] The joke, of course, was how Democratic senator and presidential candidate John Edwards had recently admitted to spending four hundred dollars on his haircuts—*one* haircut that is, not a year's worth.

Reporters following Huckabee around didn't get to see any four-hundred-dollar haircuts. He and Rick Caldwell had been going to the same Little Rock barber for years, even dating back to high school when he'd visit Caldwell there. The barber went by the name "Speedy." He operated out of a small shop with two barber's chairs and a sign stating the current price: fifteen dollars. "When he was running for president, he was still going to the same barber," Caldwell said. "People started paying attention to where Mike Huckabee went to get his hair cut, especially after the Edwards fiasco. Reporters drove over to our barber and asked Speedy, 'How much do you charge Mike Huckabee for a hair cut?' Speedy, now in his seventies, said, 'Well, it depends. Normally fifteen dollars—unless I have to give him some political advice.'"[23]

During the South Carolina debate, the moderator asked Huckabee a question about convicted rapist and murderer Wayne DuMond, a man who, when released from the Arkansas prison system, raped and murdered again in Missouri. The moderator in South Carolina asked, "[W]hen you became governor of Arkansas, you wrote convicted rapist Wayne Dumond, told him, 'My desire is that you be released from prison.' The parole board released him in 1999. The next year, he killed a woman in Missouri. Do you bear any responsibility for his release, sir?" Limited to thirty seconds, here is Huckabee's 200-word response:

I wish that he hadn't gotten out in light of what happened in Missouri. It's one of the most horrible things, I think, that I'll look back on, but I didn't let him go. The parole board did. I actually denied his clemency, which was my official action. It was my predecessor who commuted his sentence and made him parole-eligible. It's been used as a political weapon against me.

Do I regret having said that I thought that he had met the conditions for parole? I do, in light of what he did. But I don't have foresight. I have great hindsight, like everybody does.

Here's what I do know. I know that we live in a very dangerous world and we make tough decisions and we have to live by them. For 10-1/2 years as a governor, I made tough decisions and saw thousands of cases cross my desk every day. I wish I could have always made them perfect, but I can't. If I'm president—and I hope I will be—I won't be a perfect president, but I'll be one who will do my very best to not repeat mistakes or to make them in the first place."[24]

———

There are many extenuating circumstances related to the case of Wayne DuMond. Some of them are forensic and evidential, like DNA testing and clothing worn at the crime scene. Some of the factors appear to be political: the rape that landed him in jail was committed against a third cousin of then governor Bill Clinton. And even more politics entered into the story when a Baptist pastor with a radio show took it upon himself to champion DuMond's case because he was sure the whole thing had been a set-up by the Clintons. A controversial book even came out about the case: *Unequal Justice: Wayne Dumond, Bill Clinton, and the Politics of Rape in Arkansas*, by Guy Reel.[25]

And, to make things more convoluted, the more this case gets discussed by people without experience in law or law enforcement, the more the terms like *pardon*, *parole*, and *commute* get thrown around incorrectly.

There are hundreds, if not thousands of pages of material available related to this case. The facts of how he came to be released from an Arkansas prison have remained the same since DuMond was rearrested in Missouri in 2001. The story first became politicized in 2002, when Huckabee sought reelection as governor, and again in 2007, when he ran for president. Once Huckabee began gaining traction in the polls in 2007, Mitt Romney's camp brought the DuMond case to the forefront of the campaign. Huckabee found himself on his heels.

A *Washington Post* columnist wrote, "Showing mercy can be hazardous to a governor's political health, as Mike Huckabee is learning in Iowa, where his chief rival in the Republican presidential primary, Mitt Romney, is blasting the former Arkansas governor as soft on crime because he exercised his clemency power. . . , Justice is served only when it is a meaningful blend of responsibility and mercy."[26] That idea aligns with Huckabee's own published understanding of what the DuMond case had been about, in his book *From Hope to Higher Ground*. Clearly, Huckabee believed the DuMond case involved elements of injustice—and the fact that DuMond committed later crimes did not, in Huckabee's way of thinking, absolve him of the moral responsibility to be involved.

In addition, the collective decisions made by governors Bill Clinton, Jim Tucker, and Mike Huckabee all affected the chain of events—from the original crime to the deaths in Missouri.

Finally, in the process of interviewing Governor Huckabee for this book, he was asked about the DuMond case on two separate occasions, a year apart. His account of the case was identical in both interviews. What follows is a transcript of Huckabee's response to the question about this case:

What frustrates me most about DuMond is that I can live with the raw facts of the story and whatever fault I have in the facts I can live with. What's been frustrating is that the facts are never the story that's told.

For example, I don't know how many times I've read stories or headlines, "Huckabee Pardoned DuMond." Number one, I didn't *pardon* DuMond. I didn't even *parole* DuMond, because governors in Arkansas don't have the power to parole anybody. In fact, I didn't even commute his sentence. I had one action with DuMond. One. I denied a commutation. He was commuted by Jim Guy Tucker while Clinton was still governor. Which means that Clinton's staff and Clinton had to approve of the commutation. Nobody has ever talked about this, but I know how the commutation process works in the governor's office, obviously, having been in the office ten and a half years. While Clinton was out of town campaigning, Tucker commuted DuMond's sentence, making him parole eligible. Later, when I became governor, DuMond wanted me, and asked me and put in the request for me, to commute it to time served. Which meant he would have been immediately released, and he wouldn't have to go back to the parole board. Because even though he was eligible for parole, the parole board had continually denied the parole plan. And so my decision was whether or not to commute to time served or not. I finally decided I would not.

I got accused of putting pressure on the parole board, which, if anybody would think about this for one second, they would realize how ludicrous this is. Not one member of that parole board was my appointee. They were Tucker, Clinton appointees . . .

So the whole DuMond thing has always frustrated me because I never let the man go. And one of the reasons I didn't, by the way, was because if I'd commuted to time served, there wouldn't have been any reporting process. He would have been able to—no parole reports or nothing. But even that wouldn't have been a pardon. Pardon means your record is released.[27]

─────

On August 11, Huckabee came in second place at the Republicans' Iowa Straw Poll. This was considered a major victory because of how little his campaign had spent. First place went to Romney, who had spent about $1,000 per vote. Huckabee's second-place finish cost him about $60 per vote. And fellow social conservative Sam Brownback came in third after spending about $150 per vote. The low-cost nature of the second-place finish was especially sweet to Huckabee because it fit with his populist and blue-collar way of thinking. "I was grinning for a week."[28]

─────

PBS sponsored a GOP debate on September 27, held at Morgan State University, a historically black university in Baltimore, Maryland. The event marked the first time a debate panel consisted entirely of "journalists of color"—Tavis Smiley, Ray Suarez, Cynthia Tucker, and Juan Williams. Huckabee earned praise simply for showing up, as McCain, Thompson, Romney, and Giuliani all skipped the debate. Empty podiums onstage marked their places.[29]

Later in the campaign, Huckabee picked up the endorsement of fifty African-American leaders. They cited his pro-minority record in Arkansas, but also praised him for his attendance at the September debate, noting that he was the only leading candidate who had bothered to come. "I would like to declare to those frontrunners who did not participate in that debate, that if you believe that America and Americans should trust you, then why did you not show up?" asked Dean Nelson, director of the Network of Politically Active Christians.[30]

―――――

When the Republicans met in Michigan on October 9 for another debate, Huckabee talked economics in a contrarian fashion, arguing against the prevailing positive mood of the day—contrarian, because the financial crisis and recession would not arrive until the summer of 2008. "A lot of people are going to watch this debate. They're going to hear Republicans on this stage talk about how great the economy is," Huckabee said. "And frankly, when they hear that, they're going to probably reach for the dial. I want to make sure people understand that for many people on this stage the economy's doing terrifically well, but for a lot of Americans it's not doing so well."[31]

Huckabee was right, although the nation would not discover just how weak their "strong economy" was until months after Huckabee ended his campaign. Reflecting back on that debate, Huckabee later told a reporter that he was considered "a complete idiot" for his prediction: "What bothered me more than anything was the disdain that I experienced from the elites: 'Oohhhh, who does Huckabee think he is, speaking about the economy?' They treated me like a total hick. A complete, uneducated, unprepared hick."[32]

―――――

Further, some conservative groups with a focus on economic issues, such as the Club for Growth, had spent hundreds of thousands of dollars during the campaign to fight directly against Huckabee's nomination. They

261

attacked his record in Arkansas, accusing him of raising taxes and growing the size of the government. During the 2008 campaign season (and again in the pre-2012 months and now in the pre-2016 days), these groups had a near-singular focus of attack on Huckabee. Huckabee responded with statements like, "I'm not a Wall Street Republican, I'm a Main Street Republican" or "I'm not a country-club Republican. I never even set foot in a country club until the tenth anniversary reunion for my high school graduating class."[33] As for the Club for Growth, Huckabee said, "They are full of oatmeal"— employing one of those trademark Southern euphemisms. When, in 2006, the Cato Institute gave him an F on economic policies while governor, he said they "deserved an F on their grading capacity."[34]

Huckabee's pressing concern was whether Americans in poverty had any genuine opportunity to turn their own situations around in their lifetimes. Of special concern too was the plight of minorities who he believed were born with a ticket to jail printed on their diapers, given the economic realities of their childhood.

And Huckabee was concerned about the middle class—too much money to qualify for government entitlement but too poor to actually be able to fund their retirement or their kids' college tuition. "I think there are a lot of people in the Republican Party who think that there is this total disconnect between fiscal responsibility and social responsibility," he told an interviewer in 2006. "But these are not opponents. These are really elements that work together. . . . I get in trouble with my party because I've also spoken a lot about that we can't ignore poverty, we can't ignore the lack of health care available to people who are in the middle between if they're really poor, they're going to get it; and if they're really rich, they're going to get it. But if they're in the middle, they're the ones you've got to worry about because they may eventually get it, but they'll go bankrupt having it."[35]

In November, the *Christian Science Monitor* called Huckabee a "conservative with a social gospel."[36] Others began to note that the "fusion of economic and social conservatives has been a ticking time bomb for nearly 30 years. Economic and social conservatism do not naturally fit together. Their fusion has been a marriage of convenience."[37] Into this tension, Huckabee was described as "a candidate who does not force [evangelicals] to choose between their social and economic views."[38]

In October, Phyllis Schlafly, conservatism's matriarch and one of the most important influences in Huckabee's teenage political development, stated that Huckabee had "destroyed the conservative movement in Arkansas and left the Republican Party a shambles."[39] Of course, that opinion doesn't bear up under the weight of the facts. Arkansas was 90 percent Democrat when Huckabee came into office, but it is now nearly all Republican in every state-wide elected office.[40] That is to say, since the day Huckabee became governor, Arkansas has gone from being one of the bluest states to one of the reddest. Certainly factors beyond Huckabee also played a hand in this turn, but it cannot be argued that Huckabee left the party a shambles.

The *Dallas Morning News* gave Huckabee its endorsement and praised his fiscal record as governor: "Mr. Huckabee established a respectable record of fiscal responsibility in Arkansas. Rather than run up deficits, he backed raising taxes to pay for needed infrastructure, health care, and education. That's called prudence, and it was once a Republican virtue."[41]

———

By the end of November, polls in Iowa showed Huckabee either closing the gap or ahead of Romney. "The numbers show we are climbing, especially in Iowa, but also nationally," he said. "The more we get attacked, the more our numbers soar. This just proves that when you get kicked in the rear, you're really the one out front."[42]

A major profile of Huckabee, titled "My Favorite Nut Job," appeared in *Rolling Stone* magazine earlier in the year. The author, Matt Taibbi, had spent an afternoon with Huckabee and seemed surprised to discover any redeeming qualities. Taibbi headlined his objective journalism with this zinger: "Mike Huckabee is a charming, funny economic populist who seems to genuinely care about the poor. He's also a full-blown Christian kook." He wrote, *"I can almost see him as president. . . .* Then I woke up and did some homework that changed my mind. But I confess: It took a little while. Huckabee is that good."[43]

With vocal critics mounting up on the left and right, Huckabee knew if he were going to get through, he'd need a lot of help from his friends. Enter Chuck Norris.

In what became some of the most-talked-about commercials of the election cycle, Norris and Huckabee sat next to each other and gave mutual endorsements, or "HuckChuckFacts" as they were called.[44] "My plan to secure the border? Two words: Chuck Norris." "There's no chin behind Chuck Norris' beard. Only another fist." "Mike Huckabee wants to put the IRS out of business."

—————

Huckabee made an ill-advised, offhand comment to Zev Chafets in an interview for an important *New York Times* profile in December. Chafets wrote, "I asked Huckabee, who describes himself as the only Republican candidate with a degree in theology, if he considered Mormonism a cult or a religion. 'I think it's a religion,' he said. 'I really don't know much about it.' I was about to jot down this piece of boilerplate when Huckabee surprised me with a question of his own: 'Don't Mormons,' he asked in an innocent voice, 'believe that Jesus and the devil are brothers?'"[45]

The quote went viral, with accusations that Huckabee was attacking Romney's Mormon faith. Huckabee quickly backtracked off the statement and apologized to Romney, though he said the question was a genuine one—prompted by inquisitiveness, not slander.

—————

Republicans met in Miami, Florida, on December 9 for one of the final debates of 2007. Given the large Hispanic population in Miami, the topic of immigration was sure to be discussed. The chairman for Huckabee's Florida campaign, Marco Rubio, had signed on early because, as he would say, "For those of us who consider ourselves to be Reagan conservatives, Mike Huckabee is our best chance to win the nomination. People are looking for genuineness and sincerity in politics. He has those qualities as well as the positive leadership skills needed to run our country."[46]

During the debate, Huckabee explained his position on immigration, emphasizing both the rule of law but also a hand reaching out to those in the shadows: "The first step is a secure border, because otherwise nothing really matters. But I do think the pathway has to include people going to the back, not the front of the line. There can't be an amnesty policy because that's an insult to all the people who waited, sometimes, ridiculously, for years, just to be able to make the transition here. . . . When people come to this country, they shouldn't fear. They shouldn't live in hiding. They ought to have their heads up because we believe every person ought to have his or her head up and proud."[47]

This chapter utilized the GOP debates as a springboard to talk about several key themes that emerged during the 2007 pre-primary campaign season. Of course, campaigns are about much more than debates. But even among the sharpest critics of Huckabee's content, most people admitted that it was in the debates where Huckabee added credibility and gravity to his campaign by his superior performance. As he had done at Boys State three decades earlier, he differentiated himself by his communication skills and personal winsomeness. "The debates were a key factor in our gaining support," Huckabee said. "Because despite the pitiful amount of time I was given compared to some of the other candidates, my answers were obviously coming straight from my heart and not from a very carefully and cleverly rehearsed committee of consultants."[48]

In a year-end article titled "Top Ten Best (and Worst) Communicators of 2007," communications expert Bert Decker ranked Huckabee as number one. He wrote:

> A few months ago Huckabee was almost an unknown. Now he is a front-runner for the Republican Presidential nomination, and probably the fastest rise ever from relative obscurity to the cover of the weekly newsmagazines. Governor Huckabee is open in style, authentic, natural and amazingly great at thinking (and speaking) on his feet. He tells stories and connects with people. Powerful tools when you have to build trust and credibility visually, quickly and mostly through TV. And powerful tools for a leader. Although he has a conservative constituency, they alone could not get him this far this fast. It is his communicating.[49]

Would Huckabee win in Iowa? If so, would he go on to secure the GOP nomination and run against Hillary Clinton, at that time still the candidate to beat among the Democrats? Would the country give the Republican Party its third White House in a row, something the nation seems very reluctant to do? Would Huckabee pick up where George W. Bush left off?

For some people, Huckabee's campaign boiled down to this: a formerly fat, likable Southern Baptist preacher with a stupid name who also came from Bill Clinton's town and also was the governor of Arkansas. Paradoxical. Unelectable.

The early days of 2007 had begun with Huckabee in California at the Reagan Library. On the night before the Iowa caucuses, Huckabee flew back out to California to appear on *The Tonight Show* with Jay Leno. "Folks, up until a few weeks ago, my next guest was an also-ran with a funny name in the Republican campaign," Leno said. "He still has a funny name, but now he's near the top in the national polls. He's neck-in-neck with Mitt Romney in Iowa, and the caucus there will be held tomorrow. Ladies and gentlemen, please welcome Mike Huckabee."[50]

CHAPTER 28

WE ARE THE CHAMPIONS

January 3, 2008

> You know, I wasn't sure that I would ever be able
> to love a state as much as I love my home state of
> Arkansas. But tonight, I love Iowa a whole lot.
>
> **—MIKE HUCKABEE**

MIKE HUCKABEE WON THE 2008 IOWA CAUCUSES BY A MARGIN of 10,000 votes (40,954 to 30,021) over Mitt Romney. Fred Thompson came in third. If only for one glorious night—the first night of voting and the most important night in Huckabee's strategy—he and his team could belt out the rock anthem "We Are the Champions."

In the game of "historical alternatives," it is fun to ask the question, what if those numbers had been reversed and Huckabee had placed second behind Romney? After having campaigned so hard in the state, what if he did not win?

Would Huckabee have won any other states? Probably not, because the money would have dried up. After all, half of the $16 million Huckabee raised in his 2008 campaign came in the door *after* his Iowa victory. Without the win he would not have seen that spike in donations. And without the influx of money, he could have still hung on through Super Tuesday on February 5, but probably would have dropped out after that, even as Romney did.

But then what? Without Iowa and the subsequent other victories (seven states, 4.2 million votes, 20 percent of the vote total), would Huckabee have been considered an early front-runner in 2012 (though he didn't actually run)? Would he have come back around for the 2016 election? It's hard to say for sure, but probably not.

Would he have written his bestselling books, or would he have landed a popular television show—and the radio work too? The answer here is yes, given his skills behind the camera, microphone, and keyboard—though they may not have been as lucrative.

All that to say, the trajectory of Huckabee's life over the past seven years was largely determined by what happened on the third day of January 2008.

Standing before a packed room of supporters, Huckabee looked over his shoulder at his wife, Janet, smiling as she had on the day they married. Then he turned and looked over his other shoulder at . . . Chuck Norris, who was smiling like the time he fought Superman on a bet (the loser had to start wearing his underwear on the outside of his pants).

"You know, I wasn't sure that I would ever be able to love a state as much as I love my home state of Arkansas," Huckabee said. "But tonight, I love Iowa a whole lot."[1]

Exit poll results showed that 33 percent of voters said "candor" was the quality they most wanted to see in a candidate. The man whom friends describe as "Mr. Says What He Means and Means What He Says" rode that sentiment all the way to victory that night, and he'd never forget the feeling of that moment. Analysts also credited Huckabee's work ethic, which prompted him to court national press, invite reporters along for his morning runs, and appear on morning talk shows every day in the week before the vote.

To be sure, the Iowa win was a team effort. His daughter, Sarah, had directed the Iowa campaign, living in the state for months before the caucus. Bob Vander Plaats, state chairman for the campaign, had worked tirelessly for the effort, alongside what Ed Rollins called a "volunteer army" of homeschoolers, farmers, preachers, and college students. Huckabee advisor Charmaine Yoest bragged on their army, saying, "Our ragtag band of activists beat their group of super volunteers." She also emphasized the important factor of voters actually seeing and listening to Huckabee, rather than just reading about him. "We always knew our goal was for people to hear him speaking," Yoest said.[2]

Huckabee's media man, Bob Wickers, gave praise to the Christmas-themed television ad they had run in Iowa. "You can't underestimate the importance of the Believe ad," Wickers said.[3] This was the ad some people called "the floating cross" commercial, due to the positioning of a bookshelf in the background, which resembles a cross.

Huckabee, grinning from ear to ear, continued his post-caucus celebration speech to his supporters:

> I think we've learned three very important things through this victory tonight. The first thing we've learned is that people really are more important than the purse, and what a great lesson for America to learn. Most of the pundits believe that when you're outspent at least 15 to 1, it's simply impossible to overcome that mountain of money and somehow garner the level of support that's necessary to win an election. Well, tonight we proved that American politics still is in the hands of ordinary folks like you and others across this country who believe that it wasn't about who raised the most money but who raised the greatest hopes, dreams and aspirations for our children and their future.[4]

The idea that a mountain of hard work could overcome a molehill of campaign money would soon be put to the test. Though the win in Iowa brought on a deluge of donations, everything is relative. The deluge was eight million dollars, or about the same amount that Romney had just spent getting beat in Iowa. Unfortunately, for the Huckabee camp, money would play the biggest factor in the remaining sixty days of the campaign.

Huckabee concluded:

G.K. Chesterton once said that a true soldier fights not because he hates those who are in front of him, but because he loves those who are behind him. Ladies and gentlemen, I recognize that running for office, it's not hating those who are in front of us. It's loving those who are behind us.

Now we've got a long journey ahead of us. I wish it were all over tonight, and we could just celebrate the whole thing. But, unfortunately, if this were a marathon, we've only run half of it. But we've run it well.

And now it's on from here to New Hampshire, and then to the rest of the country. But I'll always be wanting to come back to this place and say, wherever it ends—and we know where that's going to be—it started here in Iowa.[5]

CHAPTER 29

IF I WERE A RICH MAN

January 4, 2008–March 4, 2008

> I spent my life raising money for both church, charitable causes, as well as political. I don't mind doing it, but I darn sure want to look someone in the eye and if I'm going to ask them to contribute something, that it's because we really need to make the contribution.
>
> **—MIKE HUCKABEE**

AS HUCKABEE EXPLAINS IT, THERE ARE FOUR THINGS YOU need if you are going to succeed in either politics or the pastorate: "You have to have a message. Secondly, you have to motivate volunteers. You have to be able to understand and work with all types of medium to get your message out, and you've got to raise money."[1]

Huckabee is correct on all four counts. But as "Huckabee 2008" left cornfields and hogs behind and journeyed into states not named Iowa, that last item would begin to reveal the major weakness of his campaign. Mitt Romney spent $7 million on television ads in Iowa alone.[2] Huckabee, though going an entire month longer into the primaries than Romney, only spent $16 million on his entire campaign. Of course, neither man won the nomination, proving Huckabee's point: you have to have all "four basic things" in order to be successful.

One of the most successful movies of the 1970s was a screen adaptation of one of the most successful Broadway plays of the 1960s. Audiences loved *Fiddler on the Roof* for its musical score, comedy, and poignant reflections on life, love, and freedom—all set in the context of a humble Jewish community in tsarist Russia. In one particularly humorous scene, Tevye, the poor yet philosophical milkman who served as the lead character, sang an answer to the question, how might my life be different if I were a rich man?

Sixty days is all that separated Huckabee's victory in Iowa from his campaign-ending concession speech after primary losses in Texas and Ohio on March 4. How might the remainder of the Huckabee 2008 campaign have been different if Huckabee had had a few more million in his campaign coffers?

———

For starters, more money wouldn't have made any difference in New Hampshire, which polls told him he had no chance to win. Pundits gave him credit for trying though, and he even won the support of the influential Ruth Griffin, then in her eighties, who for forty years had been on the receiving end of endorsement-seeking candidates. She had met Ford, Bush, and Dole in her living room, and now it was Huckabee's turn to ask for her support. Griffin gave him the endorsement and sent out thousands of postcards to tell her friends about the governor from Arkansas. Griffin appeared at a rally with the Huckabees and Chuck Norris a few days before the primary and read her favorite poem, "Somebody Said It Couldn't Be Done"—figuring those lines summed up what she thought of Mike's underfunded but plucky campaign. Griffin also took a liking to Janet Huckabee, telling reporters, "Have you ever seen her? She's 6 feet tall! She's very nice."[3] In the end, John McCain walked away with 37 percent of the vote to Romney's 31 percent and Huckabee's 11 percent.

Huckabee fared no better in the Michigan primary on January 15, once again coming in third place (16 percent) behind Romney (39 percent) and McCain (29 percent). It is doubtful that more money would have helped Huckabee win in the state Romney's father had governed. On the other hand, for lack of funds to charter an airplane, he had missed a key opportunity to meet the state's Republicans gathered at the Grand Hotel on Mackinac Island the previous fall.[4]

Why did Huckabee struggle to raise money? One might argue that donors didn't give because they didn't think he was electable—no use throwing good money after a losing campaign. While that may explain some of it, another part simply was Huckabee's reticence to ask rich people for their money. It is hard to have genuine blue-collar roots—and be proud of them—while also begging wealthy people to give you their money. Huckabee had stated that his parents gave him "a legacy of believing that character and integrity are more valuable than wealth and that what we possess is less important than what kind of people we are."[5] If that was the case, then why should he grovel for money from the wealthy? At best, it felt degrading. At worst, the money came with strings attached, as the candidate could become beholden to the moneyed class who put them in office. Huckabee simply doesn't like any of that business.

Another factor that impeded Huckabee was his frugal background. "I know a lot of people would raise millions of dollars for no particular purpose just because they could," he said. "You know, I spent my life raising money for both church, charitable causes, as well as political. I don't mind doing it, but I darn sure want to look someone in the eye and if I'm going to ask them to contribute something, that it's because we really need to make the contribution."[6] It's one thing to spend state tax revenue on bridges and books, but could the son of Dorsey Huckabee raise and spend a half billion donated dollars to promote himself into his next job?

When asked, "After the Iowa caucuses, do you think you might have won if you had an extra twenty million?" Huckabee responded, "I think less than twenty. I think if we'd had five million." Janet Huckabee added the reminder, "The whole campaign was run with eighteen million dollars." He corrected the figure, "The amount was sixteen million, less than half of which was raised before the Iowa caucuses. Half of all the money we raised came in the final five and a half weeks."[7] It's no wonder then that when Huckabee was asked in 2015 if he planned to run again, he said he'd first have to see if the money was there for him—up front. He said, "I don't want to jump in a pool that doesn't have any water in it. It doesn't make for a very pleasant swim."[8]

During the campaign, the lack of money often brought peripheral mockery—jeering at Huckabee for small symptoms of the shoestring campaign.

For example, once when Huckabee didn't know about a breaking news item that had dominated the airwaves that day, a columnist wrote, "The Huckabee campaign needs to get a subscription to a newspaper or somehow find a way to let the candidate know what the biggest political story of the day is. Maybe someone can take a peek at CNN once a day?"[9] Huckabee's volunteer army performed miracles and the paid staff was tireless, but when they were stretched too thin, perceived weaknesses would be noticed and attacked. In this case, it was a weakness in the research department. To be fair, that might have been the only news item Huckabee had been slow in hearing about during the entire campaign. But perception is often greater than reality.

Or consider the opening lines of Ross Douthat's column, "Huckabee's Amateur Hour," from December 2007. He wrote, "When I interviewed Mike Huckabee last month, the most amusing detail of the whole experience came when his (lone) aide murmured to me, apologetically, that the governor was running late to the interview because he needed to iron his own suit for a speech that afternoon." Douthat, a conservative to be sure, saw symptoms of amateurism in that Huckabee only had one aide, and that a presidential candidate was running late to an interview, not on account of something important, but because he had "to iron his own suit."[10]

The same idea was conveyed in the opening sentence of a *New York Times* profile, written just before the Douthat column. The author, Zev Chafets, wrote, "Mike Huckabee walked into the lobby of the Des Moines Marriott at 5:30 a.m. on December 3, deposited an armful of dirty laundry at the desk and checked to make sure he was being credited with Marriott Rewards points toward his next stay."[11]

Such testimony of frugality might make a group of Baptist deacons happy—"Lord, You keep our pastor humble, and we'll keep him poor"—but nobody wants to hear this kind of anecdote about their candidate for president. People say they want a president who is a normal, everyday person. A candidate who hasn't bought his own milk or driven her own vehicle for a decade seems out of touch. The populist wants a candidate who shops the clearance rack at Kohl's or JCPenney, but the elitist wants to vote for the guy wearing the Brooks Brothers tie. The elitist side of that equation is exactly what Chafets was driving at by making these the opening lines of his profile. Chafets was saying that Huckabee wasn't as legitimate as the leading candidates, with staff to iron their suits, handle their dirty laundry, and fiddle with counter clerks about hotel reward points.

Huckabee is honest about money—he'd rather have zilch than to have strings tied to a contribution. Democrats and Republicans alike can be guilty of selling their opinions and their names for a checkbook.

In December 2007, Randy Minton and Jim Holt, two former Republican members of the Arkansas legislature during Huckabee's administration, traveled to Iowa to criticize Huckabee's gubernatorial record in Arkansas. They went on the air with influential conservative radio talk host Jan Mickelson to debate two other pro-Huckabee Arkansans. Most people can't afford to take off work and pay for such an excursion from their own pockets. Apparently, neither could these two, because they each received five thousand dollars for their travels.[12] On-air, they were asked, "Who paid for your trip?" Their answer: "Ron Paul."[13]

Or, in South Carolina, Huckabee perceived that Romney was buying endorsements of key evangelicals. "When some of the evangelicals endorsed Mitt Romney, you just wonder how big of a contribution did Mitt make to them to get that. Mitt gave a lot of contributions to people and suddenly— amazingly—he got endorsements. From leaders who were so conservative. It was hard for that not to be distasteful to me because I saw a lot of people who I thought a lot better of that I thought just totally sold out. Total sell-out."[14]

Huckabee absolutely had to win South Carolina on Saturday, January 19. He didn't. Mitt Romney had not campaigned much in the state, opting to spend his efforts to win that day's contest in Nevada. Romney won Nevada easily, but also tallied 15 percent of the South Carolina vote after all. But it was Fred Thompson who hurt Huckabee's chances. Thompson had been an early favorite of many evangelicals who considered him both conservative (enough) and "electable," whereas they doubted Huckabee on one or both of those counts. Thompson polled poorly, and some speculated he was going to drop out before Iowa. Despite their denials, Huckabee remains convinced that McCain was the reason Thompson stayed in the race. "McCain convinced him to stay in," Huckabee said. "They both tried to play like that didn't happen, but members of both of their teams admitted that's exactly what had happened. They had made a deal and Fred stayed in. He stayed on the ballot in order to take some votes from me."[15]

It also snowed in the wrong places. You can't plan an entire presidential campaign around the weather working out right. But, in the strategy book of the post-Iowa Huckabee campaign, South Carolina mattered the most. Donations would either skyrocket or dry up based on whether Huckabee could secure a win there. On the day of the primary, the citizens living in the pro-McCain regions of South Carolina woke up to the sunshine. In the pro-Huckabee regions, it snowed.

When the votes were counted, McCain had 147,686 (33.2 percent) to Huckabee's 132,943 (29.8 percent) and Fred Thompson's 69,651 (15.6 percent). Thompson dropped out of the race three days later. Huckabee told MSNBC, "The votes that he took essentially were votes that I would have most likely had, according to the exit polls and every other analysis."[16]

"Not winning South Carolina really hurt us," Huckabee said. "That was the beginning of the end, even though we still fought and still won states beyond that. If we'd won South Carolina, it would have made a huge difference." When asked if he might have won South Carolina if he'd had an extra million or two to spend there, Huckabee said, "Even without the two million dollars. If Fred hadn't been in it still and it hadn't snowed in Greenville—those two things killed us."[17]

Charles Krauthammer analyzed the loss in South Carolina, and essentially the entire campaign, using an argument about Huckabee that has stuck to this day: "Mike Huckabee is not going to be president. The loss in South Carolina, one of the most highly evangelical states in the union, made that plain. With a ceiling of 14 percent among non-evangelical Republicans, Huckabee's base is simply too narrow. But his was not a rise and then a fall.

He came from nowhere to establish himself as the voice of an important national constituency."[18]

Huckabee maintains that he was, and is, more than just a candidate for the evangelical voting bloc. And he argues that if it were true that he "got the evangelical vote," then he would have won the nomination. "I hear many times this notion that 'Huckabee got the evangelical vote, but that's all that he could do.' I keep telling them, 'No if I'd really had the evangelical vote, I'd have been the nominee. No, the problem was that I couldn't get enough of the evangelicals behind me."[19]

<hr />

After South Carolina, but especially after Romney's concession on February 7, the pressure began to mount for Huckabee to follow suit and concede the nomination to McCain. "It would take a miracle for him to win the Republican presidential nomination, but former Arkansas Governor Mike Huckabee isn't going away, at least not yet," wrote columnist Steven Thomma on February 13.[20]

"They thought I should have gotten out and just handed it to him," Huckabee said. "I had a personal conversation with McCain staffers and, 'Look, guys, my whole life I've never been a quitter. I wasn't raised to be a quitter. If I had been a quitter, I wouldn't have gotten where I am today. So you can beat me, knock me to the floor, make me where I can't get up; I get that. I can handle being defeated, but I'll never be able to live with myself if I just gave up."[21]

On February 23, Huckabee appeared on *Saturday Night Live* for the "Weekend Update" skit. In a hilarious and humble bit of self-deprecating humor, Huckabee came to "explain why he has yet to concede" to Seth Myers. "I'm not a math guy. I'm more of a miracle guy. So, at this point, I'm going to focus on the miracle part." The punch line was that after Myers had finished the interview, Huckabee didn't notice the obvious cues to exit the stage.[22]

The idea that Huckabee should end his campaign shifted quickly from comedic to serious, however, and even prompted a call from the White House. "I got a call from the President of the United States, from George Bush himself. He didn't just say, 'Get out.' He said, 'Hey Huck, just kind of calling, seeing what you're thinking. Where do you think this is going?' I said, 'Well, Mr. President, I can't honestly say I know where this is going, but I know what my thinking is. When McCain gets enough delegates to claim it—and he hadn't done that yet—then, as I've said all along, I will accept that and endorse him. But I can't quit. I've gotten this far by gutting it out. My whole life I've had to fight as the underdog.'"[23]

———

Campaigns hit a candidate with stress and challenges every day for months on end—a marathon of pressure, not a sprint. When you put a campaign on a tight budget and ask everyone from the candidate on down to be frugal (some might even say miserly or cheap), then eventually tensions boil high and outbursts happen. But the aides, staff, and volunteers for Huckabee paint a different picture of what it was like to work for him. "Huckabee really is the same person behind the scenes that he is in public," Charmaine Yoest said. It's not that he's perfect and not that he doesn't lose his temper or anything like that, but he really is a man of integrity. Mike was always very even tempered. He handled the stresses on the campaign with real graciousness and he was very disciplined—sticking to his running and his schedule. There weren't the wild swings you sometimes see with people who have that outgoing personality necessary in today's culture. When ambushed by reporters, I never saw him lose his cool. He always maintained a graciousness and a dignity about him."[24]

———

Iowa and Texas held their primaries on March 4, and if McCain won either of those states, it was game over for Huckabee. McCain won both. Huckabee called and congratulated the senator on an "honorable campaign" and promised "to do everything possible to unite our party, but more importantly to unite our country."[25]

In his concession speech to his supporters, Huckabee employed an anecdote from baseball, which explained why he had stayed in the race as long as he did. Huckabee said,

George Brett was one of the greatest baseball players of all time. And in his career for the Kansas City Royals, he was asked, when he was nearing the end of his career, how he wanted his last play in the major leagues to go. Well, everyone assumed that he would say that he wanted to hit a grand slam in the bottom of the ninth to win a game, perhaps even a World Series. He surprised all of the sportswriters, because what he said was, "I want my last play at bat to be that I hit an easy [out], just one bounce to the second baseman, and they throw me out at first. But I was running as hard as I could toward the bag when they got me." And he said, "Because I want it to be said of George Brett that, no matter what, he played his best game, he gave it his best, all the way to the very end."[26]

As he closed the speech, which closed his campaign, Huckabee looked to the future:

We aren't going away completely. We want to be a part of helping to keep the issues alive that have kept us in this race. . . .

Neither Janet nor I have the words to say, "Thanks." We can only thank you with hopefully our future actions, that we will work hard for our country, we will work hard for our party and the nominee, because we love this country and that's why we got in.

And until our country is all that we hope and pray it to be, we won't be able to walk away completely.[27]

CHAPTER 30

DREAM ON

March 5–November 4, 2008

> Let me say that, as much as I appreciate this
> magnificent opportunity to speak tonight, I've got to
> be honest with you. I was originally hoping for the slot
> on Thursday night called the acceptance speech.
>
> **—MIKE HUCKABEE**

STEVEN TYLER, THE LEAD SINGER FOR AEROSMITH, RECALLED the source of inspiration for the band's original hit "Dream On." As a three-year-old, he would lie under the legs of a grand piano while his Juilliard-trained father practiced. "That's where I got that 'Dream On' chord-age," he said.[1] Released in June 1973 (the month after Huckabee graduated high school), the song is still played on radio stations every day.

Nestled in the lyrics of this rock classic is Tyler's philosophical truism that losses can prepare you for winning. That illustrates the road Huckabee traveled during the next eight months of 2008, between Huckabee's loss in the primaries and McCain's loss in the general election. Like other Republicans in the second half of the twentieth century (Nixon, Reagan, and George H. W. Bush), Huckabee lost a presidential primary. Did he learn from the experience?

Even though he had conceded that his campaign was over, Huckabee was hardly out of the media spotlight yet. McCain still needed a vice president running mate. Would he pick Huckabee? If so, would Huckabee accept? After working so hard to beat McCain (Romney had already dropped out in early February), would Huckabee now be a good sport and help the Republican Party defeat the Democrats in the fall election?

———

Pundits varied in their speculations on who McCain would choose as his running mate. By June, however, McCain's trailing poll numbers indicated he needed to shake things up and energize his campaign by choosing some-body unexpected. Columnist David Greenberg said McCain "would do well to bolster his own reputation as a maverick by choosing someone like Colin Powell or Mike Huckabee."[2]

In May, columnist Robert Novak wrote that McCain was having "a problem of disputed dimensions with a vital component of the conserva-tive coalition: the evangelicals." Novak questioned Huckabee's loyalty to the GOP team: "The biggest question is whether Mike Huckabee is part of the problem or the solution for McCain. Some U.S. Christians are not recon-ciled to McCain's candidacy but instead regard the prospective presidency of Barack Obama in the nature of a biblical plague visited upon a sinful people. These militants look at former Baptist preacher Huckabee as 'God's candi-date' for president in 2012."[3]

For his part, Huckabee had been vocal and energetic in his support for McCain, but some whispers indicated he was "capable of playing a double game." Novak, using confidential information he said had been supplied to him from a "credible activist in Christian politics," wrote that both Huckabee and conservative leader Michael Farris had spoken privately about the idea of Obama being a "plague-like presidency." In other words, if the nation wanted Obama and his terrible policies, let the nation get what it wants. Novak asked the men if this was their position and "both denied advocating that an Obama presidency should be inflicted on the country."[4] Columnist Ross Douthat countered Novak, writing in the *Atlantic* that "given the ample primary-season evidence that Huck has a major-league man-crush on the presumptive GOP nominee, I'd like to see a little more evidence before I 'embrace the concept' that the Arkansas Governor might be part of McCain's 'Christian problem.'"[5] Farris was clear about his reservations concerning McCain: "I am concerned about what judges [McCain] may name, and the test will be who he selects for vice president." Farris said Huckabee would be his choice for vice president, but added, "I understand he is not under consideration."[6]

But was there anybody in McCain's camp pushing for a Vice President Huckabee? After all, the two men had genuine respect for each other and certainly had been a common enemy against Mitt Romney in the primaries. Was VP Huckabee a possibility? "I think a lot of people assumed that I was on his short list, but I was not," Huckabee said.[7] "You've got to remember, McCain's inside circle included Steve Schmidt, a big pro–gay marriage guy." Schmidt, whose sister is a lesbian, gave support to Log Cabin Republicans in September 2008 and led the 2013 fight to overturn California's Proposition 8. Huckabee felt that some of McCain's people "were real arrogant" and "they didn't feel that I was in their league." Also, the resentment that Huckabee had remained in the race as long as he did didn't help.

"I never got even a contact," Huckabee said. "I think I could have brought something to the table, but McCain wanted to pick Joe Lieberman to be vice president, the Democrat senator. In his mind, that would be a game changer." Huckabee, like most of the state leaders of the GOP, respected Lieberman, but would have balked at the idea of a bipartisan ticket. "He's a very wonderful man. Good man. An honorable man in every way, and I like him and respect him. On defense and national security, he is a hawk and a conservative. But on virtually everything else, he's a liberal—Gore's running mate in 2002!"

Everybody understood that except John McCain, and he continued to insist that people would be okay with it. His advisors insisted that picking Lieberman ran the risk of splitting the GOP, just two weeks away at that point. "And understandably so," Huckabee said. "I mean, we'd been out there working hard to get a Republican elected. For him to turn around and say, 'I'm going to give a Democrat a job a heartbeat away from a seventy-two-year-old man, who has had cancer.' Picking a Democrat to be on the Republican ticket would be disastrous in every way." Finally, McCain gave up the fight, took Lieberman off the table, and scrambled to come up with another secret weapon for the campaign. Enter Sarah Palin.

———

Having won eight states and four million votes in the primary, Huckabee had earned the right to address the Republican National Convention meeting the first week of September in Minnesota. He addressed the convention and brought them to tears, laughter, and applause. Some even said Huckabee's speech was a highlight of the convention.

Robert Lehrman, author of textbooks on political speechwriting, analyzed Huckabee's convention speech as an example for his readers. Lehrman wrote, "Sitting through a presidential nominating convention feels different than watching it in prime time. Most of the two hundred or so speeches at each are largely ignored by the audience. There's no guarantee that a defeated candidate will excite delegations caught up in their own politicking. But during his ten-minute speech, the crowd interrupted Mike Huckabee twenty-three times with laughter or applause—and not just by his home state." Lehrman concluded, "In ten minutes Huckabee used antithesis eleven times, litany four times, and nine of the other schemes and tropes covered in the previous chapter [of his book *The Political Speechwriter's Companion*]. He didn't need to know the classical names for any of them. He knew something more valuable: how to use them to relate to his audience."[8]

Huckabee told the convention, "Let me say that, as much as I appreciate this magnificent opportunity to speak tonight, I've got to be honest with you. I was originally hoping for the slot on Thursday night called the acceptance speech." He then gave praise for his father, Dorsey, and used his home life as an explanation for his brand of conservatism: "Let me make something clear tonight: I'm not a Republican because I grew up rich. I'm a Republican because I didn't want to spend the rest of my life poor, waiting for the government to rescue me."[9]

He closed with a poignant story about remembering the sacrifice veterans—including McCain—had made to secure our liberty and give us the ability to go to school and sit behind a desk in freedom. "I pledge myself to doing everything I can to help him earn a desk, and I'm thinking the one that's in the Oval Office would fit him very, very well."[10]

McCain did not make it to the White House. On November 4, the United States elected Senator Barack Obama as president with 53 percent of the vote and an electoral victory of 365 to 173.

On November 18, Sentinel (Penguin Books' conservative imprint) released Huckabee's *Do the Right Thing*. In addition to the normal policy-related discussion expected in such books, it also contained a significant amount of firsthand reporting on his 2008 campaign, making it one of the first books to provide a retrospective look at the election that had just ended. And *Do the Right Thing* threw several punches at Mitt Romney, as Huckabee seemed to already be looking ahead to the 2012 primaries (in the event of a McCain loss).

ALL ABOUT THAT BASE

> I was raised to believe that where a person started didn't
> mean that's where he had to stop. I always believed
> a kid could go from Hope to Higher Ground.
>
> **—MIKE HUCKABEE**

WHEN IT WAS TIME FOR ANOTHER ROUND OF INTERVIEWS with Huckabee, I looked at his upcoming schedule and took note that he would be in Iowa for a few days in August 2014. He was scheduled to speak at two Christian-oriented events in two different cities, with maybe a day off sandwiched in between. I figured I could meet him at one event and interview him before he had to get down the road to the other event.

But that wasn't how his schedule was configured. After the first Iowa event in Cedar Rapids, he needed to fly to New York City to tape his television show. Then, he'd fly back to Iowa, landing in Ames for the second event. The schedule would be too tight to fly commercial, so he would utilize his charter plane services. And the only free time he would have would be on those flights.

If I were Huckabee, I'd have said, "Sorry, but I won't have time for interviews that week. Another time, perhaps."

Instead, he said, "If you can make sure to be ready to roll, and you don't mind spending a night on your own in New York while I run around taking care of business, then we can do the interviews on the flights."

That's how I was able to not only fit in another round of interviews but also see his interaction with people in New York City and Iowa (twice), all in the span of thirty-six hours. And everywhere he went, he was the same guy: to waiters, doormen, FOX colleagues, influential friends who sat in on the taping of the show, Iowan pastors, farmers, kids, seniors, and everyone in between.

We talked about the themes for the forthcoming book he had been working on—*God, Guns, Grits, and Gravy.*

"Making the Huckabee message very clear for the base of the party, right from the titling of the book?" I asked.

"Yes, it's always good to speak clearly on issues," Huckabee said. "Let people know who you really are and what you believe."

The book would speak a lot about his idea of two Americas, the cultural divide between the "Bubble-villes" of elitist culture found extensively in the coastal cities (like New York City) versus the "Bubba-villes" of rural America found mostly in the "flyover country" parts of the nation (like Iowa).

When the book hit the shelves in January 2015, controversy ensued because of Huckabee's criticism of some pop-culture celebrities. Huckabee supporters couched their agreement with statements like, "I might have said it a bit differently," though they essentially agreed with the points Huckabee had made. Those who disagreed, however, charged that Huckabee was out of touch with modern American culture. The polarization between the two groups was fascinating to observe.

———

Since John McCain's loss to Barack Obama in the 2008 election, Huckabee clearly had put himself on a path toward another run for the White House. Just as Ronald Reagan had written and delivered radio commentaries after his 1976 nomination loss, Huckabee likewise began producing radio commentaries—and added a television show too. This served as a means of income, but it also kept him in the public eye. Instead of being merely an ex-governor and a former presidential candidate, he transformed himself into a media celebrity and a go-to person for conservative commentary on breaking news events.

In the early days leading up to the nominating season for the 2012 election, Huckabee gave careful consideration as to whether or not he should run again. He looked at polls that showed him in the lead or near the top of GOP voters' choice of picks for the nomination. And President Obama seemed, at least in 2011, to be vulnerable. Would he be a one-term president? Even with those considerations, however, Huckabee felt the timing simply was not right. So in May 2011, he surprised many with his announcement that he would not be running. "All the factors say go, but my heart says no," he told the audience of his FOX News program. "Under the best of circumstances, being president is a job that takes one to the limit of his or her human capacity. For me to do it apart from an inner confidence that I was undertaking it with God's full blessing is simply unthinkable."[1]

Slowly and steadily after the 2008 election, Huckabee gained name recognition across the United States. The fame and corresponding fortune (relative to his more meager earnings as a pastor or as governor of Arkansas) didn't come without a major investment of time and effort. Friends encouraged him to relax, to learn how to play golf, or to go skydiving with Janet (something she enjoys). Instead, he flew around the nation and the world speaking to various groups, often as part of a fund-raising effort for a non-profit or a political candidate.

Just as Arnold Schwarzenegger had returned to acting after his years as the governor of California, Huckabee returned to his previous line of work—broadcasting, public speaking, writing, and mass media. He has written six books since the end of his 2008 campaign and supported the marketing of each through intensive book tours and speeches. Several of the books have earned a place on the *New York Times* bestsellers list. He has done various iterations of radio, from short, prerecorded commentaries to a daily, live call-in show lasting three hours. And the *Huckabee* television program ran on FOX News each weekend from the fall of 2008 right up to January 2015. He ended the show only when it became obvious that he was going to run for president again.

Unlike during his days as governor of Arkansas, when Huckabee found himself involved in a controversial issue, his responses now drew national attention. Yet his position in media did not give him any executive powers to direct the affairs of state in these situations. He was limited to being a commentator on action, not a player in the action itself. But whenever possible, Huckabee would create a point of action that the public could take in order to change the outcome of a developing story. He would tell his audience to write their congressman, or maybe even to run for Congress themselves.

For example, Huckabee responded to a 2012 controversy surrounding pro-traditional marriage comments made by Chick-fil-A chief operating officer Dan Cathy by calling for a "Chick-fil-A Appreciation Day" on August 1 of that year. Lines formed for blocks outside of Chick-fil-A restaurants around the country, and it was a record-setting day for sales throughout the company.[2]

Or in 2013, Phil Robertson, the patriarch of the *Duck Dynasty* family, made comments about homosexuality that created a firestorm of protest. A&E, the cable network on which *Duck Dynasty* aired, suspended Robertson from the show. Huckabee with support for the Robertsons. "What we've seen is that there is a new level of bullying of the part of these militant activist groups," Huckabee said. "I think it has come to a point in our culture where political correctness has made it so that if you want to take a point of view that is traditional, that holds to steadfast, old fashioned biblical Christian values, which are also, by the way, values of traditional Judaism, and even Islam, that somehow you're supposed to just shut up and keep that to yourself. But if you want to advocate for same-sex marriage, we're supposed to be very tolerant."[3] Huckabee then launched an online petition of support, and within weeks, the network reinstated Robertson to the show.[4]

———

As for the Huckabees' own family, Mike and Janet bought a piece of ocean-front property in the panhandle of Florida and built themselves a beautiful home. It is a wonderful place to entertain grandchildren—and that is a good thing, because five of them have been born since 2008. The Huckabees celebrated their fortieth wedding anniversary in 2014 and their sixtieth birthdays the following year.

As 2014 began to draw to a close, the Huckabees had to answer once again the question of which path they were to take next. Should they choose the path of material comfort and a leisurely calendar? Or should Mike decide to run for the president of the United States once more, with all the ensuing workload, travel stress, and limited time for relaxation? The answer was not difficult to determine.

In January 2015, when Huckabee announced he was leaving his FOX News show, he said, "I have never had so much fun in my life. But I also realize that God hasn't put me on earth just to have a good time or to make a good living, but rather has put me on earth to try to make a good life. . . . As much as I love doing the show, I love my country more, and feel that it may be time for me to leave a zone of comfort to engage in the conflicts that have almost destroyed the bedrock foundations of America. I feel compelled to ascertain if the support exists strongly enough for another Presidential run. So as we say in television, stay tuned!"[5]

———————

Five months later, May 5, 2015, Huckabee came to his hometown of Hope, Arkansas, to host his campaign announcement party. Huckabee, the forty-fifth governor of Arkansas, launched a campaign to become the forty-fifth president of the United States of America.

The audience in Hempstead Hall took their seats as the lights went dark. The announcer called for everyone to welcome "a special guest to Hope." The audience craned their necks to see a man walk briskly from the dark shadows backstage. Was it Huckabee?

No, it was . . . Tony Orlando?

Orlando's rich baritone voice immediately broke into his hit song "Tie a Yellow Ribbon Round the Old Oak Tree." He beckoned the audience to sing along with him. People *over* the age of fifty did so with gusto, not missing a word. Many would have immediately connected Orlando's appearance here with his dancing to the tune with first lady Betty Ford at the 1976 Republican National Convention, when Ford and Reagan had fought for the party's nomination.

People *under* the age of thirty, however, quickly typed a query into their smartphones: "Who is Tony Orlando?"

Huckabee, Hope's hometown son, had once again come home to celebrate with friends, just as he had done four decades earlier after winning governor at Boys State—and again later when he became the real-life governor of the state in the 1990s. Hope raised Huckabee. Now, they would baptize him with affection before sending him out once more to go make the world a better place, seeking to bring the values of Hope to the rest of America. To make that point even more explicit, Orlando sang "America is My Hometown," a song he wrote for Huckabee, whom he called "the most trusted man I've ever met in my life."[6]

A *Washington Post* columnist called Orlando "a fitting prelude, because Huckabee's campaign for the Republican presidential nomination is also a throwback: The former Arkansas governor is the candidate of the little guy at a time when big money is ascendant in politics generally, and in the Republican nominating process in particular."[7]

The *Arkansas Times*, Huckabee's old nemesis, mocked everything about the event: "Tony Orlando is warming up the crowd. Heh. This has a pro-wrestling/Vegas vibe, doesn't it? Huckabee's base is best described as 'people who vacation in Branson [Missouri].' This is actually even more schmaltzy than I was expecting. Real America!"[8]

Such a comment gives evidence that the "coastal elite" mind-set that Huckabee wrote about could also be found in flyover country. But Huckabee's choice of Orlando also revealed his political calculations about the 2016 campaign. The Republican primary would be all about the base of the party. And yes, the base of the Republican party would be happy to vacation in Branson, Missouri.

———

After speeches by the current Arkansas governor Asa Hutchinson and Huckabee's wife, Janet, the time had come for the native son to emerge and say the specific words everyone had come to hear him say.

Huckabee opened his speech, and likewise his entire campaign, with a populist message grounded in his own blue-collar biography. Even in the polarized world of American politics, he assumes the best story to tell is the true story, to show the Mike Huckabee his mother and father would recognize as their son:

It's a long way from a little brick rent house on 2nd Street in Hope, Arkansas, to the White House. But here in this small town called Hope, I was raised to believe that where a person started didn't mean that's where he had to stop. I always believed a kid could go from Hope to Higher Ground. Like a lot of Americans, I grew up in a small town far removed from the power, the money, and the influence that runs the country. . . . And it was here that I first ran for elected office when I ran for Student Council in Hope Junior High School. So it seems perfectly fitting that it would be here that I announce that I am a candidate for President of the United States of America.[9]

NOTES

Prologue

1. David Rosenbaum, "With Little Ado, Congress Put God in Pledge in 1954," *New York Times*, June 27, 2002, http://www.nytimes.com/2002/06/28/us /with-little-ado-congress-put-god-in-pledge-in-1954.html.
2. Ibid.
3. In fact, neither of the singers are from Hope, and both are already nationally known: Madison McWilliams and AJ Wray.
4. "Justin Singing So Sick by Ne-yo," YouTube video, posted by "kidrauhl," January 19, 2007, https://www.youtube.com/watch?v=csymVmm1xTw.
5. Theodore Roosevelt, "Citizenship in a Republic," speech delivered at the Sorbonne, Paris, France, April 23, 1910, http://www.theodore-roosevelt.com /images/research/speeches/maninthearena.pdf.

Chapter 1: Land of Hope and Dreams

1. Randy Sims, personal interview with the author, spring 2015.
2. "Texas Short Line. St. Louis, Iron Mountain, and Southern Railway Company, 1878," Dave Rumsey Map Collection, accessed June 1, 2015, http://www .davidrumsey.com/maps770069–22088.html.
3. Beverly J. Rowe, *Historic Texarkana: An Illustrated History* (San Antonio: Historical Publishing Network, 2009), 4–15.
4. Joshua Bradley Williams, *Hope: Images of America* (Charleston, SC: Arcadia, 2010), 55.
5. Life Expectancy Graphs, "Life Expectancy for Men and Women: 1850 to 2000," University of Oregon's Mapping History website, accessed June 11, 2015, http://mappinghistory.uoregon.edu/english/US/US39–01.html.

6. Mike Huckabee, personal interview with the author, 2014–15.

7. Mike Huckabee, *A Simple Christmas: Twelve Stories That Celebrate the True Holiday Spirit* (New York: Sentinel, 2009), 35–36.

8. Ibid.

9. "Celebrity Corner," *Hope Star*, August 3, 1973, 3.

10. "Hope Obtains Big War-Plant," *Hope Star*, June 7, 1941, 1.

Chapter 2: Small Town

1. Mary Nell Turner, "Southwestern Proving Ground, 1941–1945," *Journal of the Hempstead County Historical Society* (Spring 1986): 3–41.

2. "Hope Obtains Big War-Plant," *Hope Star*, June 7, 1941, 1.

3. Turner, "Southwestern Proving Ground, 1941–1945."

4. "Paul W. Klipsch: The Mad Man of Hope, Arkansas," Founder Biography, accessed May 31, 2015, http://www.klipsch.com/founder.

5. Ibid.

6. "Q&A with Mike Huckabee and Brian Lamb," C-SPAN, January 21, 2005, http://www.c-span.org/video/transcript/?id=7949.

7. Jennifer Shutt, "Barbara Bush Reverses on 'Enough Bushes' Line," Politico, February 13, 2015, http://www.politico.com/story/2015/02/barbara-bush-reverses-on-enough-bushes-line-jeb-bush-115200.html#ixzz3TWkEYt3K.

8. "Arkansas Election Results 2014: Governor Map by County, Live Midterm Voting Updates," Politico, December 17, 2014, http://www.politico.com/2014-election/results/map/governor/arkansas/.

9. Archives of the *Hope Star* (1930–77).

10. "Hope Watermelon Crawl-including 1926 Film of Hope, Arkansas Watermelon Festival," YouTube video, 3:06, posted by "jonkevinmck," May 22, 2009, https://www.youtube.com/watch?v=UhCx4gFZA5U.

11. "Hempstead County Has Great Year," *Hope Star* and *Daily Press*, January 2, 1930, 6.

12. "The Value of a Brand," *Hope Star*, January 3, 1930, 2.

13. "66-Year Liquor Record," *Hope Star*, December 20, 1935, 6.

14. "Hempstead Courthouse Made Possible by Federal PWA Grant," *Hope Star*, November 28, 1939, 1.

15. "New Fire Station Is Modern 2-Story Mission Building," *Hope Star*, November 28, 1938, 2.

16. Ibid.

17. Williams, *Hope*, 67.

18. "Advertisement: *Hope Star* Offers This Up-to-date Encyclopedia to Its Readers," *Hope Star*, April 3, 1936, 7.

19. Society, *Hope Star*, October 8, 1936, 3.

20. "Red Cross Roll Call Hits $4,035 for New High," *Hope Star*, December 13, 1941, 1, 4.
21. "Summer Weather Brings Out the Bathers at Hope's Pines Pool on Opening Week of the Swim Season," *Hope Star*, May 30, 1941, 1.
22. "Births: Hempstead County," *Hope Star*, September 28, 1946, 4.
23. "159 Hempstead County Men Will Report to U.S. Armed Service March 2," *Hope Star*, February 22, 1943, 1.
24. "Social and Personal: Elder-Huckabee Wedding Announced," *Hope Star*, November 3, 1948, 3.
25. Mike Huckabee, personal correspondence with the author, 2015.

Chapter 3: One Day in 1955

1. Mike Huckabee, *Living Beyond Your Lifetime: How to Be Intentional About the Legacy You Leave* (Nashville: Broadman & Holman, 2000), 13.
2. John D. Gartner, *In Search of Bill Clinton: A Psychological Biography* (New York: St. Martin's Press, 2008). Also, for more information about the relationship between Clinton and the Wright family, see George Wright Jr., interview by Andrew Dowdle, William Jefferson Clinton History Project, September 15, 2014, http://pryorcenter.uark.edu/projects/William%20Jefferson%20Clinton /WRIGHT-George-Jr/transcripts/WrightGClinton.pdf.
3. "TIME Magazine Cover: Gov. Orval Faubus, September 23, 1957," *Time*, http://content.time.com/time/covers/0,16641,19570923,00.html.
4. "Speech of Governor Orval E. Faubus, September 2, 1957," posted at http:// www.southerncolloqrhetoric.net/web/resources/Faubus570902.pdf, accessed June 1, 2015.
5. Ibid.
6. Ronald Reagan and Kiron K. Skinner, *Reagan, in His Own Hand* (New York: Free Press, 2001), 252–53.
7. Ibid.
8. Society, *Hope Star*, March 11, 1955, 3.
9. "Q&A with Mike Huckabee and Brian Lamb," C-SPAN, January 21, 2005, http://www.c-span.org/video/transcript/?id=7949.
10. Society, *Hope Star*, February 14, 1955, 3.
11. Ibid., June 18, 1955, 18.
12. *Nightline* Transcripts, "Making Hillary Clinton an Issue," *Frontline*, March 26, 1992, http://www.pbs.org/wgbh/pages/frontline/shows/clinton/etc /03261992.html.
13. "Body of Kidnapped Boy Found in River," *San Bernardino County Sun*, September 1, 1955, 12; "Mississippi's 'Wolf-Whistle' Murder Trial Opens Today," *Blytheville Courier News*, September 19, 1955, 14.

14. Mamie Mobley and Chris Benson, *Death of Innocence: The Story of the Hate Crime That Changed America* (New York: Random House, 2003); Harriet Pollack, *Emmett Till in Literary Memory and Imagination* (Baton Rouge: Louisiana State University Press, 2008).

15. Robert Smith, "All of Us, Even the Most Righteous, Had a Part in Emmett Till's Death," *Berkshire County Eagle*, January 16, 1956, 15.

Chapter 4: American Pie

1. "Star's Camera Goes to a Kindergarten Birthday Party," *Hope Star*, December 16, 1960, 8; Joshua Bradley Williams, *Hope: Images of America* (Charleston, SC: Arcadia, 2010), 120.

2. Mike Huckabee, personal interview with the author, August 2014.

3. "Dorcas SS Class Meets," *Hope Star*, July 15, 1963, 3.

4. Pat Huckabee Harris, personal interview with the author, spring 2015.

5. Ibid.

6. "Q&A with Mike Huckabee and Brian Lamb," C-SPAN, January 21, 2005, http://www.c-span.org/video/transcript/?id=7949.

7. Mike Huckabee and John Perry, *Character Makes a Difference: Where I'm From, Where I've Been, What I Believe* (Nashville: Broadman & Holman, 2007), 147.

8. "Q&A with Mike Huckabee and Brian Lamb."

9. Mike Huckabee, *Living Beyond Your Lifetime: How to Be Intentional About the Legacy You Leave* (Nashville: Broadman & Holman, 2000), 121.

10. Ibid., 3.

11. "Melrose H D Club Meets," *Hope Star*, May 13, 1964, 3.

12. Phyllis Schlafly, *A Choice Not an Echo: The Inside Story of How American Presidents Are Chosen,* 3rd ed. (Alton, IL: Pere Marquette, 1964).

13. J. Howard Crawford, "Home Demonstration Work in Arkansas," University of Arkansas, accessed May 30, 2015, http://libinfo.uark.edu/aas/issues/1951v4/v4a26.pdf.

14. Elizabeth Griffin Hill, *A Splendid Piece of Work: One Hundred Years of Arkansas's Home Demonstration and Extension Homemaker's Clubs* (n.p.: CreateSpace, 2012), 186, 260.

15. Crawford, "Home Demonstration Work in Arkansas."

16. Mike Huckabee, *From Hope to Higher Ground: 12 STOPS to Restoring America's Greatness* (New York: Center Street, 2007), 3–4.

17. Huckabee Harris, personal interview.

18. *Inquirer* Wire Services, "Former Aide Will Pay for Copter Ride," *Philadelphia Inquirer,* June 1, 1994, http://articles.philly.com/1994-06-01/news/25831747_1_golf-trip-presidential-helicopters-watkins.

19. "Giants, No Manager," *Hope Star*, May 19, 1959, 4.
20. From the book endorsement Mike Huckabee wrote for Scott Lamb and Tim Ellsworth, *Pujols: More than the Game* (Nashville: Thomas Nelson, 2011).
21. "Three Youthful Singing Idols Die in Crash," *Hope Star*, February 3, 1959, 1.
22. Don McLean, "Commentary: Buddy Holly, rock music genius," CNN, February 1, 2009, http://www.cnn.com/2009/SHOWBIZ/Music/02/01/mclean.buddy.holly/.
23. Louise Roug, "Huckabee: Republican Rock Star," *Los Angeles Times*, October 28, 2007, http://articles.latimes.com/2007/oct/28/nation/na-huckabee28.

Chapter 5: Guitars, Hobos, and Kool-Aid

1. NPR Staff, "Mike Huckabee's Musical Education," wbur.org, June 5, 2012, http://www.wbur.org/npr/154362480/Mike-huckabees-musical-education.
2. Ibid.
3. Pat Huckabee Harris, personal interview with the author, spring 2015.
4. NPR Staff, "Mike Huckabee's Musical Education," and personal interview with the author, 2014.
5. Mike Huckabee, *Living Beyond Your Lifetime: How to Be Intentional About the Legacy You Leave* (Nashville: Broadman & Holman, 2000), 67.
6. Huckabee Harris, personal interview.
7. Liz Clarke, "A Higher Power," *Washington Post*, December 15, 2007, http://www.washingtonpost.com/wp-dyn/content/article/2007/12/14/AR2007121401861.html.
8. Huckabee, *Living Beyond Your Lifetime*, 67–68.
9. "Transcript: Mike Huckabee at the RNC," NPR, September 3, 2008, http://www.npr.org/templates/story/story.php?storyId=94256318.
10. Mike Huckabee, personal interview with the author, April 2014.
11. Pat Huckabee Harris, personal interview with the author and/or the author's team, spring 2015.
12. Ibid.
13. "Hope Fireman Attends a 3-Day Study," *Hope Star*, July 1, 1966, 1.
14. Huckabee Harris, personal interview.
15. Marynell Branch (nee Huckabee), personal interview with the author and/or the author's team, spring 2015.
16. Huckabee Harris, personal interview.
17. "Q&A with Mike Huckabee and Brian Lamb," C-SPAN, January 21, 2005, http://www.c-span.org/video/transcript/?id=7949.
18. Ibid.
19. Huckabee Harris, personal interview.

Chapter 6: Fortunate Son

1. Quoted in Craig Werner, *Up Around the Bend: The Oral History of Creedence Clearwater Revival* (New York: Spike, 1998), 123.
2. "Clinton in Arkansas to Remember Mentor," *Hour* (Norwalk, CT), October 22, 2002, A2.
3. "Arkansan Is Rhodes Scholar," *Hope Star*, December 18, 1967, 1.
4. Tom Cullen, "War, Student Unrest Haunt American Scholars at Oxford," *Courier News* (Blytheville, AR), June 11, 1969, 21.
5. Mike Huckabee, *Quit Digging Your Grave with a Knife and Fork: A 12-Stop Program to End Bad Habits and Begin a Healthy Lifestyle* (New York: Center Street, 2005), 54.
6. Ibid.
7. Pat Huckabee Harris, personal interview with the author and/or the author's team, spring 2015.
8. Ibid.
9. Ibid.
10. Ibid.
11. Ibid.
12. Ibid.
13. Robert Frost, "The Death of the Hired Man," *North of Boston* (New York: Henry Holt and Company, 1915; n.p.: CreateSpace, 2012), 7.
14. Mike Huckabee, *A Simple Christmas: Twelve Stories That Celebrate the True Holiday Spirit* (New York: Sentinel, 2009), 50.
15. Heard by the author during several of Mike Huckabee's speaking engagements in 2014 and 2015. Also quoted in Mike Huckabee, "Huckabee: The GOP's Problem Is Not Being Too Conservative," Huckabee with Mike Huckabee (website), July 27, 2013, http://www.foxnews.com/on-air/huckabee/transcript/huckabee-gop039s-problem-not-being-too-conservative.
16. Ariel Levy, "Prodigal Son," *New Yorker*, June 28, 2010, http://www.newyorker.com/magazine/2010/06/28/prodigal-son.
17. Huckabee Harris, personal interview.
18. "Awards Given at Scout Court of Honor," *Hope Star*, September 14, 1967, 9.
19. "Beginning of Boy Scouts in Hope," *Hope Star*, November 16, 1972, 6.
20. "Boost the Hope Boy Scout Movement," *Hope Star*, October 7, 1937, 6.
21. Grace Leonhart, "Harlan Scout Center Opens," *Hope Star*, September 30, 2013, http://www.hopestar.com/article/20130930/NEWS/130939960.
22. "Read the Mike Huckabee Transcript," the *Life (Part 2)* page on the website of PBS, accessed May 30, 2015, http://www.pbs.org/lifepart2/exclusives/Mike-huckabee-and-1968/read-Mike-huckabee-transcript.
23. Mike Huckabee, "Huckabee: It's a Right, Wrong Thing," Fox News, March 31,

2012, http://www.foxnews.com/on-air/huckabee/transcript/huckabee-it039s
-right-wrong-thing.

Chapter 7: Bridge over Troubled Water

1. "East Second Street Blockade?" *Hope Star*, July 26, 1968, 4.
2. Michael Heatley and Spencer Leigh, *Behind the Song: The Stories of 100 Great Pop & Rock Classics* (London: Blandford, 1998), 29.
3. Harry King, "Teacher Says He Meant Every Word," *Hope Star*, May 29, 1970, 10.
4. Rick Perlstein, *Nixonland: America's Second Civil War and the Divisive Legacy of Richard Nixon, 1965–1972* (London: Simon & Schuster, 2008), 503.
5. Matt Lakin, "Protests and Progress: Nixon Visit Put Knoxville on National Stage," *Knoxville News Sentinel*, August 26, 2012, http://www.knoxnews.com/news/local-news/nixon-visit-started-70s-in-spotlight.
6. "Richard Nixon: Remarks at Dr. Billy Graham's East Tennessee Crusade," The American Presidency Project, May 28, 1970, http://www.presidency.ucsb.edu/ws/?pid=2523.
7. Escar Thompson, "Nixon Booed at Graham Crusade Talk," *Hope Star*, May 29, 1970, 1.
8. Ibid.
9. Judith Cummings, "Transcripts Vex Graham, but He Stands by Nixon," *New York Times*, May 29, 1974, https://www.nytimes.com/books/97/07/06/reviews/graham-nixon.html.
10. Falwell quoted in "The Zeal of Thy House," *With God on Our Side: The Rise of the Religious Right in America, 1969–1974*, episode 2 (PBS Video, 1996), VHS.
11. Mike Huckabee, *Character Makes a Difference* (Nashville: Broadman & Holman, 2007), 144–45.
12. Ibid., 144.
13. Joshua Bradley Williams, *Hope: Images of America* (Charleston, SC: Arcadia, 2010), 115.
14. "Mike Huckabee: Remarks to the Conservative Political Action Conference: February 9, 2008" (transcript), The American Presidency Project, http://www.presidency.ucsb.edu/ws/?pid=99340.
15. Mike Huckabee, personal interview with the author, summer 2014.
16. "Mike Huckabee: Remarks to the Conservative Political Action Conference."
17. "Q&A with Mike Huckabee and Brian Lamb," C-SPAN, January 21, 2005, http://www.c-span.org/video/transcript/?id=7949.
18. Pat Huckabee Harris, personal interview with the author, spring 2015.
19. "Mike Huckabee: Remarks to the Conservative Political Action Conference."
20. Ibid.

21. "Haskell Jones: A Hustler for Hope," *Hope Star*, August 20, 1975, 47.

22. "Mike Huckabee: Remarks to the Conservative Political Action Conference."

23. Ibid.

24. "Haskell Jones: A Hustler for Hope."

25. "All Around Town," *Hope Star*, January 17, 1969, 1.

26. Ibid.

27. "Bloodmobile Is Coming to Hope Friday," *Hope Star*, September 17, 1968, 1.

28. "Advertisement," *Hope Star*, September 5, 1969, 8.

29. Ralph Routon, "The Real Story, 40 Years Later," website of the Hope High School Class of 1970, November 9, 2010, http://www.classcreator.com/Hope-AR-1970/class_custom8.cfm (originally a *Hope Star* article).

30. Ibid.

31. Mike Huckabee, personal interview with the author, April 2015.

32. "Good Citizenship Award," *Hope Star*, February 27, 1969, 5.

33. "Student Council Elects for New Year," *Hope Star*, May 13, 1970, 2.

34. Barry Schweid, "Blackmun Likely Bends U.S. Court a Little More to the Right," *Hope Star*, May 13, 1970, 2.

35. "Students Have Goodwill Party," *Hope Star*, January 8, 1971, 10.

36. Ibid.

37. Huckabee, personal interview.

38. Lester Sitzes, personal interview with the author, April 2015.

39. "Winner of Joe Amour Award," *Hope Star*, February 9, 1971, 3.

40. "Big Crowd Expected at Fair Park," *Hope Star*, April 29, 1971, 2.

41. David Fisher and Terry Bradshaw, *It's Only a Game* (New York: Atria, 2014), 25.

42. Holly Anderson, "Duck Punt: How Phil Robertson Found Stardom After Giving Up Football," *Sports Illustrated*, March 20, 2012, http://www.si.com/college-football/campus-union/2012/03/22/duck-punt-how-phil-robertson-found-stardom-after-giving-up-football.

43. Ariel Levy, "Prodigal Son," *New Yorker*, June 28, 2010, http://www.newyorker.com/magazine/2010/06/28/prodigal-son.

44. "Q&A with Mike Huckabee and Brian Lamb."

45. See Rick Warren, *The Purpose Driven Life*, exp. ed. (Nashville: Thomas Nelson, 2013).

46. Huckabee, personal interview.

47. Levy, "Prodigal Son."

48. Marynell Branch, personal interview with the author, 2015.

49. Liz Clarke, "A Higher Power," *Washington Post*, December 15, 2007, http://www.washingtonpost.com/wp-dyn/content/article/2007/12/14/AR2007121401861.html.

Chapter 8: Rocket Man

1. Robert Harold Schuller, *The Be (Happy) Attitudes: Eight Positive Attitudes That Can Transform Your Life* (Irving, TX: Word, 1996), 104.
2. Liz Clarke, "A Higher Power," *Washington Post*, December 15, 2007, http://www.washingtonpost.com/wp-dyn/content/article/2007/12/14/AR2007121401861.html.
3. "Rotary Club Speaker," *Hope Star*, August 2, 1971, 8.
4. "Lions Club Meets," *Hope Star*, August 18, 1971, 10.
5. Jeff Foust, "A Headline Huckabee Doesn't Want to See Yet," *Space Politics*, July 23, 2007, http://www.spacepolitics.com/2007/07/23/a-headline-huckabee-doesnt-want-to-see-yet/.
6. Hugh O'Brian, "The Freedom to Choose—a Message from Hugh O'Brian," http://www.hoby.org/about-hugh-obrian.

Chapter 9: (No) Teenage Wasteland

1. Mike Huckabee, personal interview with the author, April 2015.
2. Pete Fornatale, "Woodstock 1969: High Times," *Guitar World*, September 15, 2009, http://www11.guitarworld.com/woodstock-1969-high-times?page=0,4.
3. "Hunter S. Thompson Brings 'Fear and Loathing' to Island," *Billboard*, October 26, 1996, 10, 90.
4. Mikal Gilmore, "The Last Outlaw," *Rolling Stone*, March 2005, 44–47.
5. Daniel K. Williams, *God's Own Party: The Making of the Christian Right* (Oxford: Oxford University Press, 2010), 161.
6. Paul Baker, *Why Should the Devil Have All the Good Music?: Jesus Music—Where It Began, Where It Is, and Where It Is Going* (Waco: Word, 1979).
7. *The Bobcat* (Hope High School Yearbook), 1972, 11.
8. "Hope Students Going to Alabama Meet," *Hope Star*, November 8, 1971, 1.
9. Mike Huckabee and Lester Sitzes, personal interview with the author, spring 2015.
10. "Crowd of 515 Turns Out for KXAR's 25th Anniversary Party," *Hope Star*, May 23, 1971, 8.
11. Lester Sitzes, personal interview with the author, April 2015.
12. Ibid.
13. Huckabee and Janet McCain Huckabee, personal interview.
14. Huckabee, personal interview. The comments that follow are from the same interview.
15. See Malcolm Gladwell, *Outliers: The Story of Success* (New York: Back Bay, 2011).
16. Huckabee, personal interview.
17. Rick Caldwell, personal interview with the author, spring 2015.

18. Ibid.
19. Ibid.
20. "Hope Welcomes Boys State Governor," *Hope Star*, June 13, 1972, 2.
21. "Saul Alinsky Died Monday," *Hope Star*, June 13, 1972, 2.

Chapter 10: The Christian Woodstock

1. Bill Bright, *Revolution Now* (San Bernardino: Campus Crusade for Christ, 1969), 7–8.
2. John G. Turner, "The Christian Woodstock," *Wall Street Journal*, January 18, 2008, http://www.wsj.com/articles/SB120062657590499869. Also, John G. Turner, *Bill Bright & Campus Crusade for Christ: The Renewal of Evangelicalism in Postwar America* (Chapel Hill: University of North Carolina Press, 2008).
3. Bill Bright, *Come Help Change the World* (Old Tappan, NJ: Fleming H. Revell, 1970).
4. Liz Clarke, "A Higher Power," *Washington Post*, December 15, 2007, http://www.washingtonpost.com/wp-dyn/content/article/2007/12/14/AR2007121401861.html.
5. Rick Warren, *The Purpose Driven Life: What on Earth Am I Here For?* (Grand Rapids: Zondervan, 2002); Rick Warren, *The Purpose Driven Church: Growth Without Compromising Your Message & Mission* (Grand Rapids: Zondervan, 1995). Warren and Huckabee attended the same seminary during the mid-1970s. Given the sales figures of Huckabee's own books, a case could be made that these two have sold more books in their lifetime than any other two fellow seminarians.
6. Paul Eshleman and Norman B. Rohrer, *The Explo Story: A Plan to Change the World* (Glendale, CA: G/L Regal Books, 1972).
7. Giles Wilson, "The Most Watched Film in History," *BBC News Online Magazine*, July 21, 2003, http://news.bbc.co.uk/2/hi/uk_news/magazine/3076809.stm.
8. Clarke, "A Higher Power."
9. Turner, *Bill Bright & Campus Crusade for Christ*, 144.

Chapter 11: Live and Let Live

1. Mike Huckabee, "This Past Sunday Marked the 50th Anniversary of the Beatles' Debut on the Ed Sullivan Show," Mike Huckabee's Facebook page, February 14, 2014, https://www.facebook.com/Mikehuckabee/posts/10151975922612869.
2. Roger Ebert, "American Graffiti" (movie review), RogerEbert.com, accessed May 30, 2015, http://www.rogerebert.com/reviews/american-graffiti-1973.
3. "Fire Truck Flipped Enroute to Fire," *Hope Star*, October 20, 1972, 1.
4. Mike Huckabee, "Right Now It's That Magic Time of the Year Again—School

Time!" *Baptist Trumpet*, August 22, 1973, http://baptisttrumpetarchives.
spriggsone.com/main_includes/download_pdf_file.php?rf=19730822.pdf.

5. Lester Sitzes, personal interview with the author, April 2015.

6. Ibid.

7. Alex Strawn, personal interview with the author, spring 2015.

8. Ibid.

9. Melinda Henneberger, "Shoots Bear, Submits to Husband: The Fascinating Marriage of Mike and Janet Huckabee," *Slate*, January 29, 2008, http://www.slate.com/articles/news_and_politics/first_mates/2008/01/shoots_bear_submits_to_husband.html; also retold by Lester Sitzes in personal interview with the author.

10. Strawn, personal interview.

11. Ibid.

12. "Hope High School Announces Honor Graduates," *Hope Star*, June 2, 1973, 4.

13. Strawn, personal interview.

14. Mike Huckabee, *Living Beyond Your Lifetime: How to Be Intentional About the Legacy You Leave* (Nashville: Broadman & Holman, 2000), 82.

15. "Calendar of Events," *Hope Star*, August 4, 1973, 3.

16. Mike Huckabee, "Welcome Aboard the 'RAP'ture Express!" *Baptist Trumpet*, August 8, 1973, http://baptisttrumpetarchives.spriggsone.com/main_includes/download_pdf_file.php?rf=19730808.pdf.

17. Sitzes, personal interview.

18. Mike Huckabee, "Dancing?" *Baptist Trumpet*, October 17, 1973, 6, http://baptisttrumpetarchives.spriggsone.com/main_includes/download_pdf_file.php?rf=19731017.pdf.

19. Mike Huckabee, "Smoking?" *Baptist Trumpet*, October 24, 1973, 3, http://baptisttrumpetarchives.spriggsone.com/main_includes/download_pdf_file.php?rf=19731024.pdf.

20. Mike Huckabee, "This week we'll continue our rap on dating," *Baptist Trumpet*, September 26, 1973, 5, http://baptisttrumpetarchives.spriggsone.com/main_includes/download_pdf_file.php?rf=19730926.pdf.

21. Huckabee, "Dancing?"

22. Mike Huckabee, "Fence Straddling?" *Baptist Trumpet*, October 31, 1973, 8, http://baptisttrumpetarchives.spriggsone.com/main_includes/download_pdf_file.php?rf=19731031.pdf.

23. Andrew Kaczynsk and Megan Apper, "Mike Huckabee on Old Anti-Dance Column: At Least I Wasn't in the Choom Gang," *BuzzFeed News*, February 5, 2015, http://www.buzzfeed.com/andrewkaczynski/Mike-huckabee-on-old-anti-dance-column-at-least-i-wasnt-in-t#.bhnpEG8PG.

24. Dante Chinni, "The Presidential Age Game: What's in a Number?" NBC

News, February 8, 2015, http://www.nbcnews.com/meet-the-press
/presidential-age-game-whats-number-n302356.

25. "Fact Sheet: Induced Abortion in the United States," Guttmacher Institute, July
2014, http://www.guttmacher.org/pubs/fb_induced_abortion.html.

Chapter 12: I Wish We'd All Been Ready

1. Hal Lindsey and Carole C. Carlson, *The Late Great Planet Earth* (Grand Rapids:
Zondervan, 1970).
2. Dean A. Anderson, "The Original 'Left Behind,'" *ChristianityToday.com*, March
7, 2012, http://www.christianitytoday.com/ct/2012/marchweb-only
/originalleftbehind.html.
3. John J. Thompson, *Raised by Wolves: The Story of Christian Rock & Roll*
(Toronto: ECW Press, 2000), 49.
4. Mike Huckabee, personal interview with the author, April 2015.
5. Ibid.
6. Ibid.
7. Simon Dunstan and Kevin Lyles, *The Yom Kippur War 1973* (Oxford: Osprey,
2003), 21.
8. Thomas Borstelmann, *The 1970s: A New Global History from Civil Rights to
Economic Inequality* (Princeton: Princeton University Press, 2012), 261.
9. Huckabee, personal interview.
10. Ariel Levy, "Prodigal Son," *New Yorker*, June 28, 2010, http://www.newyorker
.com/magazine/2010/06/28/prodigal-son.
11. Borstelmann, *The 1970s*, 262.
12. Hilary Krieger, "Huckabee's Visit to Yad Vashem Stirs Republicans," *Jerusalem
Post*, August 13, 2007, http://www.jpost.com/International/Huckabees-visit
-to-Yad-Vashem-stirs-Republicans.

Chapter 13: Ouachita

1. Peter Baker, "From Former Bush Aide, A Candid Assessment of the GOP
Candidates," *Washington Post*, October 10, 2007, http://www.washingtonpost
.com/wp-dyn/content/article/2007/10/09/AR2007100902064.html.
2. Mike Huckabee, personal interview with the author, April 2015.
3. Randy Sims, personal interview with the author, spring 2015.
4. Rick Caldwell, personal interview with the author, spring 2015. The comments
that follow are from the same interview.
5. Huckabee, personal interview.
6. Ibid.
7. "Former Agent, Author to Speak," *Hope Star*, September 10, 1975, 6.
8. Ibid.

9. Sims, personal interview.

10. "Hammerschmidt Appears to Be in for Tough Fight," *Hope Star*, November 1, 1974, 7.

11. "In Clinton's Race Against JPH, Campaign Spending Reflects Strong Challenge," *Northwest Arkansas Times*, November 2, 1974, 14.

12. Mike Huckabee, "John Paul Hammerschmidt Was One of the True Pioneers of the Arkansas Republican Party," Mike Huckabee's Facebook page, April 1, 2015, https://www.facebook.com/Mikehuckabee/posts/10152892201042869.

13. Sims, personal interview.

14. Huckabee, personal interview.

15. Huckabee, Sims, and Lester Sitzes, personal interviews with the author, spring 2015.

16. Sims, personal interview.

17. Caldwell, personal interview.

18. Ibid.

19. Ibid.

Chapter 14: I Walk the Line

1. Winston Churchill and Dominique Enright, *The Wicked Wit of Winston Churchill* (London: Michael O'Mara, 2001), 104.

2. Lester Sitzes, personal interview with the author, April 2015.

3. Janet McCain Huckabee, personal interview with the author, April 2015.

4. Ibid.

5. Mike Huckabee, personal interview with the author, April 2015.

6. Mike Huckabee, "This week we'll continue our rap on dating," *Baptist Trumpet*, September 26, 1973, 5, http://baptisttrumpetarchives.spriggsone.com/main_includes/download_pdf_file.php?rf=19730926.pdf.

7. Rick Caldwell, personal interview with the author, spring 2015.

8. McCain Huckabee, personal interview.

9. Melinda Henneberger, "Shoots Bear, Submits to Husband: The Fascinating Marriage of Mike and Janet Huckabee," *Slate*, January 29, 2008, http://www.slate.com/articles/news_and_politics/first_mates/2008/01/shoots_bear_submits_to_husband.html.

10. Caldwell, personal interview.

11. "McCain–Huckabee Vows Said in Saturday Home Wedding," *Hope Star*, June 3, 1974, 3.

12. Mike Huckabee, *Living Beyond Your Lifetime: How to Be Intentional About the Legacy You Leave* (Nashville: Broadman & Holman, 2000), 41.

13. Sitzes, personal interview.

14. Huckabee, personal interview.

15. Hillary Rodham Clinton, *Living History* (New York: Simon & Schuster, 2003), 69.
16. J. Everett Sneed, "Reestablishing Trust," *Arkansas Baptist Newsmagazine*, April 12, 1990, 8–9.
17. Huckabee, *Living Beyond Your Lifetime*, 73.
18. Mike Huckabee, The President's Corner, *Arkansas Baptist Newsmagazine*, April 26, 1990.
19. McCain Huckabee, personal interview.
20. Caldwell, personal interview.

Chapter 15: Born to Run

1. Peter Ames Carlin, *Bruce* (New York: Simon & Schuster, 2012), 180.
2. J. Everett Sneed, "Reestablishing Trust," *Arkansas Baptist Newsmagazine*, April 12, 1990, 8–9.
3. Mike Huckabee, personal interview with the author, April 2015.
4. Ibid. See also Gregory Tomlin, "Seminary Days Provided Ark. Governor Opportunity for Christian Growth," *Baptist Press*, May 6, 2003, http://www .bpnews.net/15859/seminary-days-provided-ark-governor-opportunity-for -christian-growth.
5. Huckabee, personal interview. The comments that follow are from this same interview.
6. Mike Huckabee, *Living Beyond Your Lifetime: How to Be Intentional About the Legacy You Leave* (Nashville: Broadman & Holman, 2000), 147.
7. Mike Huckabee and Janet McCain Huckabee, personal interview with the author, April 2015. The comments that follow are also from this interview.
8. Tomlin, "Seminary Days Provided Ark. Governor Opportunity for Christian Growth."
9. Ibid.
10. Jerome L. Himmelstein, *To the Right: The Transformation of American Conservatism* (Berkeley: University of California Press, 1990), 125; Darren Dochuk, *From Bible Belt to Sunbelt: Plain-folk Religion, Grassroots Politics, and the Rise of Evangelical Conservatism* (New York: W. W. Norton, 2011), 368.
11. Huckabee, personal interview.
12. Charles W. Colson, *Born Again* (1976; repr. Grand Rapids: Baker, 2008).
13. Randall Balmer, *Redeemer: The Life of Jimmy Carter* (New York: Basic Books, 2014), 124.
14. Huckabee, personal interview.
15. Ibid.

Chapter 16: Son of a Preacher Man

1. Carol Mason, *Reading Appalachia from Left to Right: Conservatives and the 1974 Kanawha County Textbook Controversy* (Ithaca: Cornell University Press, 2009), 44.
2. Mike Huckabee, personal e-mail to the author, April 2015.

3. Charlie Warren, "Criswell Endorses Adrian Rogers for SBC Presidency," *Baptist Press*, June 11, 1979, 4–5, http://media.sbhla.org.s3.amazonaws.com /4860,11-Jun-1979.PDF.

4. "About the Author," James Robison website, accessed May 31, 2015, http:// www.jamesrobison.net/about/.

5. *The Encyclopedia of Evangelicalism*, 1st ed., s.v. "Robison, James."

6. Daniel K. Williams, *God's Own Party: The Making of the Christian Right* (Oxford: Oxford University Press, 2010), 182.

7. William Martin, "God's Angry Man," *Texas Monthly*, April 1981, 152, 154, 223; cited in ibid., 320.

8. Mike Huckabee, personal interview with the author, April 2015. The remaining quotes in this section are also from this interview.

9. Jerome L. Himmelstein, *To the Right: The Transformation of American Conservatism* (Berkeley: University of California Press, 1990), 116–17.

10. Williams, *God's Own Party*, 140.

11. Ibid., 199–200.

12. Ibid., 183.

13. Randall Balmer, *Redeemer: The Life of Jimmy Carter* (New York: Basic Books, 2014), 112.

14. "Legal Fund Established for Evangelist Robison," *Irving Daily News* (Irving, TX), March 22, 1979, 3.

15. Balmer, *Redeemer*, 112.

16. Deal W. Hudson, *Onward, Christian Soldiers: The Growing Political Power of Catholics and Evangelicals in the United States* (New York: Threshold Editions, 2008), 13.

17. James Robison, "Freedom to Preach (part 1)," James Robison website, January 2, 2014, http://www.jamesrobison.net/freedom-to-preach/.

18. Ariel Levy, "Prodigal Son," *New Yorker*, June 28, 2010, http://www.newyorker .com/magazine/2010/06/28/prodigal-son.

19. J. Brooks Flippen, *Jimmy Carter, the Politics of Family, and the Rise of the Religious Right* (Athens, GA: University of Georgia Press, 2011), 209.

20. Balmer, *Redeemer*, 112.

21. Ibid., 117.

22. Mike Huckabee, personal e-mail.

23. *The Encyclopedia of Evangelicalism*, 1st ed., s.v. "Robison, James."

24. Himmelstein, *To the Right*, 119.

25. Hudson, *Onward, Christian Soldiers*, 15.

Chapter 17: Revolution

1. David Flick, "Dallas-Fort Worth Heat Wave of 1980 Still Seared into Memories," *Dallas Morning News*, November 26, 2010, http://www.dallasnews

.com/news/community-news/dallas/headlines/20100806-Dallas-Fort-Worth
-heat-wave-of-1868.ece.

2. Al Rossiter, Jr., "Heat Wave Cost 1,265 Deaths, Nearly $20 Billion," UPI,
October 16, 1980, http://www.upi.com/Archives/1980/10/16/Heat-wave-cost
-1265-lives-nearly-20-billion/5386340516800/.

3. J. Brooks Flippen, *Jimmy Carter, the Politics of Family, and the Rise of the Religious
Right* (Athens, GA: University of Georgia Press, 2011).

4. Garry Clifford, "After Some On-the-Job Training with Wife Betty, Jim Guy
Tucker Heads Up the Conference on Families," *People*, January 7, 1980, http://
www.people.com/people/archive/article/0,20075555,00.html.

5. "125,000 Sing, Pray in 'Washington for Jesus Rally,'" *Eugene Register-Guard*
(Eugene, OR), April 29, 1980, 2B.

6. Mike Huckabee, personal interview with the author, fall 2014/spring 2015.

7. Randall Balmer, *Redeemer: The Life of Jimmy Carter* (New York: Basic Books,
2014), 143.

8. Ibid.

9. Ibid.

10. "Prophets and Advisors, 1979–1984," *With God on Our Side: The Rise of the
Religious Right in America, 1950–1994*, episode 4, directed by Brad Lichtenstein
(PBS Video, 1996), VHS.

11. Darren Dochuk, *From Bible Belt to Sunbelt: Plain-folk Religion, Grassroots Politics,
and the Rise of Evangelical Conservatism* (New York: W. W. Norton, 2011), 393.

12. Deal W. Hudson, *Onward, Christian Soldiers: The Growing Political Power of Catholics
and Evangelicals in the United States* (New York: Threshold Editions, 2008), 14.

13. Steven P. Miller, *The Age of Evangelicalism: America's Born-Again Years* (New
York: Oxford University Press, 2014).

14. Mike Huckabee, personal e-mail to the author, 2014.

15. Paul Pressler, *A Hill on Which to Die: One Southern Baptist's Journey* (Nashville:
Broadman & Holman, 1999).

16. "Prophets and Advisors."

17. Mike Huckabee, personal e-mail to the author, June 2015.

18. Liz Clarke, "A Higher Power," *Washington Post*, December 15, 2007, http://
www.washingtonpost.com/wp-dyn/content/article/2007/12/14
/AR2007121401861.html.

19. Helen Parmley, "Religious Conservatives Launch Bid to Influence Presidential
Politics," Religious News Service, August 25, 1980.

20. *Newsweek*, September 15, 1980, http://backissues.com/issue/Newsweek
-September-15-1980.

21. Dave Swanson, "49 Years Ago: John Lennon's 'Beatles More Popular Than

Jesus' Story Is Published," March 4, 2015, http://ultimateclassicrock.com/john-lennon-beatles-more-popular-than-jesus/?trackback=tsmclip.

22. Though I do not agree with the thesis of the book, the facts of the crime scene are recounted in Fenton Bresler, *Who Killed John Lennon?* (New York: St. Martin's Press, 1989), 201.

23. Mike Huckabee, personal e-mail to the author, June 2015.

Chapter 18: A Pastor for All Seasons

1. J. Everett Sneed, "Reestablishing Trust," *Arkansas Baptist Newsmagazine*, April 12, 1990, 8–9.

2. Mike Huckabee, personal interview with the author, spring 2015.

3. "Q&A with Mike Huckabee and Brian Lamb," C-SPAN, January 21, 2005, http://www.c-span.org/video/transcript/?id=7949.

4. Sneed, "Reestablishing Trust."

5. James Robison, "Freedom to Preach (part 2)," James Robison website, January 2, 2014, http://www.jamesrobison.net/freedom-to-preach-part-2/.

6. Huckabee, personal interview.

7. Jim Harris, personal interview with the author, spring 2015.

8. Richard Pérez-Peña, "I May Be 50, but Don't Call Me a Boomer," *New York Times*, January 11, 2014, http://www.nytimes.com/2014/01/06/booming/i-may-be-50-but-dont-call-me-a-boomer.html?_r=0.

9. George M. Marsden, *The Twilight of the American Enlightenment: The 1950s and the Crisis of Liberal Belief* (New York: Basic Books, 2014), 140.

10. Ronald Reagan, "Remarks at an Ecumenical Prayer Breakfast in Dallas, Texas," University of Texas, August 23, 1984, http://www.reagan.utexas.edu/archives/speeches/1984/82384a.htm.

11. "Q&A with Mike Huckabee and Brian Lamb."

12. Sneed, "Reestablishing Trust."

13. Ibid.

14. Jodi Kantor and David Kirkpatrick, "Pulpit Was the Springboard for Huckabee's Rise," *New York Times*, December 6, 2007, http://www.nytimes.com/2007/12/06/us/politics/06huckabee.html, 1.

15. Ibid., http://www.nytimes.com/2007/12/06/us/politics/06huckabee.html?pagewanted=2&hp, 2.

16. Huckabee, personal e-mail.

17. Dwight McKissic, personal interview with the author, spring 2015.

18. Randy Sims, personal interview with the author, spring 2015.

19. Sneed, "Reestablishing Trust."

20. Ibid., 9.

Chapter 19: Texarkana

1. J. Everett Sneed, "Reestablishing Trust," *Arkansas Baptist Newsmagazine*, April 12, 1990, 8–9.
2. "Q&A with Mike Huckabee and Brian Lamb," C-SPAN, January 21, 2005, http://www.c-span.org/video/transcript/?id=7949.
3. Ibid.
4. Mike Huckabee, *Living Beyond Your Lifetime: How to Be Intentional About the Legacy You Leave* (Nashville: Broadman & Holman, 2000), 72.
5. Chris Cillizza and Dan Balz, "Interview with Arkansas Gov. Mike Huckabee," *Washington Post*, May 23, 2006, http://www.washingtonpost.com/wp-dyn/content/article/2006/05/22/AR2006052201237.html.
6. Rick Caldwell, personal interview with the author, spring 2015.
7. Sneed, "Reestablishing Trust."
8. "Advertisement for ACTS of Arkansas," *Arkansas Baptist Newsmagazine*, March 24, 1988, 7.
9. Haynes Johnson, *Sleepwalking Through History: America in the Reagan Years* (New York: W. W. Norton, 2003), 214.
10. Steve Bruce, *The Rise and Fall of the New Christian Right: Conservative Protestant Politics in America, 1978–1988* (Oxford: Clarendon Press, 1988), 193.
11. Mike Huckabee and John Perry, *Character Makes a Difference: Where I'm From, Where I've Been, What I Believe* (Nashville: Broadman & Holman Publishers, 2007), 47.
12. Mike Huckabee, "Defining Abundant Life," The President's Corner, *Arkansas Baptist Newsmagazine*, October 10, 1990, 4.
13. Colleen Backus, "President's Message," *Arkansas Baptist Newsmagazine*, December 5, 1991, 9.

Chapter 20: Can't We All Just Get Along?

1. Personal conversation with the author. Also, political scientist James Guth "showed that supporters of the Moral Majority tended to be less educated than their opponents, from less affluent churches, and less active in the life of the Southern Baptist Convention. They were, it seemed, a marginal group unlikely to have much long-term influence, even though the fundamentalist conservative wing had won the presidency of the SBC in the late 1970s after years of moderate control." That quote comes from Jerome L. Himmelstein, *To the Right: The Transformation of American Conservatism* (Berkeley: University of California Press, 1990), 121–22.
2. Jodi Kantor and David Kirkpatrick, "Pulpit Was the Springboard for Huckabee's Rise," *New York Times*, December 6, 2007, http://www.nytimes.com/2007/12/06/us/politics/06huckabee.html?pagewanted=all.

3. Mark Kelly, "Election of Officers," *Arkansas Baptist Newsmagazine*, November 23, 1989, 9.

4. Mike Huckabee, The President's Corner, *Arkansas Baptist Newsmagazine*, July 19, 1990, 4.

5. "Election of Officers."

6. Ibid., 10.

7. Kantor and Kirkpatrick, "Pulpit Was the Springboard for Huckabee's Rise."

8. J. Everett Sneed, "Stir Thy Church," *Arkansas Baptist Newsmagazine*, November 23, 1989, 1.

9. J. Everett Sneed, "Reestablishing Trust," *Arkansas Baptist Newsmagazine*, April 12, 1990, 8–9.

10. Mike Huckabee, The President's Corner, *Arkansas Baptist Newsmagazine*, August 23, 1990, 4.

11. Ibid.

12. Rob Marus, "Huckabee's Role in SBC Conflict Presaged Political Balancing Act," *Baptist Standard*, January 21, 2008, https://www.baptiststandard.com /resources/archives/48–2008-archives/7450-huckabees-role-in-sbc-conflict -presaged-political-balancing-act.

13. Mike Huckabee, The President's Corner, *Arkansas Baptist Newsmagazine*, June 14, 1990, 4.

14. Mike Huckabee, personal interview with the author, April 2015.

15. Colleen Backus, "Building God's Family: Personal Testimonies Hallmark of Harmonious Convention," *Arkansas Baptist Newsmagazine*, November 8, 1990, 7.

16. J. Everett Sneed, "The Best Ever," *Arkansas Baptist Newsmagazine*, November 8, 1990, 3.

17. Mike Huckabee, The President's Corner, *Arkansas Baptist Newsmagazine*, February 28, 1990, 5.

18. Mike Huckabee, The President's Corner, *Arkansas Baptist Newsmagazine*, July 19, 1990, 4.

19. Sneed, "Reestablishing Trust."

20. Colleen Backus, "Hope for the Home: Strengthening Families," *Arkansas Baptist Newsmagazine*, December 5, 1991, 9–10.

21. Mike Huckabee, The President's Corner, *Arkansas Baptist Newsmagazine*, July 4, 1991, 4.

22. Mike Huckabee, "Passing the Torch," The President's Corner, *Arkansas Baptist Newsmagazine*, November 7, 1991, 4.

Chapter 21: Experiencing God

1. "Huckabee's Hour with Charlie Rose," RealClearPolitics, November 1, 2007, http://www.realclearpolitics.com/articles/2007/11/huckabees_hour_with _charlie_ro.html.

2. Mike Huckabee, "Called to the Same Gospel," The President's Corner, *Arkansas Baptist Newsmagazine*, September 12, 1991, 5.

3. Henry T. Blackaby and Claude V. King, *Experiencing God: Knowing and Doing the Will of God*, rev. and exp. ed. (Nashville: Broadman & Holman, 2008), 72, 47.

4. Ibid., 219.

5. William H. Riddle, "The Interpersonal Dynamics of a Modern Political Family: An Interpretive Biography of Governor Mike Huckabee" (doctoral dissertation, University of Louisiana at Monroe, 2011), 40.

6. Mike Huckabee, personal interview with the author, April 2015.

7. Mike Huckabee and John Perry, *Character Makes a Difference: Where I'm From, Where I've Been, What I Believe* (Nashville: Broadman & Holman, 2007), 48.

8. "Q&A with Mike Huckabee and Brian Lamb," C-SPAN, January 21, 2005, http://www.c-span.org/video/transcript/?id=7949.

9. Ibid.

10. Huckabee, personal interview.

11. Ibid.

12. Mike Huckabee and John Perry, *Character Is the Issue: How People with Integrity Can Revolutionize America* (Nashville: Broadman & Holman Publishers, 1997), 125–26.

13. Huckabee, personal interview.

14. Molly Ball, "Is the Most Powerful Conservative in America Losing His Edge?" *Atlantic*, December 28, 2014, http://www.theatlantic.com/features/archive /2014/12/is-the-most-powerful-conservative-in-america-losing-his-edge /383503/.

15. Hugh Hewitt, *A Guide to Christian Ambition: Using Career, Politics, and Culture to Influence the World* (Nashville: Nelson Books, 2006), 61, 65.

16. Charmaine Yoest, personal interview with the author, spring 2015.

17. Riddle, "Interpersonal Dynamics," 39.

18. "Huckabee's Hour with Charlie Rose," RealClearPolitics, November 1, 2007, http://www.realclearpolitics.com/articles/2007/11/huckabees_hour_with _charlie_ro.html.

19. Mike Huckabee, personal e-mail to the author, spring 2015.

20. Mike Huckabee, *Living Beyond Your Lifetime: How to Be Intentional About the Legacy You Leave* (Nashville: Broadman & Holman, 2000), 162–64; emphasis added.

Chapter 22: You Can't Always Get What You Want

1. Rick Caldwell, personal interview with author, spring 2015.

2. Randy Sims, personal interview with the author, spring 2015.

3. Jim Harris, personal interview with the the author, spring 2015.

4. "The Nation. Bumpers: Watch That Killer Smile," *Time*, November 18, 1974, 10, http://content.time.com/time/magazine/article/0,9171,945093,00.html.

5. Mike Huckabee, personal interview with the author, April 2015.

6. Lester Sitzes, personal interview with the author, April 2015.

7. Sims, personal interview.

8. Sitzes, personal interview.

9. Quoted in Benjamin Hardy, David Koon, and Lindsey Millar, "The Best and Worst of Arkansas Times' First 40 Years," September 18, 2014, http://www.arktimes.com/arkansas/the-best-and-worst-of-arkansas-times-first-40-years/Content?oid=3460410.

10. Sitzes, personal interview.

11. Ibid.

12. William H. Riddle, "The Interpersonal Dynamics of a Modern Political Family: An Interpretive Biography of Governor Mike Huckabee" (doctoral dissertation, University of Louisiana at Monroe, 2011), 41–42.

13. "Transcript of Q&A Between Mike Huckabee and Brian Lamb," C-SPAN, January 21, 2005, http://www.c-span.org/video/?185230–1/qa-Mike-huckabee.

14. Harris, personal interview.

15. Mike Huckabee, *Living Beyond Your Lifetime: How to Be Intentional About the Legacy You Leave* (Nashville: Broadman & Holman, 2000), 141.

16. Sims, personal interview.

17. Huckabee, personal interview.

18. Seema Mehta, "AIDS Statements Haunt Huckabee," *Los Angeles Times*, December 12, 2007, http://www.latimes.com/news/la-na-huckabee12dec12-story.html.

19. Colleen Backus, "Building God's Family: Personal Testimonies Hallmark of Harmonious Convention," *Arkansas Baptist Newsmagazine*, November 8, 1990, 12.

20. Max Brantley, personal interview with the author, spring 2015.

21. Michael Kranish, "Gay Comments Haunt Huckabee's Rise in Iowa, US Polls," Boston.com, December 12, 2007.

22. Sitzes, personal interview.

23. Ibid.

24. Riddle, "Interpersonal Dynamics," 42–43.

25. Sitzes, personal interview.

Chapter 23: *Even the Losers Get Lucky Sometimes*

1. "Q&A with Mike Huckabee and Brian Lamb," C-SPAN, January 21, 2005, http://www.c-span.org/video/transcript/?id=7949.

2. Mike Huckabee, personal interview with the author, April 2015.

3. Ibid.

4. Frontline, "Interview with George Stephanopoulos," PBS, July 2000, http://www.pbs.org/wgbh/pages/frontline/shows/clinton/interviews/stephanopoulos.html.

5. Rex Nelson, "Clinton's Hired Gun Gives Huckabee Hand: Lieutenant Governor Shooting for Senate," *Arkansas Democrat-Gazette*, July 2, 1995.

6. Ibid.

7. Huckabee, personal interview.

8. Ibid.

9. Mike Huckabee, *Living Beyond Your Lifetime: How to Be Intentional About the Legacy You Leave* (Nashville: Broadman & Holman, 2000), 19–21.

10. Huckabee, personal interview.

11. These stories have been retold in many places, but especially in chapter 3 of Mike Huckabee and John Perry's *Character Makes a Difference: Where I'm From, Where I've Been, What I Believe* (Nashville: Broadman & Holman, 2007).

12. Mike Huckabee and John Perry, *Character Is the Issue: How People with Integrity Can Revolutionize America* (Nashville: Broadman & Holman, 1997), 62–63.

13. Huckabee and Perry, *Character Is the Issue*, 62.

14. Roy Maynard, "Arkansas' Mister Clean," *World*, July 6, 1996.

Chapter 24: Under Pressure

1. Mike Huckabee, *Living Beyond Your Lifetime: How to Be Intentional About the Legacy You Leave* (Nashville: Broadman & Holman, 2000), 119.

2. Pat Huckabee Harris, personal interview with the author and/or the author's team, spring 2015.

3. Rick Caldwell, personal interview with the author, spring 2015.

4. "Decade of Duty: Governor Mike Huckabee, July 15, 1996–January 9, 2007" (video), broken into six parts and posted on YouTube by "bosscog," February 21, 2007. All six videos can be accessed via "Mike Huckabee—Decade of Duty" (playlist), posted by "Joseph Parks," March 1, 2009, https://www.youtube.com/playlist?list=PLBB082E7A3EC9D3A0.

5. Caldwell, personal interview.

6. "Decade of Duty."

7. Steve Barnes, "Arkansas Governor Resigns After Furor," *New York Times*, July 15, 1996, http://www.nytimes.com/1996/07/16/us/arkansas-governor-resigns-after-furor.html.

8. "Decade of Duty."

9. Ibid.

10. Ibid.

11. Ibid.

12. Mike Huckabee, personal interview with the author, April 2015.

13. "Q&A with Mike Huckabee and Brian Lamb," C-SPAN, January 21, 2005, http://www.c-span.org/video/transcript/?id=7949.

14. "Arkansas Governor Blocks Medicare Payment for an Abortion in Incest Case," *New York Times*, August 9, 1996, http://www.nytimes.com/1996/08/10/us/arkansas -governor-blocks-medicare-payment-for-an-abortion-in-incest-case.html.

15. "Pact Reached on Abortion in Arkansas Medicaid Case," *New York Times*, August 13, 1996, http://www.nytimes.com/1996/08/14/us/pact-reached-on -abortion-in-arkansas-medicaid-case.html.

16. Huckabee, personal interview.

17. William H. Riddle, "The Interpersonal Dynamics of a Modern Political Family: An Interpretive Biography of Governor Mike Huckabee" (doctoral dissertation, University of Louisiana at Monroe, 2011), 51.

18. Caldwell, personal interview.

19. Jim Harris, personal interview with the author, spring 2015.

20. Randy Sims, personal interview with the author, spring 2015.

21. "Time names the five best governors in America," *Time*, November 13, 2005, http://content.time.com/time/press_releases/article/0,8599,1129509,00.html.

22. Amanda Little, "An Interview with Mike Huckabee About His Presidential Platform on Energy and the Environment," *Grist*, October 3, 2007, http://grist .org/article/huckabee/.

23. Ibid.

24. Chris Cillizza and Dan Balz, "Interview with Arkansas Gov. Mike Huckabee," *Washington Post*, May 23, 2006, http://www.washingtonpost.com/wp-dyn /content/article/2006/05/22/AR2006052201237.html.

25. Harris, personal interview.

26. Ibid.

27. Max Brantley, personal interview with the author, spring 2015.

28. Huckabee, *Living Beyond Your Lifetime*, 34.

29. Brantley, personal interview.

30. Huckabee, personal interview.

31. Ibid.

32. U.S. Department of Commerce, NOAA, and National Weather Service, "March 1, 1997 Arkansas Tornado Outbreak," September 1997, http://www .nws.noaa.gov/os/assessments/pdfs/ark61.pdf; TornadoHistoryProject.com, accessed June 18, 2015, http://www.tornadohistoryproject.com/custom /5821142; *The Encyclopedia of Arkansas History & Culture*, s.vv. "Tornadoes," accessed June 18, 2015, http://www.encyclopediaofarkansas.net/encyclopedia /entry-detail.aspx?entryID=2377; *Wikipedia*, s.vv. "Tornadoes of 1997," accessed June 18, 2015, https://en.wikipedia.org/wiki/Tornadoes_of_1997.

33. Frank Rich, "Journal; Lord of the Flies," *New York Times*, March 27, 1998, http://www.nytimes.com/1998/03/28/opinion/journal-lord-of-the-flies.html.

34. Mike Huckabee and George Grant, *Kids Who Kill: Confronting Our Culture of Violence* (Nashville: Broadman & Holman, 1998).

35. Brenda Turner, personal interview with the author, spring 2015.

36. "Arkansas State of the State Address for 1997," C-SPAN, January 14, 1997, http://www.c-span.org/video/?78036-1/arkansas-state-state-address.

37. Dwight McKissic, "Why I'm Voting for Mike Huckabee," February 13, 2008, https://dwightmckissic.wordpress.com/2008/02/13/why-im-voting-for-Mike -huckabee/.

38. Huckabee, personal interview.

39. McKissic, "Why I'm Voting for Mike Huckabee."

40. Huckabee, personal interview.

41. Ibid.

42. "Central High School Desegregation Anniversary," C-SPAN, September 25, 1997, http://www.c-span.org/video/?91570-1/central-high-school-desegregation -anniversary.

43. Ibid.

44. "Huckabee: Never Again Be Silent When People's Rights Are at Stake" (transcript), September 25, 1997, Arkansas Online, http://www .arkansasonline.com/news/1997/sep/25/huckabee-never-again-be-silent -when-peoples-rights/?news-arkansas-specials-central_crisis.

45. Lerone Bennett Jr., "Chronicles of Black Courage: The Little Rock 10," *Ebony*, December 1997, 140.

46. Kevin Sack, "On 40th Anniversary of Little Rock Struggle, Clinton Warns Against Resegregation," *New York Times*, September 26, 1997, http://events .nytimes.com/learning/general/specials/littlerock/0926little-rock.html.

47. Mike Huckabee and John Perry, *Character Makes a Difference: Where I'm From, Where I've Been, What I Believe* (Nashville: Broadman & Holman, 2007), 8.

Chapter 25: Life Is a Highway

1. Brian Skoloff, "Governor: Highway Improvements Helping Roads, State Reputation," Associated Press, January 25, 2002, http://thecabin.net/stories /012502/sta_0125020047.shtml#.VYy0seuBZqs.

2. James Jefferson, "Highway Bills Pass House," Associated Press, March 4, 1999, http://thecabin.net/stories/030499/sta_0304990005.shtml#.VYy1f-uBZqt.

3. Mike Huckabee, "On Behalf of Fix Our Roads Committee," (letter), April 10, 1999, accessed at the Mike Huckabee collection of archives at Ouachita Baptist University in Arkadelphia, Arkansas.

4. Alice Stewart, personal interview with the author, spring 2015.

5. Mike Huckabee, personal interview with the author, spring 2015.

6. William H. Riddle, "The Interpersonal Dynamics of a Modern Political Family: An Interpretive Biography of Governor Mike Huckabee" (doctoral dissertation, University of Louisiana at Monroe, 2011), 49–50.

7. Kenneth Vogel, "Huckabee Rivals Unearth Ethics Complaints," Politico, November 21, 2007, http://www.politico.com/news/stories/1107/7000.html.

8. Ibid.

9. Vogel, "Huckabee Rivals Unearth Ethics Complaints," 2, http://www.politico .com/news/stories/1107/7000_Page2.html.

10. Max Brantley, "The Dark Side of Mike Huckabee," *Salon*, November 13, 2007, http://www.salon.com/2007/11/13/huckabee_5/.

11. Ibid.

12. Ibid.

13. Andrew DeMillo, "Huckabee Defends 'Wedding' Gift Registry," *Washington Post*, November 14, 2006, http://www.washingtonpost.com/wp-dyn/content /article/2006/11/14/AR2006111400724.html.

14. David Firestone, "Little Rock Journal; Governor's Mansion Is a Triple-Wide," *New York Times*, July 18, 2000, http://www.nytimes.com/2000/07/19/us/little -rock-journal-governor-s-mansion-is-a-triple-wide.html.

15. James Jefferson, "Leno, Arkansas Governor Trade Barbs," Amarillo.com, August 11, 2000, http://amarillo.com/stories/081100/usn_leno.shtml# .VYLpq_lVhBc.

16. Mike Huckabee and John Perry, *Character Is the Issue: How People with Integrity Can Revolutionize America* (Nashville: Broadman & Holman, 1997), 135.

17. Tom Bevan, "Interview with Mike Huckabee," RealClearPolitics, March 27, 2007, http://www.realclearpolitics.com/articles/2007/03/interview_with _mike_huckabee.html.

18. Mark Leibovich, "Fire in the Belly Arkansas Gov. Mike Huckabee, Dedicated to Fighting Obesity, Could Have a Meaty Opportunity Ahead," *Washington Post*, January 17, 2006, http://www.washingtonpost.com/archive/lifestyle /2006/01/17/fire-in-the-belly-span-classbankheadarkansas-gov-mike-huckabee -dedicated-to-fighting-obesity-could-have-a-meaty-opportunity-aheadspan /2ac2d3ce-9a2f-41c7-bd20-22883923b8d6/.

19. Andy Barr, "Huck's Humor," *Politico Live*, September 17, 2010, http://www .politico.com/blogs/politicolive/0910/Hucks_humor.html.

20. Ariel Levy, "Prodigal Son," *New Yorker*, June 28, 2010, http://www.newyorker .com/magazine/2010/06/28/prodigal-son.

21. Huckabee, personal interview.

22. Ibid.

23. Janet McCain Huckabee, personal interview with the author, April 2015.

Chapter 26: Another Brick in the Wall

1. Ariel Levy, "Prodigal Son," *New Yorker*, June 28, 2010, http://www.newyorker
   .com/magazine/2010/06/28/prodigal-son.
2. "Governor Huckabee's News Column: Subj.: Lake View Case," February 22,
   2003. Arkansas State Library Archive, http://worldcat.org/arcviewer/1/AST
   /2006/06/20/0000021102/viewer/file1.html.
3. "Arkansas Governor Huckabee's Educational Plan," accessed June 18, 2015,
   http://www.wpaag.org/Huckabee's%20Ed.%20Plan%20–2%20Parts.htm.
4. Levy, "Prodigal Son."
5. "Gov. Mike Huckabee: Strafford County Republican Picnic/Pig Roast: Three
   River Farm: Dover, New Hampshire" (transcript), August 27, 2005, http://
   www.gwu.edu/~action/2008/huckab082705spt.html.
6. Dan Balz, "Microsoft's Gates Urges Governors to Restructure U.S. High
   Schools," *Washington Post*, February 27, 2005, http://www.washingtonpost
   .com/wp-dyn/content/article/2005/03/23/AR2005032302395.html.
7. Richard Fausset, "Huckabee Breaks the GOP Mold with Idiosyncratic Stands,"
   Los Angeles Times, December 2, 2007, http://articles.latimes.com/2007/dec/02
   /nation/na-huckabee2.
8. Doug Thompson, "Immigration Bill Un-Christian, Anti-Life, Governor Says,"
   Arkansas News Bureau, January 28, 2005, http://web.archive.org/web
   /20070704122041/http://www.arkansasnews.com/archive/2005/01/28/News
   /316347.html.
9. Chad Gallagher, personal interview with the author, spring 2015. The
   remaining quotations in this section are also from this interview.
10. "Time Names the Five Best Governors in America," *Time*, November 13, 2005,
    http://content.time.com/time/press_releases/article/0,8599,1129509,00.html.
11. Ibid.
12. "Inspire Awards: Volunteering, Celebrity Activists, Making a Difference," on
    the website of the AARP, accessed June 26, 2015, http://www.aarp.org/politics
    -society/advocacy/inspire_awards/. See also "Governor Mike Huckabee,
    Health Crusader," *AARP the Magazine*, August 20, 2009, http://www.aarp.org
    /politics-society/advocacy/info-2005/impact_awards_huck.html.
13. Alan Greenblatt, "2005 Honoree: Mike Huckabee—Trim Waist, Hefty
    Record," *Governing* magazine, 2005, http://www.governing.com/poy/Mike
    -Huckabee.html.
14. Michael D. Tanner, "Huckabee: The Biggest Big-Government Conservative,"
    CATO Institute, http://www.cato.org/publications/commentary/huckabee
    -biggest-biggovernment-conservative.
15. Levy, "Prodigal Son."
16. Mike Huckabee, personal interview with the author, April 2015.

17. Ibid.

18. Ibid.

19. Associated Press, "Ark. Governor Embraces Covenant Marriage," NBC News, upd. November 9, 2004, http://www.nbcnews.com/id/6440961/ns/us_news /t/ark-governor-embraces-covenant-marriage/.

20. Shaila Dewan, "The Slenderized Governor, with Advice to Share," *New York Times*, September 9, 2006, http://www.nytimes.com/2006/09/10/us/10weight .html.

21. Stella Prather, "Ark. Governor, 6,400 Others Take Stand for Covenant Marriages," *Baptist Press*, February 15, 2005, http://www.bpnews.net/20148 /ark-governor-6400-others-take-stand-for-covenant-marriages.

22. Melinda Henneberger, "Shoots Bear, Submits to Husband: The Fascinating Marriage of Mike and Janet Huckabee," *Slate*, January 29, 2008, http://www .slate.com/articles/news_and_politics/first_mates/2008/01/shoots_bear _submits_to_husband.html.

23. Levy, "Prodigal Son."

24. "Q&A with Mike Huckabee and Brian Lamb," C-SPAN, January 21, 2005, http://www.c-span.org/video/transcript/?id=7949.

25. Mark Leibovich, "Fire in the Belly," *Washington Post*, January 17, 2006, http://www.washingtonpost.com/wp-dyn/content/article/2006/01/16 /AR2006011601380.html.

26. "Q&A with Mike Huckabee and Brian Lamb."

27. Alice Stewart, personal interview with the author, April 2015.

28. Ibid.

29. Huckabee, personal interview.

30. Ibid.

31. Ibid.

32. Ibid.

33. Ibid.

34. Ibid.

Chapter 27: With a Little Help from My Friends

1. "MTP Transcript for Jan. 28, 2007," NBCNews, January 28, 2007, http://www .nbcnews.com/id/16785556/ns/meet_the_press/t/mtp-transcript-jan/# .VVUEYvlViko.

2. Mike Huckabee, *Do the Right Thing: Inside the Movement That's Bringing Common Sense Back to America* (New York: Sentinel, 2008).

3. Tom Bevan, "Interview with Mike Huckabee," RealClearPolitics, March 27, 2007, http://www.realclearpolitics.com/articles/2007/03/interview_with _Mike_huckabee.html.

4. Ibid.

5. Ibid.

6. Huckabee, *Do the Right Thing*, 51.

7. Alan Cooperman, "Evangelicals at a Crossroads as Falwell's Generation Fades," *Washington Post*, May 22, 2007, http://www.washingtonpost.com /wp-dyn/content/article/2007/05/21/AR2007052101581.html.

8. Tim Alberta and Tiffany Stanley, "Inside Jeb Bush's Stealth Campaign to Woo Christian Conservatives," *National Journal*, March 28, 2015, http://www .nationaljournal.com/magazine/jeb-bush-religious-christian-conservatives -20150327.

9. "Press Release—Huckabee campaign sets the record straight with Paul Weyrich," The American Presidency Project, November 6, 2007, http://www .presidency.ucsb.edu/ws/?pid=93364.

10. Huckabee, *Do the Right Thing*, 56.

11. Ibid.

12. Ibid.

13. Warren Cole Smith, "Divided We Stand," *World*, April 5, 2008, 1, http://www .worldmag.com/2008/04/divided_we_stand.

14. Mike Huckabee, personal interview with the author, April 2014.

15. Ibid.

16. Ibid.

17. Robert Novak, "Baptists Not on Board," *Washington Post*, December 20, 2007, http://www.washingtonpost.com/wp-dyn/content/article/2007/12/19 /AR2007121901856.html.

18. Dwight McKissic, "Wm. Dwight McKissic, Sr," March 12, 2012, https:// dwightmckissic.wordpress.com/2011/03/.

19. Huckabee, personal interview.

20. Smith, "Divided We Stand."

21. NBC, "Republican Presidential Candidate Mike Huckabee on *The Tonight Show with Jay Leno*," January 2, 2008, http://usatoday30.usatoday.com/news/pdf /Huckabee-on-Leno-1-2-2008.pdf.

22. "GOP Candidates Go for the Jugular in Feisty Primary Debate," Fox News, May 16, 2007, http://www.foxnews.com/story/2007/05/16/gop-candidates -go-for-jugular-in-feisty-primary-debate/.

23. Rick Caldwell, personal interview with the author, spring 2015.

24. Mike Huckabee, "Republican Presidential Debate in South Carolina," *New York Times*, May 15, 2007, http://www.nytimes.com/2007/05/15/us/politics/16repubs -text.html?#59;oref=slogin&_r=4&pagewanted=all.

25. Guy Reel, *Unequal Justice: Wayne Dumond, Bill Clinton, and the Politics of Rape in Arkansas* (Amherst, NY: Prometheus, 1993).

26. Marc Fisher, "Marc Fisher—The Gift of Justice Doesn't Cost a Dime," *Washington Post*, December 23, 2007, http://www.washingtonpost.com/wp -dyn/content/article/2007/12/22/AR2007122201549.html.

27. Huckabee, personal interview.

28. Jill Lawrence, "Straw Poll: Huckabee Spent Just $58 per Vote for 2nd Place and Revived Prospects," *USA Today*, August 12, 2007, http://content.usatoday.com /communities/onpolitics/post/2007/08/163446/1#.VXRrFNJVhBc.

29. Gerhard Peters and John T. Woolley, "Republican Candidates 'All-American Presidential Forum' at Morgan State University in Baltimore," September 27, 2007, The American Presidency Project, http://www.presidency.ucsb.edu /ws/?pid=75913.

30. Joy Lin, "Huckabee Courts Black Vote," CBS News, January 21, 2008, http:// www.cbsnews.com/news/huckabee-courts-black-vote/.

31. "The Republican Debate," *New York Times*, October 9, 2007, http://www .nytimes.com/2007/10/09/us/politics/09debate-transcript.html?pagewanted =all.

32. Ariel Levy, "Prodigal Son," *New Yorker*, June 28, 2010, http://www.newyorker .com/magazine/2010/06/28/prodigal-son.

33. Huckabee, personal interview.

34. W. James Antle III, "Huckabee: 'I'm a Main Street Republican,'" Politico, August 8, 2007, http://www.politico.com/news/stories/0807/5428.html.

35. Chris Cillizza and Dan Balz, "Interview with Arkansas Gov. Mike Huckabee," *Washington Post*, May 23, 2006, http://www.washingtonpost.com/wp-dyn /content/article/2006/05/22/AR2006052201237.html.

36. Gail Russell Chaddock, "Mike Huckabee: A Conservative with a Social Gospel," *Christian Science Monitor*, November 7, 2007, http://www.csmonitor .com/2007/1107/p01s04-uspo.html.

37. David Madland, "What Would Jesus Tax?" *Think Tank Town* (blog), January 19, 2008, http://www.washingtonpost.com/wp-dyn/content/article/2008/01/18 /AR2008011802936.html.

38. Ibid.

39. "Phyllis Schlafly comments on Huckabee's lack of conservatism," Eagle Forum Legislative Alerts, October 26, 2007, http://blog.eagleforum.org/2007/10 /phyllis-schlafly-on-huckabee.html.

40. Kevin Bumpus, "Before Mike Huckabee was Governor," C-SPAN, January 24, 2015, http://www.c-span.org/video/?c4528649/Mike-huckabee-governor.

41. "We Recommend Mike Huckabee for the Republican Nomination," *Dallas Morning News*, December 23, 2007.

42. Gerhard Peters and John T. Woolley, "Statement by Mike Huckabee on Latest Polls—New Rasmussen Poll Shows Huckabee Ahead of Romney in Iowa,"

November 28, 2007, The American Presidency Project, http://www
.presidency.ucsb.edu/ws/?pid=91284.

43. Matt Taibbi, "My Favorite Nut Job," *Rolling Stone*, March 25, 2011, http://www
.rollingstone.com/politics/news/my-favorite-nut-job-20110325#ixzz3a08wTGuX.

44. "Mike Huckabee Ad: 'Chuck Norris Approved,'" YouTube video, 1:00, posted
by "Veracifier," November 18, 2007, https://www.youtube.com/watch?v
=MDUQW8LUMs8.

45. Zev Chafets, "The Huckabee Factor," *New York Times*, December 12, 2007,
http://www.nytimes.com/2007/12/12/magazine/16huckabee.html?pagewanted
=all&_r=0.

46. Jeremy Wallace, "When Marco Rubio Was Firmly on Mike Huckabee's Team,"
HT Politics, January 31, 2015, http://politics.heraldtribune.com/2015/01/31
/marco-rubio-firmly-mike-huckabees-team/.

47. "Presidential Forum Transcript," December 9, 2007, Univision, http://www
.factcheck.org/UploadedFiles/Univision_Republican_Forum_Transcript.pdf.

48. Huckabee, *Do the Right Thing*, 60.

49. Bert Decker, "Top Ten Best (and Worst) Communicators of 2007," Decker
Communications, December 31, 2007, https://decker.com/blog/top-ten
-best-and-worst-communicators-of-2007/.

50. NBC, "Republican Presidential Candidate Mike Huckabee on The Tonight
Show with Jay Leno."

Chapter 28: *We Are the Champions*

1. "Mike Huckabee: Remarks Following the Iowa Caucuses," January 3, 2008,
American Presidency Project, http://www.presidency.ucsb.edu/ws/index
.php?pid=76230.

2. Charmaine Yoest, personal interview with the author, spring 2015.

3. Michael Shear and Perry Bacon, "GOP Victor Calls for 'New Day' in Politics,"
Houston Chronicle, January 4, 2008, http://www.chron.com/news/houston-texas
/article/GOP-victor-calls-for-new-day-in-politics-1785169.php.

4. "Mike Huckabee: Remarks Following the Iowa Caucuses."

5. Ibid.

Chapter 29: *If I Were a Rich Man*

1. Jodi Kantor, "Pulpit Was the Springboard for Huckabee's Rise," *New York
Times*, December 5, 2007, http://www.nytimes.com/2007/12/06/us/politics
/06huckabee.html.

2. Alexander Mooney, "$40 Million Spent to Tout Candidates on Iowa TV,"
CNN, January 1, 2008, http://www.cnn.com/2008/POLITICS/01/01/iowa
.ad.spending/.

3. Kevin Merida, "Her Motto: 'I Like (M)Ike,'" *Washington Post*, January 4, 2008, http://www.washingtonpost.com/wp-dyn/content/article/2008/01/03/AR2008010304129.html.

4. Michael Scherer, "The GOP Gets Gaudy in Michigan," *Salon*, September 24, 2007, http://www.salon.com/2007/09/24/mackinac/.

5. Mike Huckabee, *Living Beyond Your Lifetime: How to Be Intentional About the Legacy You Leave* (Nashville: Broadman & Holman, 2000), v.

6. Chris Cillizza and Dan Balz, "Interview with Arkansas Gov. Mike Huckabee," *Washington Post*, May 23, 2006, http://www.washingtonpost.com/wp-dyn/content/article/2006/05/22/AR2006052201237.html.

7. Mike and Janet Huckabee, personal interview with the author, April 2014.

8. Philip Elliott, "Huckabee Poised to Jump into GOP Primary (Video)," *Christian Science Monitor*, April 18, 2015, http://www.csmonitor.com/USA/2015/0418/Huckabee-poised-to-jump-into-GOP-primary-video.

9. Joel Achenbach, "Huckabee's Big Whiff; Plus, Luckiest Man Alive?" *Achenblog* (*Post* blog), December 5, 2007, http://voices.washingtonpost.com/achenblog/2007/12/luckiest_man_alive.html.

10. Ross Douthat, "Huckabee's Amateur Hour," *Atlantic*, December 12, 2007, http://www.theatlantic.com/personal/archive/2007/12/huckabees-amateur-hour/55135/.

11. Zev Chafets, "The Huckabee Factor" (Correction Appended), *New York Times*, December 12, 2007, 9, http://www.nytimes.com/2007/12/12/magazine/16huckabee.html?pagewanted=9&_r=0.

12. Andrew DeMillo, "Paul Brings Huckabee Critics to Iowa," *USA Today*, December 13, 2007, http://usatoday30.usatoday.com/news/politics/2007-12-13-783485599_x.htm.

13. Mike Huckabee, personal interview with the author, April 2015. The audio is available at: "Four Arkansas GOP Legislators Discuss Huckabee on Iowa WHO Radio," ARRA News Service, December 15, 2007, http://arkansasgopwing.blogspot.com/2007/12/four-arkansas-gop-legislators-discuss.html.

14. Huckabee, personal interview with the author.

15. Ibid.

16. Adam Nagourney, "Thompson Ends Campaign for G.O.P. Nomination," *New York Times*, January 22, 2008, http://www.nytimes.com/2008/01/23/us/politics/23thompson.html.

17. Huckabee, personal interview.

18. Charles Krauthammer, "Losing Ugly," *Washington Post*, January 25, 2008, http://www.washingtonpost.com/wp-dyn/content/article/2008/01/24/AR2008012402799.html.

19. Huckabee, personal interview.

20. Steven Thomma, "Huckabee Keeps on Running, but Why?" McClatchy DC, February 13, 2008, http://www.mcclatchydc.com/2008/02/13/27578/huckabee -keeps-on-running-but.html#storylink=cpy.

21. Huckabee, personal interview.

22. "SNL Weekend Update: Mike Huckabee on Why He's Not Conceding the Republican Nomination from Saturday Night Live on NBC.com," NBC, February 23, 2008, http://www.nbc.com/saturday-night-live/video/gov -huckabee-on-update/n12193.

23. Huckabee, personal interview.

24. Charmaine Yoest, personal interview with the author, spring 2015.

25. Michael Shear and Peter Slevin, "McCain Clinches GOP Presidential Nomination," *Washington Post*, March 5, 2008, http://www.washingtonpost .com/wp-dyn/content/article/2008/03/04/AR2008030401984.html.

26. "Transcript: Huckabee Concedes Nomination to McCain," WP Politics (blog), March 4, 2008, http://www.washingtonpost.com/wp-dyn/content/article /2008/03/04/AR2008030402801.html.

27. Ibid.

Chapter 30: Dream On

1. Brian Hiatt, "The Emancipation of Steven Tyler," *Rolling Stone*, January 17, 2012, http://www.rollingstone.com/music/news/the-emancipation-of-steven -tyler-20120117#ixzz3ZvpJYZpw.

2. David Greenberg, "Usual Wisdom on V.p. Choices Is Full of Errors," June 8, 2008, http://www.deseretnews.com/article/700232354/Usual-wisdom-on-vp -choices-is-full-of-errors.html?pg=all.

3. Robert Novak, "McCain's Christian Problem," *Washington Post*, May 12, 2008, http://www.washingtonpost.com/wp-dyn/content/article/2008/05/11 /AR2008051101786.html.

4. Ibid.

5. Ross Douthat, "Huckabee vs. McCain?" *Atlantic*, May 13, 2008, http://www .theatlantic.com/personal/archive/2008/05/huckabee-vs-mccain/54064/.

6. Novak, "McCain's Christian Problem."

7. Mike Huckabee, personal interview with the author, April 2015. The remaining Huckabee quotes in this section are also from this interview.

8. Robert A. Lehrman, *The Political Speechwriter's Companion: A Guide for Writers and Speakers* (Washington, DC: CQ Press, 2010), 94–100.

9. Mike Huckabee, "Mike Huckabee 2008 Convention Speech," C-SPAN, September 3, 2008, http://www.c-span.org/video/?280790–8/mike-huckabee -2008-convention-speech.

10. Ibid.

Epilogue

1. Jim Rutenberg, "After Hinting Otherwise, Huckabee Says He Won't Run for President," *New York Times*, May 14, 2011, http://www.nytimes.com/2011/05/15/us/politics/15huckabee.html?_r=1.

2. Leon Stafford, "Chick-fil-A Keeps Growing Despite Uproar," *Atlanta Journal-Constitution*, January 29, 2013, http://www.ajc.com/news/business/chick-fil-a-keeps-growing-despite-uproar/nT85n/.

3. Rebecca Kaplan, "Huckabee Weighs In on 'Duck Dynasty' Controversy," CBS News, December 22, 2013, http://www.cbsnews.com/news/huckabee-weighs-in-on-duck-dynasty-controversy/.

4. "Huckabee Launches Petition to Support 'Duck Dynasty' Star," video clip, Fox News, December 23, 2013, http://video.foxnews.com/v/2966031995001/huckabee-launches-petition-to-support-duck-dynasty-star/?#sp=show-clips.

5. Mike Huckabee, Facebook post, January 3, 2015, https://www.facebook.com/mikehuckabee/posts/10152701857157869.

6. Ben Gittleson, "Huckabee Announces 2016 Presidential Bid," ABC News, May 5, 2015, http://abcnews.go.com/Politics/mike-huckabee-announces-2016-presidential-bid/story?id=30816392.

7. Dana Milbank, "Mike Huckabee's Ill-Fated Quest," *Washington Post*, May 5, 2015, http://www.washingtonpost.com/opinions/mike-huckabees-ill-fated-quest/2015/05/05/15fa7330-f35e-11e4-84a6-6d7c67c50db0_story.html.

8. David Ramsey, "Mike Huckabee Is Running for President," *Arkansas Times*, May 5, 2015, http://www.arktimes.com/ArkansasBlog/archives/2015/05/05/mike-huckabee-is-running-for-president.

9. Mike Huckabee, "Huckabee Announces," C-SPAN, May 5, 2015, http://www.c-span.org/video/?c4536668/huckabee-announces.

ACKNOWLEDGMENTS

My heart is full of gratitude:

To Pearl, my best friend. Every day with you is another reminder of God's smile.

To the greatest kids—Josiah, Nathanael, Isaac, Benjamin, Savannah, and Aaron. You are God's gifts—first to us, then to the world. You're all growing up way too fast, especially when I'm in the middle of a book project. So thanks for bringing such joy into my life on days which otherwise were full of deadlines and pressure.

To my parents, Walter and Rexanna Lamb, for all your encouragement to me throughout the years. And for your help moving our family to Tennessee while in the middle of this writing project.

To Mike and Janet Huckabee, for the unending openness of your heart and home. You gave, and never asked for anything in return.

To the board of directors of the Presbyterian Lay Committee and my colleagues: Carmen Fowler LaBerge, Paula Kincaid, Susan Andrews, and Jessica Lalley—people who combine great talent and accomplishment with kindness and civility.

To David and Cindy Lane of the American Renewal Project, who open doors and spread joy to others.

To John Solomon of the *Washington Times*, who believes that truth can still hold its own ground in the public square.

To the incredible team at Thomas Nelson: Matt Baugher, Lori Cloud,

Nicole Pavlas, Caroline Green, and Kristi Smith. And an extra word of thanks to editors Joel Kneedler and Meaghan Porter for the generous use of their incredible talents, helping direct the vision for this book.

To all the people who were interviewed, understanding Mike Huckabee would have been impossible without your input. Thank you so much for being interviewed by me or one of my journalist friends.

To my friends who helped me conduct or transcribe the interviews: Jeff Robinson, Tim Ellsworth, Bethany Blankley, Michelle Smith, Patricia Latham, and Jennifer White. And thanks to Caleb Yarbrough of the *Arkansas Baptist News* for the work in your archives.

To Dr. Wendy Richter and Dr. Phil Hardin of Ouachita Baptist University, for their assistance and hospitality while conducting research in the archived political records and papers of Governor Mike Huckabee, housed there at his alma mater—a beautiful and friendly campus!

To Lester Sitzes for his hospitality in Hope, and for the pictures. I had a great evening of fajitas and fun stories about your best friend since first grade.

To Jim and Pat Harris—your stories about your kid brother had me laughing and crying. Thank you for opening your home to me—and for all the pictures.

To Clay Smith and family and Klay Aspinwall and family—for prayer and encouragements over the past two decades. (What? Are we that old now?)

And thank you to God for giving me salvation through the work of the Holy Spirit in my life, bringing me to faith in Christ and repentance of my sin. *Soli Deo Gloria!*

ABOUT THE AUTHOR

W. Scott Lamb serves as the executive director of the Presbyterian Lay Committee and the president of Reformation Press in Nashville, Tennessee. He is an ordained pastor who has led churches in Alabama, Missouri, and Kentucky. He and his wife, Pearl, are the parents of five sons and a daughter. With Tim Ellsworth, Scott coauthored *Pujols: More than the Game* (Thomas Nelson, 2011). With David and Jason Benham, Scott coauthored *Whatever the Cost* (Thomas Nelson, 2015). Under the banner of "Jesus in the Public Square," he produces and curates news stories and analysis for the *Washington Times*.

INDEX

Index